120 Ways
To
Market
Your
Business
Hyper
Locally

Tried and True

Tips and Techniques

Sue Ellson

Published by
๏ 120 Ways Publishing PO Box 65, Surrey Hills, Victoria, Australia, 3127
120ways@120ways.com

Printed by
IngramSpark, Unit A1/A3, 7 Janine Street, Scoresby, Victoria, Australia 3179
ingramsparkinternational@ingramcontent.com

Copyright
All text and technical diagrams copyright © Sue Ellson 2016 The moral rights of the author have been asserted. All rights reserved.

Photocopying and reproducing in print or digital format
If recommending the content in this book to friends, family, clients or colleagues, please keep in mind that the original rights belong to the author only. The content has been generously provided and it is only fair that the reward be returned to the author to recover the cost of production, distribution and future editions.

If you wish to reproduce, store or transmit any part of this book, please email the publisher 120ways@120ways.com for written permission rights. All quotations need to be referenced to Sue Ellson.

National Library of Australia Cataloguing-in-Publication entry
Ellson, Sue, 1965 – Author
120 Ways To Market Your Business Hyper Locally
Tried And True Tips And Techniques / Sue Ellson
ISBN-10: 0-9942875-6-9 ISBN 13: 978-0-9942875-6-4 (paperback)
Includes index. Books – Business, Books – Self-Help

Please note
All care has been taken in the preparation of this book. The publisher and the author have no liability to any person or entity with respect to any loss or damage alleged to have been caused directly or indirectly by the information contained herein, which was correct at the time of writing, and is based on past experience, but is subject to change. This content has not been approved or endorsed by any social media or online platform provider. Trademark information has been omitted from the main text to assist readability. All trademarked brands are owned by their respective corporations.

DEDICATION

For my children,
Carmen and Peter,
whom I love more
than words can say.

ACKNOWLEDGEMENTS

When I set out to finish three books within 12 months, I really had no idea what was in store for me. I simply chose my book titles - '120 Ways To Achieve Your Purpose With LinkedIn,' '120 Ways To Attract The Right Career Or Business' and '120 Ways To Market Your Business Hyper Locally' and set book launch dates and went for it.

Personally, I thrive on deadlines, in fact they usually drive my efforts, but when I changed the goal posts along the way, I now realize that I probably bit off slightly more than I could chew.

For example, when I first thought about writing three books, I assumed that they would be about 45,000 words each. It turns out they are all around 80,000 words each. I originally thought about 120 ways, but the books include hundreds of ways sorted into 120 summaries. I thought it would be easy to continue writing because I developed comprehensive writing plans, but I often found myself unable to focus thanks to the distractions of my business and personal life. I thought I would outsource some of the tasks but ended up learning how to do everything myself.

However, the experience has been cathartic. I have finally managed to put on paper so many of the tried and true tips and techniques I have been using for years and it is such a relief to remove them from my internal unsorted catalogue.

It has also enabled me to produce three comprehensive publications that enable you to take selected actions with your LinkedIn Profile, your career, your business and/or your marketing, either on your own or with a friend, colleague, coach or mentor.

As a learning junkie who also likes teaching, this book writing process has given me an enormous sense of achievement. Knowing that I will be able to help you and others from all over the world achieve your goals is super exciting!

This particular book may not have ever reached your hands if it wasn't for the constant encouragement and reminders I received from Suzanne Dunlop - so I would like to personally acknowledge her significant contribution.

Throughout this three books journey, I have also received support from Euan Mitchell (my author advisor), Aaron Brendel (my website designer), various business clients and colleagues and several friends - most notably, Grace Guo, Ângelo Klin, Colin Freckleton and Gefferson Heemann. My children have also endured a few high pressure moments - but thankfully, our relationship has survived!

I have several ideas about what I will write next. So please consider staying fully updated in relation to this book and other publications by joining the 120 Ways Publishing Membership Program at http://120ways.com/members.

Contents

Preface xi

Introduction 1

1. Our Global Village 5
1.1 Marketing, Selling And Networking 6
1.2 Location Attachment And Choice 7
1.3 Defining Hyper Local Marketing 10
1.4 The Benefits Of Hyper Local Marketing 12

2. Personal Context 15
2.1 Self Evaluation 15
2.2 Self Management 17
2.3 Management And Leadership 20
2.4 Succession Planning And Exit Strategy 21
2.5 Personal Principles 23
2.6 Community And Business Congruency 25
2.7 Business Ethics And Self Regulation 27
2.8 Staffing And Outsourcing 28
2.9 Effective Hyper Local Recruitment Techniques 30

3. Business Context 35
3.1 Business Choice 35
3.2 Consumer Choice 38
3.3 Sustainable Business 40
3.4 Business Type And Differentiation 42
3.5 Business Pricing 43

4. Product And Service First Or Target Audience First? 45
4.1 Securing Referrals From Existing Clients And Customers 47
4.2 Other Sources Of Clients And Customers 48
4.3 Maintaining Clients And Customers 50

5. Market Analysis 55
5.1 Site Or Location Setting 55
5.2 Market Size 56
5.3 Competitor Analysis 57
5.4 Online Competitor Analysis 57

5.5 Collaborator Analysis 59

6. Location Context 61
6.1 Fixed Address 61
6.2 Online Address 62
6.3 Platform Presence 64
6.4 Collective Marketplace Address 66

7. Market Presence 71
7.1 Business Premises Look And Feel 72
7.2 Business Website Development 73
7.3 Personal Authority Website Development 76
7.4 Real World Marketing And Advertising 79
7.5 Currency, Recency And Relevancy 83

8. Online And Digital Marketing 85
8.1 White Hat Search Engine Optimization (SEO) Techniques 86
8.2 Search Engine Ranking Factors 87
8.3 Content Marketing Strategies That Work 88
8.4 Amplifying The Value And Conversions From Your Content 90
8.5 Developing Viral Content And Conversions 91
8.6 Sending The Right Signals 94
8.7 Sourcing Hyper Local Website Links 96
8.8 Improving Overall Online Performance 99
8.9 Website Ranking Threats 102

9. Paid Marketing 105
9.1 Search Engine Marketing (SEM 106
9.2 Social Media Marketing (SMM) 108
9.3 Online Advertisements 110
9.4 Aggregator Websites 112
9.5 Professional Body, Industry Group And Association Memberships .. 115
9.6 Gifts 117
9.7 Donations 118

10. Database Marketing 121
10.1 Email Newsletter Marketing 123
10.2 Joint Ventures And Strategic Alliances 126

10.3 Partnerships 128
10.4 If / Then Scenarios 130
10.5 Follow Up And Feedback 132

11. Program Marketing 135
11.1 Award Programs 136
11.2 Affiliate Programs 139
11.3 Formal Recognition Programs 142
11.4 Rewards Programs 143
11.5 Surveys, Quizzes And Research Programs 145
11.6 Accreditation And Certification 146

12. Public Marketing 151
12.1 Generating Content 152
12.2 Reviews 153
12.3 Recommendations 155
12.4 Referrals 156
12.5 Reputation 159
12.6 Testimonials 162
12.7 Feedback 163
12.8 Advocacy 164

13. Events Marketing 167
13.1 Free Events 167
13.2 Hosting Paid Events 171
13.3 Speaking At Events 174
13.4 Teaching 178
13.5 Expos, Trade Fairs And Conferences 179
13.6 Online Summits, Podcasts And Webinars 182

14. Media Marketing 185
14.1 Editorial 187
14.2 Advertorial 188
14.3 Publicity And Public Relations 189

15. Community Marketing 193
15.1 Networks 194
15.2 Bartering 196

15.3 Exchanges 196
15.4 Local Suppliers 197
15.5 Location Sharing 198
15.6 Naming Rights, Sponsorships And Advertising 199

16. Incentive Marketing 203
16.1 Competitions 204
16.2 Gamification Programs 205
16.3 Loyalty Programs 206
16.4 Relationship Marketing Programs 207
16.5 Thank You And Gratefulness Initiatives 209

17. Future Options Marketing 211

18. Marketing Measurement 215
18.1 Digital Asset Value 215
18.2 Goodwill 217
18.3 Performance Assessment 218
18.4 Performance Improvement 219
18.5 Top 20 Tips And Techniques 220

19. Full List Of 120 Actions 225

20. Bonuses 241

Index 243

Author 263

Preface

'120 Ways To Market Your Business Hyper Locally: Tried And True Tips And Techniques' is for:

- defining your target audience
- aligning your marketing with your local community
- building your lifetime and dynamic asset value
- integrating online and offline marketing techniques
- collaborating effectively with complementary businesses
- encouraging learning, growth, social democracy and investment

It includes information for:

- marketers, salespeople and advertisers
- freelancers, entrepreneurs, business and franchise owners
- advisers, consultants and thought leaders
- coaches, trainers and mentors
- community leaders and initiative instigators

This thorough, practical and detailed guide provides you with the key strategies and techniques, based on your business values, that you can implement today for your success in the future.

Get started and take action now!

**Special free bonus offers at http://120ways.com/members

This book is a companion book to '120 Ways To Achieve Your Purpose With LinkedIn' and '120 Ways To Attract The Right Career Or Business' also written by Sue Ellson.

Introduction

Are you clear about the value your business provides?

If the answer is yes, well done!

If the answer is no, don't worry, it will come - or you will modify it!

Do you already know how to market your business hyper locally?

If the answer is yes, fantastic, you are about to learn a lot more!

If the answer is no, I am so happy that you are willing to learn!

'120 Ways To Market Your Business Hyper Locally' has been written to help you choose what actions you can implement to develop a sustainable business within a local context or location – and give you the courage to complete the right steps to achieve results.

So get ready to take action!

GENERATIONS

Openness generates Opportunity

Gratitude generates Generosity

Commitment generates Connectedness

Resourcefulness generates Referrals

Consistency generates Collaboration

Significance generates Sustainability

Inclusiveness generates Intellect

Purpose generates Performance

Wisdom generates Willpower

Enquiry generates Enterprise

Reflection generates Resilience

Bravery generates Beauty

Learn to Generate

Achieve your Goals

Sue Ellson August 2016

After growing up in the city of Adelaide, South Australia and spending many childhood vacations on Kangaroo Island, I have developed an acute sense of the value and meaning of place.

This was enhanced even further when I moved to the 'big smoke' of Melbourne, Victoria, Australia (triple the population of Adelaide at the time). I found the transition extremely difficult, so a few years later, I developed Newcomers Network http://newcomersnetwork.com to help make it easier for other people in the future.

Over time, Newcomers Network has morphed into many different online and real life formats, but it has always been based on the principle of connecting new arrivals with existing resources and teaching newcomers from all walks of life the strategies that will overcome the challenges associated with moving.

Right now, we all know that the rate of change in technology and lifestyle is increasing at exponential speed. As human beings existing within our natural (and unnatural) environment, we need to adapt to be able to survive.

What we have seen throughout history is that the people who have survived and prospered are those that have joined forces. The people who see the value of the group rather than those who pander to the indulgences of an individual.

What I have learnt from all of my interactions with thousands of newcomers is that location makes up a huge part of our personal identity. It gives us a framework for the context of our life, career and business.

Whilst affordable travel has given many people the opportunity to explore the world and some people have chosen to be 'location independent' with their business or career, I have found that the happiest and most contented people are the people who live in a 'location by choice,' even if that is more than one location.

That doesn't mean that these people do not travel and explore, it just means that for the majority of their time, they choose to live, work and play in a particular location/s.

So this book is dedicated to and designed for locals. In particular, hyper locals. The people who are happy to spend most of their year in one location or one context, for any reason. Your presence enhances that place and has inspired me to write this book.

If you can implement the tips and techniques in this book, you will feel more connected, be more content and make an even bigger contribution that will reward both you, your loved ones, your community and the environment.

1. Our Global Village

There is an African Proverb that says 'It takes a village to raise a child.'

In my view, it takes a community to enjoy your life.

And it takes perseverance and commonsense to run a successful business.

Whilst some people strive for a business that is 'location independent,' other people choose to run a business in a 'location by choice.'

This does not mean that your business needs to only serve people within a certain geographical radius. It is possible to have an international business in a local community. It is also possible to have an international community in a local business.

If you have completed any form of training or education in business, you will already know that most business startups will not be in business five years later. We also know that some types of business only exist for a certain duration.

For example, you probably wouldn't get much work as a blacksmith making horse shoes in the city of São Paulo in Brazil! Thanks to the rapid changes in modern society, very few Fortune 500 companies are in the same list 50 years later.

So before you start thinking that this book can make any business viable with hyper local marketing, think again. None of these tips and techniques will work if there is no demand for your business's products or services.

It is of course important to remember that even though you may have some amazing products and services, and everyone might 'need' them, not everyone will buy them.

After the 'greed is good' mantra of the 1980's, I am pleased to see that more and more people and communities are adopting a minimalist approach to life - reducing the size of their ecological footprint by utilizing local food sources, travelling less (or walking, riding a bike or taking public transport), reducing their consumption of products and services and recycling as much as possible (even clothing).

Being in business is not about taking from your community and ultimately destroying our global village in the long run. It comes with both rights and responsibilities. Just as the native birds and bees only consume what they need, so too should you and your business.

In fact your business will be even more successful if you approach it with an attitude of value exchange and social investment. If I expect a particular product or service for a certain price and you provide it willingly and offer me a value that is way above that price (perceived or real), then you are much more likely to generate more business in the future. Remember that up to 85% of business is generated through referrals.

So a quick disclaimer right up front. I don't know the nature of your business or the context in which you operate - so if you are not absolutely clear about what you offer and the genuine opportunities that are available, you will need to do some soul searching first.

Let me give you an example. I was running a workshop on 'How to promote your website free of charge.' One woman was travelling around the world and wanted to start a travel blog. I asked her, why? She couldn't answer. She didn't know if she wanted to make money out of it (difficult in this crowded space - you may be old enough to remember 'slide nights' when friends and family would gather in the main room of the house, turn off the lights and look at slides on a portable screen, usually images of the person's last holiday - most people would become restless within five minutes). I suggested it might be best to create the website as a hobby rather than a business in the initial stages.

Another person in the same class loved gardening. He lived in a nearby local suburb and had decided that he wanted to grow plants. But he hadn't decided which plants (indoor or outdoor), who to sell them to (consumers or businesses) and where to (from his home or all over the city).

By asking a few quick questions, we quickly determined that he would like to offer indoor plants to local businesses within a 10 kilometer radius and that he would deliver them to the premises. Now we had a niche business idea that we could market effectively. More importantly, the narrowing of his niche was in alignment with his personal ability and market demand and I could easily demonstrate how he could market this business hyper locally.

Action 1: *Define your niche business idea based on a realistic assessment of market demand and personal ability. If there is no existing or future demand, there is no business opportunity*

1.1 Marketing, Selling And Networking

Marketing hyper locally can be good for saving time, money, energy and your community. It can also be more environmentally friendly and sustainable. It is not something to fear. I do understand that a lot of people just want to do what they love - they don't want to do marketing, selling or even networking.

The irony is that we have all been marketing, selling and networking since we were born. We have managed to collect family, friends and acquaintances. In our working life, we have collected colleagues, mentors and friends. In business, we network locally, nationally and internationally.

If we have a 'normal' job, then someone else has had to sell something to generate the income to be able to pay us. Even if the role is an 'essential service,' the right marketing needs to be done so that the service funding can be maintained. Our networks are now our 'net worth' as job security has virtually vanished.

So rather than fear the demands of marketing, selling and networking, especially if they are tasks that you prefer to outsource, try re-framing your perception of the tasks involved and as you read through this book, choose the options that are most aligned with your values. Some will be much more appealing than others.

However, remember that success usually involves being willing to do things that are just slightly outside of your comfort zone. I defy anyone to live their life without ever completing a task they don't like. What is important is making sure that around 80% of your time is spent aligned with your values. That leaves 20% for the necessary items. Of course, if you adopt a flexible approach to how you see the 20% of necessary tasks, you can still gain 100% contentment.

Notice that I didn't say happiness. Happiness can be a trap - because we can automatically assume that if we are not happy, things are bad. For me, contentment is about enjoying the journey, understanding that there will be a few bumps on the road, but regardless, I will recover and continue travelling until my time on the journey ends.

Action 2: *Marketing, selling and networking are part of being in business. Accept that 20% of your time will be spent doing tasks that are either just outside of your comfort zone or necessary rather than fun. Aim for contentment rather than happiness*

1.2 Location Attachment And Choice

I often tell people that I am a Victorian, Australian, from South Australia and thanks to my education and technology, I am a citizen of the world.

The same applies to you. Whether you have lived in one location or many. I know that in many indigenous cultures, the place where you are born is a very strong influence on who you are as a person and the pull is sometimes so strong that even decades later, people are drawn to a particular location. Some indigenous cultures also insist that when you die, you must be buried where you were born.

I have experienced the feeling of attachment to a place on several occasions. As a child, when I was holidaying on Kangaroo Island (colloquially known as KI), I always wanted to be the person saying farewell rather than be the person who was leaving - I put this experience down to having my father's DNA as he spent most of his formative years on KI. Many years later when my daughter visited for the first time, she said that she felt she had just come home.

Years later after living in Melbourne, I went on a trip back to my hometown of Adelaide and whilst I was there, I felt very disoriented. When I got back to

Melbourne, I felt that the 'gravity' was back to normal and I was home. More recently I received a message from a colleague who has been living in China and Brisbane, Queensland, Australia for several years now (regularly commuting between both countries) and he made the comment that whenever he is on the plane travelling to the other location, he always feels as if he is 'going home.'

Some regional communities have very strong feelings about whether or not someone is a 'local.' My grandfather was not born in the country and yet despite living in the same country town for many decades, he never felt that he was a local.

After extensive experience working with newcomers, I usually say that it takes three years to feel 'normal' in a location and 10 years to feel like a local - but this can vary depending on the your level of cultural adaptability and the nature of the community that you have joined.

Some communities still insist that unless you were born there, you will never be a local. I would like to think that we will eventually understand that whilst you are living in a location, you are a local, especially if you are willing to respect, understand and learn about the local customs and traditions.

I had a rather overwhelming experience when I moved to Melbourne. When I was in Adelaide and I went out and about, I would usually always see someone I knew or recognized and we would always say hello to each other. When I arrived in Melbourne, I started work and I would walk around the city at lunch time and it felt very strange.

I felt as though everyone was staring at me and they were all wearing black (it is still a bit of a trend to wear black in Melbourne). One day, to my surprise and delight, I saw someone I recognized. I smiled and he smiled back - I was ecstatic. Then it took me nearly three days of careful thinking to try and remember who he was. As it turns out, he was an actor off television! So I didn't really know him at all, but I was so desperate to see someone I recognized to feel normal in my new location that I simply searched for any face that was familiar.

To help newcomers, I suggest that they make friends as quickly as possible. This is quite easy. It is as simple as visiting the same shop most days and saying hello to the staff on each visit - the staff will eventually ask for a name and be more friendly. Once the first friend is found, all of the others will appear.

When I visited Sydney in my teenage years, I sat on a park bench near a busy street for about an hour one day and during that time, I saw many of the same people walk past multiple times. I have even read stories about how internet dating has helped introduce single people who live in the same street! It is not the size of the community that makes a difference, it is your approach to meeting the people in the community that makes a difference.

Sadly I have also met people who have lived in multiple locations across the world and they have felt that they don't belong anywhere. They often feel as if a little piece of them is 'left' in all of these places and to overcome this sensation of not belonging and settling in just one location, they usually just pack up and move on to the next location. Whenever I hear their stories, I feel an awful sense of sadness as I cannot imagine what it is like to feel as if you do not belong anywhere.

Ultimately, where you are living now is based on many factors. It could be by choice or circumstance. It may be desirable or undesirable. You may be longing to move elsewhere or dreaming of where you will go next. Regardless, the principles you learn in this book are portable across locations and communities around the world.

However, I do not know how every community operates and there may be some local customs that will find the suggestions here inappropriate. So if you are uncertain as to how some techniques will be perceived in your present location, seek opinions from at least three other local people who are qualified to give appropriate unbiased advice.

It could be that the principle listed here can simply be adjusted slightly - or perhaps implemented in a different way. If in doubt, I usually always say don't try it - or battle test it with a small sample before implementing the concept more broadly.

If you are having difficulty accepting the reasons for living in your current location, this will come across to the other locals. Subconscious motives are extremely difficult to hide. If you continually say you are an outsider, people will be more likely to treat you as an outsider. If you say that you are willing to learn and adapt, people are usually willing to teach you and forgive any mistakes you make (provided you are willing to apologize).

Regardless of how you have arrived in your location, why you came or how long you are going to stay, I encourage you to make the most of the opportunities in front of you. It is never too late to learn and adapt. That said, if you really do want to move on in two years time, please don't broadcast that information right now as most people will try to protect themselves from a future loss. If you are asked how long you are planning to live there, say, "I don't know."

Action 3: *Regardless of the reasons why you are in your current location, do your best to learn and adapt to the norms of the local community. Understand that it is normal to take some time to feel like a local, but there are many ways to connect with locals and make new friends*

1.3 Defining Hyper Local Marketing

I originally came up with the concept of 'Hyper Local Marketing' after attending an event where it was identified that the only printed newspapers that were either surviving or growing were those with hyper local content. It seems that many people who live in a local area like to know what other people are doing in the local area. A lot of movies and television programs have featured 'nosy neighbors' peeking over the fence to see what is going on next door.

One day I checked out the term on Google and I found that the term 'hyper local marketing' had already been defined in marketing circles.

Here is my definition for the purposes of this book.

Hyper local marketing is marketing that is designed to reach a defined area - that could be a geographical radius from a central point or a defined group of people connected by context, geolocation or time.

In my mind, in a city location, hyper local marketing would probably include a radius anywhere within 10 kilometers of a central point. In a regional location, it could be a defined region within a 100 kilometer boundary on the longest side. In digital marketing, it could target people currently in a particular geolocation tracked by their mobile device (for example, people attending a concert).

For a defined group of people, it could include any community that is connected via one database or purpose. This could include all members of a professional association or club, everyone within an organization (even if it is a worldwide organization) or anyone with a shared interest in a particular topic.

It can also include people who are currently completing a particular activity or are in a particular situation. For example, it could target everyone who visits a particular store or who buys particular products or services or is part of an upcoming celebration. We have seen plenty of enterprises that have capitalized on the loyalty of same store purchases, timed promotions (like home delivered take away on a Friday night) or Mother's and Father's Day special occasions.

Before our societies were mobile, the most popular form of marketing was always hyper local marketing (it just wasn't called hyper local marketing). There was no alternative. Now, with the advent of the internet, social media, mobile devices and advanced advertising systems, there are many ways to target a hyper local audience.

The main benefit of adding in the word 'hyper' local rather than just 'local' marketing is that it is designed to reach a very specific audience. As a business decision maker, you need to be able to define your target audience and the clearer you are about your ideal client, how they can be reached and how you can serve them effectively, the closer you are to success.

Some people associate the word 'hyper' with 'hyperactive.' I do not want to encourage this type of approach! I have seen a lot of businesses crash and burn because they were hyperactive in the beginning and they simply could not sustain the effort or cope with the demand. I have always believed in growing a business enterprise organically, at least for the first part - that way you have a greater vested interest in making it work - you cannot blame someone else if it doesn't work out!

I should also add that I am going to assume that you possibly have a zero budget for purchasing above the line advertising, expensive sponsorships or hiring a marketing and public relations expert. You may also not be willing to give up control of how things are run in your business if you are in the early setup stages. So wherever possible, I will make recommendations that most secondary school educated people could implement.

Let me state up front that this book will share everything I know at this point in time. I am not holding back any information for my next book (I work especially hard to make sure that each book I write has brand new content that has not been recycled from a previous book). You can check out all of my books at anytime at http://120ways.com and all of my publications at http://sueellson.com

That said, we also know that creating an 'evergreen' book is tricky nowadays - so I will make every effort to provide the best tips and techniques that I believe will stand the test of time. The way that the tips and techniques are completed is very likely to change, so please don't get hung up on perfection - understand why I am sharing these suggestions so that you can implement them in a way that is congruent with your values, your target audience and your current context.

Finally, be willing to constantly re-learn and un-learn what you already know. I have noticed over the years that a huge range of trends in business have come and gone, but the simple concepts of creating assets, reducing liabilities, maintaining cash flow, planning, measuring and constantly learning and improving have never changed. The way we do it has changed, but the principles have not changed.

Ultimately I believe that most people want to be in business because they believe it will be fun, it fits with their values, they are seeking a higher quality of life or they want to try something new.

I truly believe that it is possible for most people to create a sustainable small business. As the world of work changes and more jobs will be completed with some form of technology, I would like to think that you can also apply the principles in this book to a job role, a social enterprise, not for profit initiatives and community development.

Regardless of what happens in the future in the world of work, most people will still want to do something every day, so even if you are not generating an income, you can make a positive difference to your community (for example, you could apply all of these tips and suggestions to your local sporting club)!

Action 4: *Hyper local marketing is marketing that is designed to reach a defined area - that could be a geographical radius from a central point or a defined group of people connected by context, geolocation or time. Now is the time to define your target audience*

1.4 The Benefits Of Hyper Local Marketing

Globalization has created an enormous range of opportunities for consumers and businesses. Economies of scale have made products that were once considered a luxury accessible to average wage earners.

However, mass production and distribution has its own flaws - too many travel miles, non-tailored services and decreased competition to name just a few.

On the other hand, hyper local marketing provides a range of benefits. It can:

- be more sustainable

- be environmentally friendly

- help people feel more connected to their community

- save time

- save money (fuel, transport, storage, parking)

- support local people (not just corporate organizations)

- develop your community

- encourage smiling – because your life is just so much simpler (even if it costs a few dollars more, your sanity will be restored – who knows, you might even enjoy riding your bike to a meeting and the extra walking will shed a few kilograms!)

As a service based business without any family living close by, I have found that connecting with my local business community has helped me feel as if I am a valued member of my community. I have been able to share my knowledge, skills and networks and have passed on many gigs to other locals.

Likewise, I have received many referrals (and I have always personally thanked each person who has given me a referral). These opportunities would never have happened if I did not create a hyper local marketing strategy.

The value of quality relationships cannot be underestimated. Walking into a discount store or buying something online simply doesn't have the same sensation as sourcing products and services through a local provider and knowing that you have helped support their family.

This extends even further as ultimately, you can target the people that you know, like and trust (not just the ones that know, like and trust you). Many new business owners start out thinking that they can sell their products or services to everyone.

As time goes by and the business develops and adjusts to the market conditions, successful entrepreneurs will ultimately make decisions about the types of people that are most interested in purchasing their products and services. Working with these clients and customers creates enormous harmony and ultimately, the entrepreneur will learn how to turn away the 'maybe' clients and customers or offer them an alternative.

For example, I receive enquiries from all over the world and I can tell by the nature of the correspondence that the person expects to receive free assistance and support. So I have created a huge amount of content that is freely accessible on my website at http://sueellson.com and I select specific links for their purpose and reply with the details. If they are genuinely interested in professional paid assistance, they respond in their own time. I can still serve them but not lose too much of my own time.

I have also attracted a second tier of 'wrong' clients and I have learnt how to verify their fit for my business by going through a selection process and politely referring them to someone else if they don't fit with what I offer. Interestingly, the more 'wrong' clients I decline, the more 'right' clients appear. However, this is not an entirely black and white solution. I still look at each situation on its merits. At this point, I just want to encourage you, if you have a service rather than a product, over time, become selective about who you serve.

As another example, I complete quite a lot of work that is outside of the normal principles of business and classify it as paid marketing. For example, I teach at a much lower rate than my professional consulting rate - but this regularly leads to paying clients and I get to enjoy my interest in training and sharing knowledge! This also means that I must keep myself up to date with current technology and new information on my teaching topics - so I have created another process to maintain my commitment to constantly learning and growing.

By sharing these examples, you can start to think about the systems and processes you can implement to keep you and your business fresh and moving forward. The enterprises that succeed are the ones that constantly adapt, persevere, learn and improve. If you need an analogy, think of the local cafe that offers exactly the same food and drinks without ever changing. Would you visit them as frequently as the one that has some well-loved staples and a few new items every so often?

At the end of the day, wherever possible, I always 'shop local.' I don't think about saving $5 on an item by going to a discount store further away. I believe that by spending local I will be able to continue buying local - and be able to support my local community. There is a little quote that I have seen that helps reinforce this idea - and I encourage you to spend locally too!

When you buy from a small mom and pop business, you are not helping a CEO buy a third vacation home. You are helping a little girl get dance lessons, a little boy get his team jersey, a mom or dad put food on the table, a family pay a mortgage, or a student pay for college. Thank you for supporting small businesses! - Unknown

---

Action 5: *There are many benefits to creating a hyper local marketing strategy. Write down the three main reasons that will help you and your business in the future, based on your values*

_____

_____

_____

2. Personal Context

Before you can really move forward with new information, you need to understand a little bit more about where you have come from. This section provides you with an opportunity to understand a little bit more about yourself and how you can really maximize the tips and techniques in this book. We will consider you, your business and the key stakeholders.

Let's begin.

2.1 Self Evaluation

Have you ever received any form of business or life coaching in the past? Have you noticed that the main tool they use to help you achieve your goals is to align your mindset with your desired results? For you to change your story to one that will help you get there?

I have been given the title of 'skills coach' by a very experienced coach and I believe that this is a good description of how I personally help each of my clients. I focus on teaching people new skills - but in the process, I incorporate a number of specific coaching techniques to help them learn.

I encourage you to find someone you can work with so that you can do something similar or you could even go through the following steps on your own and coach yourself:

- create a safe environment so you can share your story openly (if you are on your own, talk to yourself and use the voice recorder facility on your phone to say what you think without correcting yourself or thinking about what you are saying)

- listen extremely carefully to what you have said and identify any false beliefs (replay the recording and listen for the false beliefs and write them down - once completed, you can delete the voice recording or even listen to it again in six months time)

- discuss the false beliefs and remember that no time is ever wasted (look at your written list and ask yourself, are these all absolutely true or just 'true from my perspective.' Look for the lessons in each one)

- identify any of your known 'blockages' (if these are a little deeper and more significant, you may need to seek some professional support)

- acknowledge your past achievements (write them out and give yourself a big pat on the back)

- identify your natural strengths and use these when learning (decide if you learn best by watching, reading, doing or listening)

- create a list, mind map or chart of what needs to be done in the short, medium and long term

- start with some steps that are manageable and complete them quickly

- identify some slightly more difficult steps and complete them soon (remember success is usually achieved just outside of your comfort zone - start with three that you can complete relatively quickly)

- review your list and plan your process with target dates included

- find an accountability partner, mentor, coach or skills coach to help you complete the various tasks

- record all of your achievements (even the small ones)

- reflect on your progress, modify appropriately and continue

During this process, reflect on the marketing components that you have in mind for both you and your business. Yes, I did say YOU as you are the face of your business - and I realize that this is difficult news for a typical introvert (who usually gets their energy by spending some quiet time on their own rather than an extrovert who usually gains their energy by spending time with other people).

Ultimately what I am trying to encourage you to do here is to really start thinking about some of the things that you need to do in your business to start marketing in a new ways. This exercise is something that you may wish to do twice, both right now and after reading the book - but don't forget to do it if you postpone it until later.

Any improvement in your business will require you to take action of some sort. You may like to make notes as you read this book!

Action 6: *Identify what has happened up until this point with you and your business and identify any false beliefs and personal blockages. Acknowledge your past achievements. Focus on using your strengths to learn new skills and complete some actions now, soon and later. Review, reflect and record what needs to be done and find someone else to keep you accountable for taking action*

2.2 Self Management

Have you often found yourself saying, I know how to help others and I can tell them what to do, but I can't do what I want to do myself?

Do you find that your level of motivation comes and goes? Are your motivation levels influenced by other factors? Do you sometimes say to yourself, if only...?

I have already mentioned that perseverance is a very important part of being in business. However, I want to remind you not to beat yourself up every time something doesn't work out quite right. We all make mistakes.

Mistakes are often a timely reminder or a little red flag that reminds us that we need to constantly lift our game. Mistakes help us learn lessons and if we bypass a small mistake, we often find a bigger mistake will appear or the same mistake will appear again.

If I make a mistake, I always own up to it and I apologize as soon as possible (even if it is difficult or I wasn't totally in the wrong) and I try and make amends. It is important to be gracious and resilient and not let big or small mistakes destroy your ability to keep going (although it is perfectly okay to take a little time out to 'lick your wounds').

To manage yourself more effectively, I am going to remind you of the most obvious self management principles that are required for business success.

- eat healthy food, drink water, exercise regularly and make sure you get enough rest

- create a manageable routine that can be flexible and source help if you need it

- build in systems and processes to overcome your weaknesses

- host regular celebrations to acknowledge your achievements (being in business can be very lonely)

- implement reliable measurements of performance, reflect regularly and follow up with action

- cultivate a burning desire to keep learning, growing and improving - even by just 1%, on a regular basis

- align your values and sense of purpose with achieving your goals - your why will pull you towards your results, a push requires willpower and that can fade

- develop resilience in the face of adversity - regardless of how the challenge occurs or what it takes to overcome it - some of my biggest challenges have generated the best rewards (both personally and professionally)

- the ability to see each new day as a new opportunity, but also the willingness to let some things go when they have reached their expiry date (but make sure you have evaluated this logically - some people give up right before they could have achieved success, others push well past the point of reality)

In a job, someone else has the ultimate responsibility for making sure there is enough money in the business to pay your wage. When you are in your own business, the buck stops with you. So ultimately, you have to be able to manage yourself.

In your own business, you will find that on many occasions you will not have someone instantly available to provide assistance and you may have to learn how to do many more tasks on your own (my friend in IT told me that 'Google is my friend' and I have used Google many times to find a solution for my IT issues).

I have found that the biggest challenge for me is the lack of genuine feedback and discussion. Like many women, when I discuss a situation, I usually resolve the issue. When there is no-one to talk to on a daily basis (that you trust), how will you resolve your challenges? How will you receive recognition for your efforts? How will you maintain your sense of self worth?

What are your challenges likely to be? Will you be able to adjust to a new working routine or a different income? Will you get out of bed in the morning when there isn't a defined start time? Will you be able to tolerate multiple 'bosses' (also known as customers, clients and staff) rather than just one boss? Are you ready to be completely accountable for all of your actions?

Don't panic if you are unsure about any of these challenges. Most business owners who choose to go into business overcome these challenges very quickly - or they find people, systems and processes that will help them. All I want to do at this point is just remind you to seek assistance if you need it.

Here is another quick story from my past. My first full time job was working in a major well-known bank. When I met people for the first time and they asked me where I worked, I could easily tell them and then the conversation would quickly move on (by the way, I still find this to be a rude question because not everyone has a job and asking this question to someone who is unemployed can be very distressing - I usually ask people what keeps them busy during the day).

When I started working on my own and mentioned the name of my business, I could see their eyes glaze over in less than a second. I felt like I had lost my value overnight. I remember another story of a woman who held a very high position in local government, Deputy Lord Mayor, and when she lost an election, she simply couldn't get out of bed in the morning. Many people find that a job helps provide a part of their identity and purpose so when they go into business, they often feel a little bit lost and confused.

This process was explained to me when I interviewed a very successful relocation consultant. She said that in your home country, the people around you provide a personal mirror, reflecting your own image back to you. When you move to another country, this mirror disappears and your sense of identity vanishes. When you go to the hairdresser for the first time in a new location, you will probably look in the mirror and have to make a choice. Will you choose the same hairstyle again or will you choose a different one for your new location. How will you create a new circle of friends as a personal mirror?

So when you are in your own business, you need to create your own identity and be able to describe what you do to the people that you meet. Eventually, it becomes quick and easy and your passion and belief will mean that their eyes will not glaze over as soon as you talk about something they may recognize at all.

That said, I have found that using some familiar language in the description of my business helps enormously. A few years ago, I was offering a wide range of different consulting services and the work simply wasn't coming in. So I looked at the situation and thought, out of all of the things that I do, which particular component combined most of my skills effectively and included a word that most people already knew?

That's when I chose to call myself an 'Independent LinkedIn Specialist.' By working with LinkedIn, I can combine my training, marketing, business, information technology, recruitment, human resources and general knowledge skills through the one vehicle. Most professionals (my ideal clients) already knew about LinkedIn.

That enabled people to 'remember' what I did and then they started sending me referrals (even though they could have probably used my services themselves!) When people meet me and realize that I can help them with a range of other consulting services, I collect even more work - so it didn't stop me from getting any work, it actually gave me more work.

To sum up, self management is critical to business success and it is also an important component of personal branding and this will be discussed in more detail later.

Action 7: *Whether you are new to your own business or you have been running your business for some time, you need to be able to manage yourself and source people, systems and processes to overcome your challenges. Make sure you create your own personal identity within and with the people around you. Describing your value is part of your personal branding*

2.3 Management And Leadership

In your own business, there will be times when you manage others (task driven) and lead others (vision driven). They are distinctly different skill sets and many former specialists who end up in a management or leadership position often find the transition difficult, particularly if they haven't received any training.

Let's start by askingan important question. Are you in business or are you self employed?

I used to always think that I was in business, but then it was put to me that if I cannot go away and leave the business to someone else to run, I am really only self employed. To be honest, I am actually happy to be self employed. I am not someone who can easily give away control or delegate tasks to others when I don't believe that they will complete the tasks adequately. I also don't want to go down the path of having an office, multiple staff to support, more complex systems etc - but this is entirely my personal choice. I still use business principles in everything that I do.

You on the other hand may love the idea of having a team of employees either located in one spot or connected remotely. Your business may require you to have staff because you cannot do everything at once (for example, a 100 seat a la carte restaurant cannot be staffed by one person).

Whether you are self employed or in business, I would like to remind you of some important management and leadership principles that are required for business success.

- managers and leaders must say thank you regularly

- managers and leaders need to listen regularly and respond appropriately

- managers and leaders that can work with a diverse range of people have been proven to generate better results (smiling regularly helps too as that crosses every cultural background)

- managers and leaders need to set a good example

- managers and leaders need to be open to effective communication and be able to provide useful feedback

- managers and leaders need to understand the needs of all stakeholders and set realistic expectations and where possible, under promise and over deliver every so often (for example, promise to deliver a result by Friday but deliver it two days earlier)

- managers and leaders need to adequately recognise and reward achievement

- managers and leaders need to be able to admit mistakes and apologize and make amends

- managers and leaders need to have their own sources of support available at all times

Whilst I have been referring to the whole business with these principles, similar concepts apply to your marketing efforts. Although you may choose to outsource some of the marketing tasks, you will still need to make the final decisions on what will or will not be implemented, you will need to monitor the performance and make decisions about what to continue or change in the future.

In my view, successful managers and leaders do not try to be an expert on everything. However, they do make a conscious effort to understand the fundamentals and they are willing to ask questions for clarification. Most successful decision makers know how to assess results - and not just short term gains but long term results.

Action 8: *Managers are task driven and Leaders are vision driven. As the business owner, decide whether you will be self employed or in business. Remember that managers and leaders need to be able to supervise people, processes and performance. Make sure you have enough knowledge to make effective decisions for long term results*

2.4 Succession Planning And Exit Strategy

Several years ago, I worked with a CEO who sold off a large part of the business and this looked fantastic on the very first Balance Sheet after the transaction occurred. Unfortunately, this decision also ruined the revenue generation potential of the organization and it collapsed soon after. Thousands of people lost their jobs.

Another executive team acquired a profit making startup enterprise and used its profits to balance out the losses of another part of the business. Once the loss was absorbed, the startup enterprise was wound up. The person who had created this startup enterprise had invested a huge amount of his time, money and dedication and he took several years to recover from losing his enterprise to 'a balance sheet transaction.'

One of my longest clients has decided that when she dies, so will her business. This is a great shame as she has produced a huge amount of useful evergreen content that could continue to help many people if it remained published. I am trying to help her create an independent income stream from her products so that it can be sold as a going concern or provide a new income stream for her beneficiaries.

As the manager or leader for your business, you need to make a decision as to what will ultimately happen to your business when you are no longer a part of the business. This will also determine what marketing strategies you will ultimately implement. For example, if the business is heavily dependent on your expertise, there could be more marketing around your skills rather than the name of the business.

Let's look at the most common options for transferring a business:

- **Acquisition** - another person or enterprise pays money to purchase your business. This could be a direct sale to a friendly purchaser (often negotiated through a business broker), a special offer received from an interested party that believes your enterprise would add value to theirs (very common with smaller specialist practices) or a negotiated takeover (for example with a business partner)

- **Merger** - another business merges with yours and the new enterprise continues in either the same name or a different name

- **Liquidation** - the business is closed and ceases to trade. It may be possible to sell some of the assets of the business but the business is not acquired as such. Any outstanding creditors must be paid

- **Become a public company** - where you have an Initial Public Offering (IPO) and are ultimately listed on the stock exchange. This is more common with enterprises that have received some form of venture capital or investor support

- **Managed enterprise** - where you set up a legal structure where you or your family trust is a part of the business but the day to day operations are conducted by a paid leader. You may still be called on as a Non Executive Director

As you can imagine, the way you market the business will be very different depending on which exit strategy you have chosen. Many business owners don't think about these options until a crisis occurs and this can make it very difficult to prepare the business for the best option.

Serial entrepreneurs know that before they even start a business, they will be planning their exit strategy. It is never too late to start this important work. If you are ultimately planning to create an income producing asset that will either be acquired, merged, listed or managed, you need to have the business ready for the takeover with systems and processes functioning without your direct involvement.

An important part of modern business development is your digital asset strategy and I will be incorporating a lot of tips and techniques to develop your digital assets in this book.

Action 9: *Consider which succession planning or exit strategy you will use when you are no longer a part of your business and consider this objective when selecting your marketing strategies*

2.5 Personal Principles

I have noticed that some business owners are still stuck in the past and still believe that:

- every action must lead to a return on investment

- secrecy is more important than sharing

- profit is more important than value

- isolation is more important than collaboration

In my view, the world has CHANGED. As business owners, we all need to understand that the widespread availability of information has democratized many aspects of the business world.

I am very grateful that more people can publish and share their views and that the majority of the younger generation in the Western world have benefited from significant advances in education.

There has also been a significant shift in the collective moral compass. In Australia, our culture has traditionally operated on the concept of every individual having both rights and responsibilities - every person is entitled to a certain standard of living but they are also responsible for making a contribution to their community (many Australians participate in voluntary work on a regular basis).

When I share all of my intellectual property both online and in print, the only fear that I have is that the information will be used for an individual person's personal advantage and not for the benefit of their community and our amazing planet.

For people who have had a difficult past and very little personal security, I can understand that they may be tempted in the future to accumulate material wealth and a luxury lifestyle. However, this comes at a price and our planet cannot sustain a relentless mass pursuit in this popular culture direction.

Just for a moment, I would like you to have a serious look at what you really need versus what you currently want. In my opinion, many people have been seduced by advertising and the media to find meaning and purpose through possessions - but as many people have said before, possessions have the ability to possess you - they will not necessarily create a contented life.

When a crisis occurs in a person's life, most people will suddenly realize that they want to be with their family and friends or be living according to their highest values. Take a short moment to write down the three things that are most important to you in your life right now and how much of your week is spent doing those things (there are 168 hours in a week and if you spend 10 hours a day sleeping and eating, you are left with 98 hours per week).

1. _____ ____ hour/s per week

2. _____ ____ hour/s per week

3. _____ ____ hour/s per week

If your total number of hours for your highest value items is less than 49 hours, you may not be living according to your highest values. There are certain times in your life when your personal circumstances dictate that you must spend more time at work, or caring for family members or recovering from an illness or something else that is not in alignment with your highest values.

Ultimately though, to live a contented life, I believe that you need to be spending up to 80% of your time in alignment with your highest values. If your family is important to you, it is tempting to think that providing an income is the best way to support them - but I would disagree. I believe that both time and money are important to support a family (and most young children would rather play with their parents than play on their own with a shiny new toy - and this is also a great opportunity for you to have some fun).

If you find yourself trapped in a situation where you are not living according to your highest values, it is time to start making small changes. Don't beat yourself up over past mistakes, simply start doing more things that are in alignment with your values. You could even start by making your current experiences just 1% better. You could also look at why you are doing it and see the bigger picture rather than the regular annoyances.

You can plan an exit strategy, even if it takes six months for you to leave or accept the situation and prepare for some form of transition. You can also put some more things into your life that are aligned with your values. Have you always wanted to sing, or play music, dance, participate in sport, draw, paint, explore the world?

There are many ways to gain access to these opportunities on an exchange basis (without payment) so don't assume that you need to produce a huge income to start moving in new directions. Start today by doing just one thing different - like getting into bed from the other side or changing what you eat for breakfast. Realize that you can make simple changes to your life and lots of little changes will ultimately lead to big changes.

Action 10: *Review how you spend your time each week and see if the majority of your time is aligned with your highest values. If it isn't, start making small changes today as a lot of little changes will ultimately lead to big changes*

2.6 Community And Business Congruency

You may already be part way along the path to complete personal and community congruency. Where you look at every situation according to your highest values and the common good. Where your intention is always to provide service and value to your fellow man and the planet. Where you complete actions that will leave the world a slightly better place thanks to your contribution.

I am always inspired and excited when I meet people who are living according to their purpose. When I hear a talented musician that can pursue his passion because he is fairly paid for his performance. When an emergency services person can provide genuine care in a crisis and still receive professional support if they are having difficulty coping with witnessing so much trauma. When a person who is passionate about the environment or animals can show me ways to preserve these amazing wonders for future generations.

Please take a moment right now to write down the three highest values you would like to live by within the next six months and how much of your time will be spent doing each of them every week. If there is only time in your life for one of your values to be completed for one hour per week, that is not an issue, so long as it is on your list and you make at least some time available.

1. _____ ____ hour/s per week

2. _____ ____ hour/s per week

3. _____ ____ hour/s per week

Now that we know what you will be doing, let's take a moment to look at your business. If you have decided to consider hyper local marketing for your business, you will need to be thinking about your community as well as your business. You will need to be consistent and congruent to generate trust, respect and credibility.

Let's take a moment to record how you are supporting your local community right now. Are you attending local events? Are you volunteering for a local group? Are you shopping locally? Do you walk or ride a bike rather than drive? Do you recycle most of your waste? Do you save power by turning off unnecessary heating, cooling or lighting? Do you provide hospitality to family and friends?

Write down at least three things that you are doing to support your local community right now:

1. _____

2. _____

3. _____

Now I would like you to think about three things that you have seen other people do in your community that you admire or respect, even if it is not something that you would normally do either now or in the future:

1. _____

2. _____

3. _____

What I am trying to do here is to increase your awareness about what is already happening around you. It will give you clues as to how you can incorporate your skills, talents and abilities into your local community.

You do not need to take on everything yourself - but you do have unique gifts that you can share and what is easy for you could be very difficult for someone else. When you share your gifts, you enable others to share their gifts. This is what helps create a cohesive and supportive community.

Whilst this concept is fresh in your mind, please write down three things that you could offer to your community in the future. Please make sure that they are realistic and manageable options based on your values and skills rather than just what you think you should do based on someone else's opinion:

1. _____

2. _____

3. _____

Fantastic and well done. I will not keep you accountable to these - but I sincerely hope that you will be able to implement at least one of these options in the next six months.

Action 11: *Review how other people currently contribute to your community and choose ways that you can contribute in the future based on your skills, talents and abilities. Make realistic and manageable choices for implementation within the next six months*

2.7 Business Ethics And Self Regulation

In my university degree I studied a subject called 'Business Ethics.' It opened my eyes to a completely different way of seeing the world and how to make decisions.

Personally, I live with an optimistic faith that despite various challenges, if I behave ethically at all times, the greater good can be served (even if that means that I am worse off in that moment). It has created a very simple framework for me to make decisions. It has been hard sometimes admitting my mistakes and missing out on a quick win, but fortunately for me, it has always led to more growth and opportunity.

However, I am well aware that many people are still living with self interest as their highest value, so I am a firm believer in regulation that enforces the common good.

For example, just 100 years ago, people with disabilities were kept out of sight. Today they have a chance to live, work and contribute independently thanks to successive changes in legislation.

I do understand that market forces can create competition and that this can be healthy within a managed system (for example, government regulation that prevents monopolization). What I cannot accept is any form of exploitation - of individuals or communities.

What I would like to see more of is self regulation - where each individual gratefully acknowledges what they already have and is willing to support their community and the environment throughout their life.

There is enough for all of us if we are willing to share and live cooperatively. There is even a movement called Cooperativism and I am really excited by this business model as in my view, it combines the best of the old with the new.

Cooperativism has several basic principles. Firstly, local cooperatives are established and they are jointly-owned and democratically-controlled (formal legal agreements ensure that everyone understands the management process). They have systemized the values of self-help, self-responsibility, equality, equity, democracy, and solidarity. People, not profit, are at the center of a cooperative's economic activity. Profits are essentially recycled into the community group to ensure that the entire group benefits rather than an individual.

I like to think of Cooperativism as a business model that provides a 'hand up' philosophy rather than a 'hand out' approach to business development.

In the recent past, various governments have provided grants to kick start new programs and initiatives. However, I see this model as an extension of welfare rather than a tool for sustainable economic and community development.

I have been running a social enterprise since 2001 and I have found various ways to maintain its existence without hand outs. It has been empowering to me and the people I have served to be able to do this in a sustainable fashion for over 15 years.

Just as policy makers need to implement sustainable programs for the less fortunate, so too do you as a business owner need to create a sustainable enterprise. However, there is no need to believe that you must do it all on your own. There is help, guidance and assistance available to you if you simply investigate a little further.

For example, I asked a successful businessman who told me that he was able to 'retire at the age of 28' whether or not he had ever had a mentor or adviser. He initially said 'no.' Then he remembered that a senior executive would regularly meet with him just for a chat and looking back, he can now see that this man had been guiding him to success.

So whether you choose a person, a process or a business model to build your enterprise, understand that there is help available, that there are tried and true techniques that you can implement and that there is no need for you to do it all on your own or 'reinvent the wheel.'

Ultimately, I encourage you to adopt an ethical approach to both your personal and business life with the ultimate goal of living a self regulated life based on ethical principles.

Action 12: *Understand that to be a successful business owner, you need to abide by ethical principles in both your personal and business life. On your business journey, you can source assistance from people, processes and business models. Ultimately, your goal is to self regulate your actions for the benefit of your community and the planet*

2.8 Staffing And Outsourcing

Whether you are self employed or running a business with some form of staffing or outsourcing, there will be a time when you need to make the next big leap.

If you are at the point where you are thinking about bringing in your very first type of support, I encourage you to consider the least risky option first.

Although I have managed staff in my professional career and recruited many people for various roles, when it was time for me to hire my first contractor, I had to think very carefully about what would work for me and my business.

With the hyper local philosophy in mind, I chose to hire someone who lived locally (my number one priority). As the role was for only a few hours here and there, I wanted to make sure that the person could walk to my office within 30 minutes. I also started with a short term agreement (the first 10 hours were at a slightly lower rate so that we could both assess whether it would work for both of us as a significant portion of this time was spent training my new recruit).

Our business relationship developed and the hours increased over the next year. Unfortunately my new recruit moved to a new home that involved up to an hour of public transport travel time and I noticed a significant drop in her productivity and performance. It was okay as my business was moving in a different direction so we parted ways on friendly terms.

I then experimented with a virtual assistant from another country at a much lower hourly rate and we connected online. This was helpful in some ways, but for me personally, it simply didn't work. I found it difficult to manage this person remotely as I like working directly with people. There were significant cultural differences and she kindly offered to continue working for free but I couldn't accept her generous offer as I felt it would be exploitative.

Thanks to my ability to learn and manage various IT based solutions, I decided that for me, it would be better to just manage my time a little better and outsource the difficult tasks to local contractors on an hourly basis. I do not waste as much time explaining tasks and managing people when in many cases, I could simply complete the task quickly and easily myself. I also stopped spending time trying to learn things that were too difficult to master quickly.

I am also the type of person who cannot think clearly if too many things are swimming around in my thoughts at the one time. Unlike many women, I don't like multi-tasking!

The end result is that I no longer waste my time trying to work out everything myself. When I find someone in my community with the expertise I need, I bring them in! When the job is finished, we both move on. I have increased my efficiency enormously and I have been able to maintain my focus and keep writing (this is my third book in one year).

I am well aware that I pay a slightly higher hourly rate by employing other local people living close to me in Melbourne, but I also gain more because they understand the local conditions and they often provide excellent suggestions for improvement.

I also have another set of eyes and ears watching out for me and I also source more referrals. So what I lose in terms of dollar spend, I gain in terms of more clients and business opportunities. This point is often over looked by people only interested in measuring dollars spent.

As I have been in recruitment, I am well aware that diversity is a key to business success. I make an effort to choose people who will challenge my current thought processes and will be willing to share their ideas and suggestions. I treat all of my contractors with respect and whenever possible, I also refer work to them. Whilst I cannot guarantee them more billable hours through my business, I can share their talents around the community.

If their work doesn't meet my requirements, I don't continue to work with them, but I always try and give them some extra tips and advice before they leave. This was quite difficult when one of the people was a sister of a friend, but as I am still technically 'self employed,' I simply could not afford to carry the expense of someone who was extremely accurate but incredibly slow. This person needed to upgrade her skills as soon as possible, so I provided her with a range of useful information for progressing further.

What I also like about this model of hyper local recruiting is that the people who love doing what they do get to keep doing it! My IT guy does IT. My original assistant still helps me out when I am exhibiting at expos and she can work with people rather than in front of a computer screen. My tax accountant can keep doing my tax. I can keep control of the quality of my published content (which is extremely important to me). I can source specific advice when I need it and only pay for it when I need it.

Action 13: *Whether you are just starting out in business or you have been in business for a while, you will need to think about your staffing and outsourcing requirements and be able to identify reliable sources of new recruits. If you manage this process effectively, you can also reduce your total costs and source more referrals*

2.9 Effective Hyper Local Recruitment Techniques

You may be wondering - how did I find my staff and contractors? In most cases, it was whilst I was out and about at events.

I set up Camberwell Network http://camberwellnetwork.com in November 2012 and I have been hosting monthly events ever since. Camberwell is a nearby suburb with a good range of shops, businesses, residences and public facilities. Whenever I host the event, I talk to local business owners and always come away with new knowledge, ideas and quite often, referrals.

I also attend the Melbourne SEO Meetup Group http://www.meetup.com/Melbourne-SEO/ on a regular basis (and have done so for more than three years).

I have provided three informative presentations to this group and once again, I have sourced new knowledge, ideas and referrals from group members.

This Meetup Group meets on the other side of town, but it is full of like-minded people who are willing to share what they know. I have developed good business relationships with several group members and referred multiple gigs to them.

So to my earlier point, hyper local can be hyper local in terms of geographic location but it can also be hyper local in terms of context.

The major benefit of participating in these real world groups is that I meet real people in real life. I am able to develop trusted relationships because I go there frequently. I can align myself with people with similar values and diverse experience. I can assess their suitability in a non-threatening environment and measure their performance over time (rather than try and assess someone who is completely unknown in am artificial job interview situation).

There is also an implied requirement that they deliver what they promise. As they are part of a group, they would be well aware that if their performance is good, I will rave about them and encourage other group members to utilize their skills.

If things don't work out, I still maintain my friendliness and professionalism but I do not hire them again. I would never complain about their performance to other group members as that is simply gossip, but their accountability is implied.

I do realize that for some people reading this book, your ability to source the expertise you require from your local area or context may be difficult. For this reason, I would suggest that you still try and use referral techniques or be willing to work with someone who is keen to learn where you both accept some of the risk.

For example, you may have a local school, college or university that has students who are studying a related subject. You could encourage these students to work with you on a solution which will give them relevant practical experience and will give you some professional assistance. They may know enough to be able to work out a solution on the go - with your expert direction. Again, there is no need for you to do everything on your own.

If you already have a number of employees working in your business, I encourage you to do most of your recruitment through their networks. The people who are recruited through existing employees consistently record higher levels of performance and retention. The second option would be to use the methods outlined above.

You could also source some assistance via other local networks. Perhaps there are local groups of recent retirees who would love an opportunity to do a small project on a part time basis. If you don't have the time to go to events and network regularly, make a few phone calls and ask around or delegate this responsibility to someone who is a good networker and has already done the legwork.

If you do receive a referral, make sure that you still undertake your own due diligence and complete the necessary research and assessment processes before making a hiring decision.

One of the best tools I have used is a 'real life example' of what they would be doing in the future and I invite the candidate to complete the task within an agreed time frame. This way I have a reliable sample of their capability.

If you would like to use an online tool, given the nature of my background, I would recommend LinkedIn. To date, this is the largest database of professionals in the world. The key factors in your search query would include:

- keywords around the skills you need

- shared connections (so you can complete effective due diligence)

- relevant experience and achievements (past behavior is a good predictor of future performance)

- overall presentation (is it in alignment with your enterprise?)

I would always recommend a more general Google search and going beyond page one of search results, but these points are a good start.

What I really want to emphasize is that for your business to grow significantly, you will ultimately need more regular assistance through people or systems. In some cases, you may think that you would be better off with a computer based application, but with up to 85% of business still being generated by referral, I would still advocate that real people can make a real difference to your success.

That said, if you do choose an electronic solution, make sure you get it installed and implemented by an expert so you can maximize its value.

To find the right people, you need the right recruitment techniques. If you interview more than three people in person for one position, your selection and assessment processes are probably out of date and you are ultimately wasting your time and the candidate's time (sorry if that sounds harsh, but I really don't like wasting anyone's time and for most people, it takes a lot of emotional energy to perform well in a job interview).

If you need some recruitment advice, please get it! You cannot be an expert in every aspect of your business, but you can manage every aspect of your business.

The best businesses continue to grow and develop over time, in manageable and realistic steps, with a bit of faith, innovation and imagination thrown in! Good recruitment can make the journey more rewarding in every sense.

Action 14: *It is possible to find good staff and contractors via hyper local recruiting based on geographic location or context. Real world groups enable real life assessment and accountability, online tools enable a wider reach and alternative verification methods. Remember that you cannot be an expert in every aspect of your business but you can manage every aspect of your business*

3. Business Context

Most people would assume that we have moved past the industrial age and we are now in the technological age. Digital disruption has already occurred and we are now in the digital era. How does business adjust to such a rapid transformation of choice? How do consumers decide what to purchase? What are the essential ingredients of a sustainable business?

The first thing to consider is demand. Is there a reasonable level of demand for your products or services within the context in which you operate?

If your local market is already saturated or not willing to adopt something new, you are probably taking a huge risk. You may need to re-evaluate how you will move forward and even consider removing some products or services from your current range. If you simply need better marketing to reach willing purchasers, then read on.

Action 15: *Consider the current level of demand within your local context to make a valid risk assessment of your business. If necessary, re-evaluate what is worth keeping in your range of products and services*

3.1 Business Choice

On a regular basis, you will be faced with decisions on what to keep in your range of products and services and what to add or remove. The first priority is of course demand, but a close second is whether or not the business is aligned with your values.

Let's start with a quick look at a family business. There is a bit of a joke that the first generation makes money from the business and the second generation spends it. Have you met someone who is reluctantly running the family business because they felt they 'had to' rather than because they 'wanted to?'

My children have always told me that they don't want to work in my business and I have accepted their choice. Every now and then, I ask for some casual assistance and fortunately, they do help me out. I also know that by watching what I have done over the years, they have acquired many useful skills that they can use in their own career and business life, so I do not feel as if I have lost anything by not having them in the business. I would rather work with someone who wants to be in my business than someone who doesn't want to be. I can still enjoy social time with my children and we often have chats about our different business experiences.

If you are in business because you are driven by a financial reward rather than a core belief, it can be harder to engage with an ideal client. If a person senses you are not passionate about your enterprise, they often sub consciously make a choice to go somewhere else.

For example, a new cafe opened in a quaint little shopping strip close to my home. The decor was not to my taste and the personality of the husband and wife owners who had come from another country was extremely quiet and unassuming. I often wondered about their ongoing viability because although they cooked with passion and flair, their personal demeanor was very reserved.

I decided to visit this cafe for lunch with my two children and my daughter made an unsolicited comment about the personality of the business owners and she made it clear that she did not feel as if the business would survive. Interestingly, during our meal, several older patrons came in and I overheard them say how much they liked it there because it was quiet.

On that day, more than 50% of the chairs were unoccupied. Meanwhile, another cafe that we visited in the same street for lunch on a similar day and time just two weeks prior was fully occupied and everyone was eating and drinking. It is owned and operated by a young father who was previously an employee.

Whenever I visit the second cafe, I have a sense that the owner and staff are motivated to provide an amazing experience. It is a little too noisy for me, so I prefer a third cafe.

The third cafe has excellent coffee - a wonderful benefit of living in Melbourne. It is never too noisy and they have a loyalty card system so every now and then, I enjoy a free coffee. What I like most of all is the friendliness of the staff. They smile, make polite conversation and never rush you even if you are only having coffee.

They don't begrudge providing a free coffee and they don't push me into buying something I don't want, but they always politely ask if there is anything else I would like (and I have splurged every now and then). When I visit this cafe, I feel as if the business is being run by people who are aligned with their highest values and whenever I have a choice between these three cafes, I return to this cafe every time.

However, there are still some other ways that this cafe could improve. It has a fairly small range of savory items on its lunch menu. The business may have chosen to focus on the 'coffee and cake' range - but to increase patronage and turnover, it may choose to adjust the menu in the future as its occupancy usually sits at around 75%.

Interestingly, there are at least six other cafes in the same street. I have been to all of them, but I still prefer my favorite cafe. Sadly, the first cafe in this story closed just one month after I had lunch there with my children.

As I have mentioned earlier, I have been running the social enterprise Newcomers Network since 2001. A few years ago, I participated in a group coaching program and one of the participants was so impressed with what I was trying to achieve, he asked me straight out, how much money do I need to continue to grow and develop?

When someone offers you a 'golden' opportunity like this, it is natural to react and say 'woo-hoo!' Unfortunately, I had to say 'no thanks.'

Whilst financially this would have helped me enormously, the money came from the profits of the pharmaceutical industry. This is an industry that I know very little about but I have heard many people complain about what prescription medicines have done to their health. I do not know what is true or not true (and let me add, I am very grateful for antibiotics that helped me recover from pneumonia several years ago).

But in accordance with my highest values, I didn't want to take the risk. I decided to keep growing organically over time and maintain my independence. I have never regretted this decision.

If you are not sure about whether or not your business is aligned with your highest values, try answering the following questions:

- do you believe that your products or services are helpful and provide value to your customers or clients?

- does your business enable you to grow and develop in positive ways?

- do you enjoy working in your business?

- do you receive some form of feedback that makes your efforts feel worthwhile (compliments, companionship, financial rewards, bonuses)?

- do you reminisce about how much easier it was to have a normal job?

Try not to over think your answers. If you have had a bad week, the last question may make you want to stop your business tomorrow! The reality is that we can never go back to exactly what we had in the past and if you are like me and have been in your own business for several years, it can be very difficult to go back to a 'normal job.'

One larger than life person I met at a networking event told me that he was 'unemployable.' He has successfully created and launched multiple startups so his ability to work in the same place every day now is virtually impossible. He is also handsomely rewarded for his consulting services so he has no desire to change.

If your business is more susceptible to changes in technology (for example, an accountancy practice), you may need to provide additional services. I have seen more accountancy practices offer business advisory, insurance, superannuation, financial planning, bookkeeping and even contract or interim inhouse chief financial officer services as a way to add value to their existing clients. As so many of their previous services have been replaced by inhouse accounting systems, they have had to constantly reinvent their service offering to remain financially viable.

If you feel as if you need some guidance to clarify your business purpose and products and services in alignment with your values, I encourage you to seek some professional advice. It can be exhausting to continually 'make it up as you go.' Whilst you may initially need to make some changes, you can ultimately end up with a much more aligned enterprise and it can all become much easier rather than harder.

Action 16: *Make sure that your business products and services match market demand and are in alignment with your values. If you need assistance to clarify your business direction, seek some professional advice*

3.2 Consumer Choice

Have you noticed that over time, you have changed the way you decide what to buy? Have you noticed that you rely more on referrals and recommendations from people you know? Or have you been more tempted to complete a range of online research before making a buying decision entirely on your own?

Personally, I do a combination of all of the above and I believe that other well educated consumers are likely to do the same. Our society hasn't quite managed to cross over to exclusive online shopping, but I am quite sure that every year, more purchases are being made via online methods.

As a business owner, you need to be aware of how consumer behavior is changing. One of the most significant changes is the use of mobile technology - phones and tablets in particular. These 'everywhere' devices are encouraging more people to make buying decisions on their own.

There is also a greater range of sophisticated artificial intelligence (or machine learning) systems that are tracking our behavior online and in real life (several of these systems rely on our mobile phones to collect data). Have you noticed how advertisements for the items you have previously searched for online now appear in your social media news feed? Have you also been offered special offers in alignment with your areas of interest? It is not simply a coincidence.

A quick reminder here that most of us no longer have very much privacy. If you have a credit card and you use it for purchases, there is a record of what you have spent. If you are on a mailing list, there is a record of your interest. If you have a mobile phone, you are essentially carrying a mobile tracking device.

We are long past the stage where we can control this collection of information about our behavior and interests. In some respects, it can save us a lot of time and effort (for example, we can be prompted to purchase a logically compatible product at the same time and save on postage).

Despite all of these changes to consumer choice, many individuals still want to have a good experience when they make a purchase. Most people will ultimately have a preferred method for making purchases and it may vary according to what they are purchasing.

For example, I am not a big shopper. In fact, I find shopping a waste of productive time. However, I still need to shop to buy the essentials for my household. So I have worked out a few systems to make this as quick and efficient as possible.

Firstly, I make sure that for essential items, I always have two items in the cupboard. The one I am using and a spare. That way if I run out between visits to the shop, I start using my spare item and I just add the details to my shopping list so that I am not time bound to make a repeat purchase.

Like most people, I have a freezer so that I don't have to go shopping for perishable items as frequently. I also purchase my fruit and vegetables from a green grocer with an extremely high turnover so some of the fresh food items last more than two weeks as they haven't been on display for a week before my purchase.

I also time my trips to the shop and normally schedule a visit to a friend who lives close by - and that means I have something good to look forward so that I can tolerate the shopping part!

You probably have your own idiosyncrasies too. You may only like one particular brand of bread or coffee. You may have a preference for locally produced organic fruit and vegetables. Just as you have these preferences, so too do your clients and customers purchasing your products and services.

Sometimes consumers appear to make very irrational choices. One in particular that frustrates me enormously is that some consumers can 'afford' to spend $300 when they go out for one meal over three hours, but they cannot afford to spend $300 for professional advice on their career (where they spend many hours per week). That said, if you are a restaurant owner, you probably have a different perspective!

As a business owner, it is extremely easy to become frustrated and angry when you know that your products and services can provide amazing value but your potential customers cannot see it. If this regularly occurs in your business, you need to think about the buying process in a little more detail and realize that just like a personal relationship, it takes time to develop into an ongoing relationship - and it can take many touch points before a final sale occurs.

I will talk more about this throughout the book, but for now, just remember that most consumers still walk to the beat of their own drum.

Before I move on though, I want to share a quick comment about pricing. When I was working in real estate, my boss would always tell me that the reason a property wouldn't sell was the price. I would often think it was not only the price, it was the approach the business was using to find the person willing to pay that price. In an auction situation, you only need two people who are interested to 'fight' each other with higher bids to secure a good sale price.

I have a personal view that everything is worthless unless someone wants to buy it. You could own an amazing historical artefact worth 20 million dollars, but if no-one wants to buy it, it is essentially worth zero. Although I generally have a minimalist approach to life, I encourage you to think about your purchases before you assume that you can liquidate the items in the future at a moment's notice. This includes stock if you work with products and the investment you make in time or money if you are developing services.

Action 17: *Consumers now have a much greater variety of ways to select and purchase products and services. As a business owner, you need to be able to build a buying relationship over time and provide the best touch points that will lead to a sale. Some of these touch points are likely to be facilitated by mobile or online technology*

3.3 Sustainable Business

I believe that every business owner should be aiming to have a sustainable business. When I think of sustainability, I think of an enterprise that can stay in business in a manageable and productive way without harming the environment and yet still make a profit so that everyone involved can receive a fair reward for their efforts.

A more common definition involves an enterprise having a minimal negative impact on the global or local environment, community, society, or economy. I would like to think that a business can have a positive impact in all of these areas!

Over the years, there have been many different business methodologies that have improved the efficiency and effectiveness of business. Just in time manufacturing. Business process improvement. Minimal inventory levels and smarter logistics. Revised performance feedback systems. Too many to mention here.

I conducted a small survey of local business owners in July 2016 and it was fascinating to see the results come in. The question was, "What are most local businesses interested in?"

Developing a sustainable business	100%
Increasing profit	75%
Improving work/life balance	50%
Increasing market share	42%
Expanding the business	33%

The questions were not listed in this order (in fact the Sustainable Business option was number four on the list). So I am extremely pleased to see that the concept of sustainability is currently more important than profit. I suspect some people still have not worked out how to create a good work/life balance in their business. It seems that there are also several people like me who do not have grand plans for expansion and world domination!

The next question was about what would most significantly help a local business?

More marketing	67%
More support from local authorities	58%
More business education	33%
Cheaper rent	33%
Cheaper advertising	25%
Cheaper labor	16%

This is congruent with another workshop that I went to with Reg Eustace who mentioned that there are three aspects to business - Marketing, Operations and Finance. Apparently Marketing is the most important as without it, you don't have a business! (Operations and Finance are second and third).

The third question was what would encourage more people to utilise local businesses?

More networking and relationship building	75%
More local events	50%
More targeted advertising and marketing	33%
Increased social media presence	25%
Better transport and car parking	25%

I truly believe that hyper local marketing and hyper local business activity can provide a positive impact on the local environment, community, society and economy. I believe that there are many quantitative and qualitative results that can be directly attributed to a hyper local approach. Some of the qualitative results can never be measured, but they can sometimes be the most valuable - somehow, serendipity just makes things happen.

I am not suggesting for a moment that we cease mass production or distribution as this creates other economies of scale. However, I would like to see countries all over the world implement the best of both systems and create a well balanced social democracy. I would like to see this create a more egalitarian share of resources and lifestyle that ultimately leaves our planet in good condition for future generations.

Even if you implement all of the ideas in this book in your business, it will not guarantee you business success (although I am sure it will help!). Please remember that responsible business owners accept responsibility for all aspects of their business - not just the marketing. Remember, you need to think very carefully about streamlining your business processes, pricing your products and services appropriately, managing your staff and stakeholders, maintaining your cash flow, following up on outstanding invoices, strive for continuous improvement etc.

Action 18: *Developing a sustainable business can help create a positive impact on the local environment, community, society or economy. Combining mass production systems with hyper local systems can create a more egalitarian share of resources and lifestyle. Business owners need to combine the best of both worlds to leave our planet in good condition for future generations and accept full responsibility for managing all aspects of their business, not just the marketing*

3.4 Business Type Differentiation

I have already touched on a range of differentiators when defining the model for your business. Understanding yourself and the market conditions and the overall impact of your business is extremely important.

Now it is time to look at your business in a bit more detail. How will you:

- be distinctive and create your own character?
- reflect your personality and values?
- appease your own dragons and false beliefs?
- identify the business avatar or ideal client or customer?
- share your business story to journalists?
- create timeless narratives for yourself and your clients or customers?
- determine what will work before you do it? (not always possible)
- determine what people will pay for?
- record your achievements over time?
- remain fresh, new and flexible in a changing world?

Most successful business owners will tell you that along their journey, they received exceptional help from suitably qualified and experienced mentors or coaches who have a successful track record in the current market.

The world we live in is no longer linear. Our time honored chronological and linear traditions are undergoing a massive transformation. Many of the basic fundamentals of business (and people) will never change, but the way that business occurs is constantly changing and even what is traded in business is also changing exponentially (both products and services).

I encourage you to continually learn and grow with professional qualifications but also hands on experience from multiple experiences and product and service iterations. You need to be able to adapt to the changing market and continually find ways to improve but be mindful not to follow shiny object style new marketing ideas without testing them first.

Clarity leads to conversion - so being clear and remaining clear is extremely important. If you need professional assistance, I encourage you to source it!

Action 19: *Clarify the exact nature of your business and how you will differentiate yourself from other enterprises. Understand that the world is constantly changing and that you will need to continually learn grow and adapt - with professional assistance if required*

3.5 Business Pricing

Most business owners realize that they need to provide a product or service at a price where the consumer believes they are receiving amazing value. So essentially, in their mind, it is worth $1,000 but they are only paying $500.

However, it is not always a dollar cost analysis. The perception value amount is also included in this example of $1,000 of value for $500.

For example, I could purchase a watch for $5 and have a watch. Some people choose to spend $50,000 on a watch because in their mind, it is worth at least $50,000, if not, a whole lot more, even if the materials only cost $500.

Another trap I have seen people fall into over time is not charging enough for their products or services. For example, they may buy an item for $100 and think that by selling it at $150, they have made a reasonable profit. However, if they are not making many sales and their overheads are quite high, they may need to sell the item at $180 just to break even. Cash coming in doesn't necessarily mean a profitable business - all of the costs need to be included and there has to be an allowance for profit.

This is probably a bigger trap for service based businesses. In an effort to source work, they often reduce their price to win the first opportunity. Unfortunately, they often bring down the charge out price for everyone in the industry - and worse still, the people paying for the service expect more.

I have seen this happen in the training industry. In the past, trainers were usually paid for creating the course content (and they maintained ownership of the content), setting up and packing up the room and delivering the course. Now, they are often only paid for the course delivery and they have to 'give away' their time to create the content - and worse still, they either have to give their content to the company receiving the training or have their course recorded on video so they only receive one payment but the video collects revenue from multiple students.

If your products or services fall into the category of being replaced by another product or service, then you need to think about additional products or services you can offer - but also set realistic time frames on your product life cycles.

If you can build in a 'currency' or 'recency' factor, this will help maintain demand and is a marketing and pricing strategy in its own right. For example, I regularly publish my past courses online because what I am teaching is changing so frequently, I can sell my course content on the basis that what has already been published will be out of date very quickly.

Likewise, if you have a product based business, try and keep your stock levels as close to demand as possible so that you are not stuck with unsaleable items. Provide discounts when there is still some margin to be made. If your discount incentives can help your hyper local community, fantastic!

The final aspect of pricing is the convenience amount. A good example is painting your house. Sure, you could probably do the job a whole lot cheaper than the painter, but do you want to? How much time do you have? How long would it take you compared to the painter? How many items do you need to buy to do the job? What skills do you need to learn and can you be safe on a ladder? What is your time worth and what would the total cost be if you added all of these items to the bill?

Here, the price is not about 'value for money' as such. It is more about convenience and letting the expert do the best job rather than you trying to do everything. You can still shop around, make sure you get at least three quotes, source the business from a referral etc, but at the end of the day, the price you choose to pay will be dependent upon how much you do versus how much is done by the service provider and it may be more worthwhile and better value overall to pay the painter instead of doing it yourself.

Action 20: *Ultimately, pricing is dependent upon dollar cost value, perception value and convenience. How you price your products and services needs to be aligned with your business costs and market conditions. If you can incorporate a 'currency' or 'recency' value, this can maintain demand for your products and services*

4. Product And Service First Or Target Audience First?

Another big shift that has occurred over recent years is either creating the product or service first or connecting with the target audience first.

There will always be room for innovators and entrepreneurs who create products and services that we don't even know that we need or want right now.

For example, Henry Ford famously said, "If I had asked people what they wanted, they would have said faster horses." Instead, he offered the world a motorized car.

But that was in the manufacturing era. The technological era is slightly different.

Now consumers have the opportunity to create exactly what they want. Even the fast food chain McDonald's allows you to 'Create Your Own Taste' and order your hamburger with the ingredients you choose. Three dimensional printers enable you to personally manufacture tailor made solid objects that you have designed - you can essentially create your own prototype.

So what we have now is the eternal question, what came first, the chicken or the egg? The product or the service - or the customer?

Successful sustainable businesses usually start with some form or product or service, but they are increasingly finding that they need to adjust their products and services to the needs of their target audience, the client or customer.

Sometimes they need to create a product or service based on a specific customer request or feedback.

There are many ways to find out what your target audience needs and wants. You can:

- use predictive analysis based on sales or income

- ask your customers in person or with some form of survey or feedback process (ask long term loyal customers as well as new customers)

- create test versions and run trials to assess viability before implementation

- create special offers and see if these are accepted by your current customers

- establish focus groups of ideal customers with an external provider so that you can gain anonymous insights and answers (which may be slightly more accurate because they can contribute anonymously)

- observe your direct competitors' behavior (what they are offering that is new, discounted, being run out etc)

- constantly improve your business operations and observe what additional products or services are purchased by existing clients

- attend trade fairs, expos and conventions to identify new trends

As with most business practices, I encourage you to consider your overall values and purpose first, but to remain vigilant and aware at all times as to how your customers are responding to your offerings. Attracting interest from consumers that are constantly bombarded with messages from many sources requires a planned strategic approach.

Be careful not to make a radical decision based on your loudest 1% of customers. It can be very tempting if you are aggravated emotionally by someone who complains. You need to be able to assess whether or not their particular view is the view of the majority or they are just a specific individual who may never be happy regardless of the quality of the product or service you have provided.

As a general rule, I prefer to stick with tried and true base products and services and then provide tailor made adjustments depending on the value of the purchase. This is why most businesses offer different levels of products and services - low, medium and high cost with a greater exchange value as the price increases.

This is also a good technique for sorting out the people who are genuinely interested in paying for your premium products. Have you ever noticed how very expensive luxury stores usually have a small price point item so that people with a lower budget can still have the experience of luxury without the million dollar price tag (like a miniature Ferrari key ring?). It also creates a natural pathway to a greater spend in the future and as the risk increases, so does the price (for both parties).

I have mentioned this point in my first book '*120 Ways To Achieve Your Purpose With LinkedIn.*' There are three types of people. The people that no matter how good your product or service is, they will not buy it. The second type will buy your product or service in conjunction with you and perhaps take care of some aspect themselves (for example a good relationship with a professional adviser who gives you templates and homework to complete between appointments). The third type of person is the one who wants a product or service to do everything for them.

If you want to run a sustainable business, you need to be polite towards the first group of people as they may still refer other people to you. You also need to decide which of your products and services will meet the needs of the other two types of people. If you have a service based business, there can be different price points for partial service versus full service. However, if you offer a 'full service' option, make sure that the information you require for that full service is collected before you promise to deliver it!

Managing expectations is one of the most critical success factors for a successful business. Remember that people who receive good products and services will tell a few people. People who receive bad products and services will usually tell lots of people!

Action 21: *When selecting your products and services, always think about the needs of your target audience. Provide low, medium and high cost options so that you can create a natural pathway to a bigger total spend over time. Manage expectations at all times as bad news will be spread further than good news*

4.1 Securing Referrals From Existing Clients And Customers

Let's take a quick overview of the business relationship cycle in the technological era.

Firstly your potential client or customer has a trigger of some sort that helps them realize that they would like to purchase your products or services. They may not know anything about you at this point.

Then they will look for further information and insights and they will often seek advice from someone they know, like and trust and this person will possibly give them a referral to you.

Many clients and customers will then complete some form of due diligence. Although they have received a direct referral, they will often look for further information online about you and your business. If your business provides the right experience that matches their expectations, they are likely to consider purchasing your products and services.

At this point, the person is in a 'friendship' relationship with your business. If they choose to make more purchases over time, they develop into a 'companion.' If they are particularly happy with your offerings, they could become a 'crusader' and regularly mention your business when they are talking to other people who have expressed a specific interest in the same product or service.

If you constantly deliver on your promises and provide even more value, beyond the actual delivery of your standard products and services, the customer can become an 'advocate' and be willing to promote a range of your products and services whenever a suitable opportunity arises.

Ultimately, if you can establish a true commitment with your clients and customers, they can become an 'ambassador' and personally represent you on a more regular basis and actually start conversations or represent your business in various situations.

As you can imagine, with so much business secured via referral (up to 85%), if you can build these highly developed relationships with your existing clients and customers who are already part of your target audience, you will be able to attract an even greater range of ideal clients and customers.

As you go through this process, be realistic. Not every client or customer will eventually become your business ambassador. Some may simply remain business friends. However, marketing 101 has always said that it is easier to sell an extra product or service to an existing client or customer than it is to sell a product or service to a new client or customer.

By building a longer term relationship with your clients and customers, you are much more likely to generate more referrals and more business. Don't spend time worrying about the clients and customers you didn't get - work with the ones you did get! For a start, they already 'like' you to some extent because they have already made a purchase.

A number of the tips and techniques in this book will show you how you can develop this business relationship over time. For more suggestions, please read my companion book *'120 Ways To Attract The Right Career Or Business'* and don't forget to join the 120 Ways Publishing Membership Program at http://120ways.com/members.

Action 22: *With up to 85% of business being sourced via a referral, your business needs to build a strong relationship with your existing clients and customers over time so that they can become your target audience ambassadors, willingly representing you and your business in various situations*

4.2 Other Sources Of Clients And Customers

As I have mentioned earlier, some business owners start with the false assumption that everyone in their community will be interested in their products and services.

I have personally referred several potential clients to other businesses. This is not just because I didn't offer the specific product or service they were seeking. If I cannot see a reasonable level of congruency and alignment with my ideal client profile, I politely refuse to work with them.

This may seem counter intuitive, particularly to a business startup, but in the long run, it works. It gives another business the chance to service their needs and wants and it means that I can focus on my ideal clients needs and wants. Even if the referred business does not send me any clients in return, it still creates goodwill within my industry and profession.

Now, a quick word of warning. As I list the following sources of clients and customers, I want you to critically evaluate whether or not you would definitely find your target audience in each of these locations.

There is absolutely no point in you spreading yourself too thin and wasting time on techniques that will not deliver the right results.

That said, I never put all of my eggs in one basket. My best clients are usually sent to me by one man who constantly refers individuals to me for personalized consulting services. But these referrals alone are not enough to keep me in business. I have multiple effective strategies all running at the same time and every six months, I review what is working best and consider all of my options for the next six months based on past performance and future possibilities.

If you look at the following list and see some sources where you could create an aligned business presence without necessarily spending a lot of time or money, this is an excellent business strategy. By increasing your overall brand penetration, you can build your attraction power (but please remember to maintain accurate business details in each of these locations).

- reaching out to local or international influencers in your business specialty and inviting them to share details of what you do to their audience (this could involve some form of payment for the endorsement or appearance)

- inviting a well known and aligned celebrity (you may know someone directly) to participate in some form of activity and using this as part of a media or marketing campaign where you re-use their appearance on multiple channels (print, online, television, radio, podcasts etc)

- aligning yourself with other local identities - either individuals or businesses - this is particularly relevant in regional communities where local clients and customers associate with local icons that have been in the area for a long time

- participating in regional community initiatives - cooperatives, business incubators, co-working spaces, community groups, industry groups, professional associations, chambers of commerce, government programs, sporting clubs (one of my personal favorite techniques)

- directly networking with your suppliers, other retailers in non-competing locations or distributors - these people usually have a wealth of knowledge, experience and ideas to share

- identifying local business conditions and responding accordingly - is there a high proportion of people visiting the area for special events, lunchtime trade or seasonal activity where you can tap into that unmet demand?

- establishing some sort of affiliate program with a non-competing business that services a similar or the same target audience. You may be able to set up an exchange arrangement either personally or online and help each other

- developing a consistent and current brand both online and offline that directly reaches your target audience when they are looking for your services and when they are not looking for your services (provided it doesn't become annoying). Remember to balance perception and reality - you do not want to be perceived inappropriately

- online platforms and apps - there are a variety of online platforms and apps you can join however, you need to make sure that there is a significant number of members overall and a reasonable number of people from your target audience participating regularly

- online and offline listings and directories - there are an enormous range of local listings and directories where you can create a presence. Any with a large number of records or traffic are good, as are those with a 'high authority' online profile (for instance local government listings)

- classified advertisement listings - these can either be the general buy/sell listings or they can be specific portals around a theme (jobs, real estate, cars etc). Again, look for traffic numbers and reach. Some small listings in specific locations do better than large listings in a popular location. Consider local newspaper listings (but again, only if they have a good level of circulation and readership)

I will share specific examples from these various options throughout the book.

Action 23: *Identify other quality sources of clients and customers by doing some research in to what is available in your local area or context. Make sure that each source either has a high volume of participants, high online authority or a direct link to your target audience. Maintain the accuracy of all of your profiles over time and review each option's suitability as a client source every six months*

4.3 Maintaining Clients And Customers

Every business owner knows that to stay in business, you have to maintain relationships with new and existing clients and customers.

The target audience clients who comply with your service offerings or frequently purchase your products are especially important.

For example, if you provide professional services to a client, did you know that you can sometimes be more effective by communicating remotely or as part of a group than you can by meeting one-on-one in person? This is because the client has already accepted some of the responsibility for completing the work. They realize that it is not possible, in most cases, for you to do everything for them so they are more motivated to take action independently (or spend money for you to do it for them later).

This is why a number of business coaches are encouraging business owners to offer 'one-to-many' services at the lower end of the budget range and offer 'one-to-one' services at the higher end of the budget range. In this situation, additional motivating power comes from the cost of the advice! If you are paying $5,000 per hour, are you more likely to take action than if you are paying $500 per hour? Be honest!

On some occasions, your clients and customers will ask for additional products and services. Rather than say 'no' outright, think about whether or not their suggestion is in alignment with your values and purpose. They may be providing a logical segway to a new business opportunity or a higher total spend.

You may also bring in a new product or service and realize that some of your existing clients and customers would really benefit from your new offering. Don't be afraid to provide a personal suggestion directly to that person. The worst that can happen is that they say 'no.' If you decide to do this on a regular basis, make sure you keep accurate records so that you don't double up the same invitation at any point (particularly if you outsource the direct contact).

Some clients and customers try to get away with what my mother would call, 'blue murder.' They seem to want everything for nothing. These are the sorts of clients that always ask for a discount, or who prolong a one hour appointment, or expect a refund after they have taken advantage of your products or services. These are the sorts of clients and customers that you need to handle politely and firmly. If they comply, they can continue to be a client or customer. If they do not comply, it is time to let them go (but again, always politely).

Business is about a fair exchange and you cannot provide a fair exchange if the customer is taking advantage of you.

The most effective strategy for customer and client relationship management, above everything else, is following up with your clients and customers. If your sales process provides a way for you to keep in touch, this is a direct way for you to constantly re-sell more products and services in the future.

There are different ways to follow up and it is important to be able to systemize them as much as possible so that all clients and customers can expect a similarly high level of service. You could:

- keep in touch via a monthly or quarterly communication (email, SMS, letter or phone call)

- create an automatic follow up stream by encouraging your clients to connect via an online platform or app which automatically sends appropriate news, offers or reminders

- recognize special occasions or high value transactions with a suitable gift or personal hand written card (provided you meet ethical governance rules)

- provide a personalized invitation to an exclusive 'client only' event that is either free or low cost and provides even more value (very common in the financial planning and investments industry)

- utilize your inhouse Customer Relationship Management (CRM) system with IF/THEN processes and follow up with a relevant offering throughout the customer lifecycle

- do something that offers 'surprise' value. Include a bonus for no reason at all, give an unexpected discount, listen carefully and follow up with either information, a product or a service that they were not expecting (I always like receiving chocolate for no reason!)

- provide an offer that they can utilize for their own benefit but also share with someone else. So the next time they purchase your product or service, a friend can receive the same benefit

There are probably several other ways you can think of in your industry or profession to follow up with your clients and customers. Make a few notes right now so you can implement them in the future:

_____

_____

_____

Even if you do not have time to offer personalized customer relationship management techniques for every transaction, client or customer, make sure that your customer service standards are always maintained and that your high value clients and customers receive a little extra value at least once a year. If you are worried about the time or cost, think about the extra value you can receive from the referrals that they send to you!

Some of the simplest ways to maintain a client or customer relationship over time are:

- personalize every interaction with their name (remember Dale Carnegie's book 'How to win friends and influence people')

- always say thank you every time you communicate

- apologize for any mistakes and make amends

- smile whenever possible

- respond promptly to all requests (this is becoming critical, particularly in the online world where response times are being measured and recorded)

- always allow the other person to maintain their dignity, even if they have made a mistake

- treat everyone respectfully and politely (even if you find their behavior offensive)

- be prepared to be firm and clear rather than weak and vague - confusion can lead to chaos

All of the above suggestions need to be approved by you as the business owner before implementation. I worked with one client who hired a university student with no experience in his industry to do some online sales, marketing and social media and it was a disaster. The low quality content that was produced didn't offer any useful information, it did not generate any likes, comments or shares and it didn't trigger any enquiries or leads. In short, it was a waste of time and money.

As a general rule, outsource business tasks that don't require specific knowledge of the business first and only outsource sales, marketing and follow up tasks if you can provide very specific guidelines and instructions and you can closely monitor the performance and feedback.

Action 24: *Identify ways that you can maintain the relationship with your clients and customers over time. Always maintain your customer service standards and incorporate customer relationship management processes in your business processes so that it is automatically implemented for most of your transactions*

5. Market Analysis

Finding information about your local market opportunities is vital if you want to be successful in business. There are several specific areas where you need to source reliable quantitative and qualitative information so that you can make informed decisions.

5.1 Site Or Location Setting

As you may already know, when large multinational enterprises consider expanding into new countries, cities or towns, they complete a lot of market research to find out if there is sufficient demand for their products and services in that location.

There are also companies that specialize in geospatial analysis where they investigate a range of geospatial and statistical data, the future plans for the community, local demographics, pedestrian traffic, tenant mixes, food offerings, car parking and public transport, other competitors etc.

You can be quite sure that if a large company is prepared to pay for this professional advice before selecting a site or location for their business, there are many good reasons for doing so!

Many startups will often start from a home base and this certainly saves on setup costs. Whether you are in a location or moving soon, please keep these concepts in mind. Selecting a property that has cheaper rent but no passing traffic or car parking for staff could create challenges.

For example, I have previously worked for a client who had an office and warehouse close to the city. He was the son of the original owner and had made a few bad decisions within the last two years.

He was then offered the opportunity to lease purpose built premises a long way from the city and the real estate agent was forcing him to make a decision within 24 hours. I had to remind him that although he may save on storage and even distribution costs, he ran the very real risk of losing most of his staff who would not travel further out of the city to the new premises.

I am pleased to report that the business moved to bigger premises that were still close to the city and they now have offices in six countries and a local presence in over 40 countries on six continents. I can't say that this result came from that one decision, but I am pleased to see that the business has grown over the years and I am very pleased that they chose to maintain a local presence.

I also went to a very interesting workshop where a new startup signed a lease with a 'first right of refusal' at the end of the term of the first lease. This meant that if their first three years of operation were successful, they would not have to compete against other interested parties at the end of the lease term. They turned out to be extremely successful and renewed the lease for another three years, without any complications or a significant increase in rent.

Action 25: *If you are planning to operate a business in a particular location, you need to understand the local geospatial data and make an informed choice before selecting your site. If you have already chosen a site, investigate what other opportunities might be available in the future by collecting reliable local quantitative and qualitative data*

5.2 Market Size

Yes, as I have mentioned previously, you can do international business in a local area and you can have people with international experience and connections in a local business. This is a good thing to remember if your local market is very small and you need to attract work from another larger population location. This is also a side benefit of us living in an electronically connected world!

However, if you would like to grow the size of your market in your local area, you need to think beyond a larger market elsewhere. You need to have a growth mindset rather than a scarcity mindset.

I recently visited my dentist and I was talking about this book and she told me that she wanted a copy but she didn't want any other dentist in the local area to know about the book as a number of new dentists had recently started new practices in the local area. I politely told her that this was old school thinking.

I suggested that a better way to look at this situation was to encourage more local residents to visit the dentist regularly! Then every dentist would have more work. Rather than marketing the painful experience of major dental work (I have had a root canal and it was horrendous), a better strategy to grow her business and increase the supply of patients would be to educate local residents about regular checkups, dental hygiene, preventative treatments and cosmetic options.

Another way to increase your market size in the local area is to increase your presence in the local community. Firstly, imagine where your target audience is most likely to be found and then find a way to appear where they meet.

For example, if your main target audience is mothers of children aged 6 - 12, you could consider supporting local school events in cash or in products and services and supply items for auctions, art exhibitions, sports days, fairs or fetes. If you are also a parent of similar aged children, consider becoming involved in voluntary activities at the school - canteen duty, literacy support, school administration etc. Most people will ask you when they meet you in this situation, "and what do you do?" and then you can explain the nature of your business (without the hard sell).

Action 26: *To increase the potential size of your target market, consider international markets and connections, increasing demand through education, contributing to your community and adopting a growth mindset*

5.3 Competitor Analysis

I do not believe in reinventing the wheel. I also believe that there is enough opportunity for all businesses to coexist and support specific target audiences in a responsive economy. If demand drops significantly in a particular area, all businesses need to respond, not just the leading businesses.

If two businesses operate almost identically on opposite sides of the same street (right next to a traffic light crossing where people can pause before crossing the road), some people will always choose to go to the business on the north side and some people will always choose to go to the business on the south side (or east and west depending on the location).

Logistically, it is probably easier to see what is going on across the street than it is to see what is going on two blocks away, but ultimately, if you want to run a successful business, you need to constantly improve, as a miniumum, by 1% at a time on a regular basis.

To do this, you need to look a lot further than across the street. You need to look online, two blocks away, in local suburbs, in other states, countries and continents and see what new ideas you can incorporate into your offering.

Action 27: *Every business needs to respond to changes in the economy and find ways to constantly improve over time. Aim to make at least a 1% improvement on a regular basis*

5.4 Online Competitor Analysis

In the online search engine results world, your business needs to rank in search queries, both desktop and mobile for:

- your location

- your primary and secondary keywords

- your name (as the business owner)

- your business name

Your online presence can be supported by your activity on other social media platforms, apps, reviews etc but this is only part of the puzzle.

If you have identified a particular business as similar to yours, you should conduct incognito online searches through your internet browser when you have cleared your cookies and browser history and are logged out of every other online resource, for all of the search queries related to your competitor (location, keywords, name, business name etc).

This exercise worked particularly well for one of my clients who was about to purchase a franchise with 170 locations as well as one of her own locations. She conducted a location search with her keywords and found a similar business in page one of search results listed before her own business (despite the fact that the franchise company had implemented a significant search engine marketing strategy for the 170 locations). She then looked at the keywords on the competitor's website and she also searched for the business owner's name and the business name.

As a result of this competitor analysis, she was able to identify multiple additional hyper local marketing strategies that she could implement in her own business. She found additional high ranking local directory websites that would accept a free listing. She identified some excellent social media hashtags and posting formats. She even discovered new venues, potential target audience networks and product suppliers.

A word of warning though - the time to activate these options is right now. With the increase in voice activated search queries through mobile devices, the increase in advertisement results in search engine results and the development of wearable devices, it is becoming more important than ever to 'cover multiple bases' in the online world.

If you want to complete a very quick analysis, look at the competitor's website, survey the content they have and how it is structured and what techniques they use to encourage the visitor to perform a particular task or tasks.

Right click with your mouse on the website where there is not a function or link (yes, it is better to do this research on a laptop or desktop computer), and choose the 'View Page Source' option so that you can view the HTML code behind the website. This will give you clues as to the search engine optimization techniques they are using on that page - the page title, the keywords, meta description, tags etc. It can also give you some great clues as to what to prioritize on your website (and remind you about how you can differentiate what you offer).

Another favorite website of mine is http://archive.org. This is a website that will allow you to look at previous versions of websites and you can get even more clues by looking at past versions of their website (make sure you add your own website at http://archive.org/web).

Action 28: *Complete an online competitor analysis for at least one business that is competing for the same target audience. As a minimum, visit their website, right click with your mouse, view the source code and see how they are optimizing their content. Visit http://archive.org for historical website information. Ultimately, look at multiple competitors' online presence across various platforms*

5.5 Collaborator Analysis

This idea really needs to be implemented at the same time as the Competitor Analysis. As you go through your various online and offline research, you may find that there are other enterprises that operate in the same location or context and they offer either similar or complementary products and services.

You have multiple options. You could:

- identify or redefine your unique points of difference and refer people who are outside of your target audience to the other enterprise

- discuss options with the other enterprise for sharing economies of scale and working collaboratively in the future

- discuss a referral or exchange program that incorporates some of the other suggestions from this book

When thinking about potential collaborator enterprises, you need to make sure that you understand each other and the nature of the exchange. Ideally, you would both share a similar value system and both be willing to give more than you take and constantly think about ways you can support each other.

However, not everyone operates on this basis. I have heard of so many failed partnerships where one person took advantage of another and where expectations were not met.

As always, there are at least two sides to a story (often more!). Whilst one person may feel as if they were treated unfairly, the other person may feel as if they were not given what they were promised.

So whilst I truly believe in the value and benefit of collaborating with other people, I also like to manage risk and make sure that I will not be disappointed in the future. I recommend that if you are willing to try a collaborator arrangement, you need to make sure that both parties expectations are extremely clear.

You may or may not feel the need for a formal legal agreement, but I believe that one way to keep both sides honest is to make sure that either party can walk away at any time. The concept being that ideally, you will both benefit if you support each other but if one person does not contribute, you can go elsewhere without justification. This means that a certain level of quality performance and accountability is required to maintain the collaborator arrangement.

Alternatively, you may choose to maintain a loose collaborator arrangement even if there is not an equal exchange. This concept is very exciting to me. It is similar to the 'pay it forward' movement. Whilst you may not derive a direct or even long term benefit by collaborating, you do so anyway because you understand that at some other moment in time, someone will refer an opportunity to you.

This is similar to the 'if you can't tie knots, tie lots' philosophy that I discuss in the book '*120 Ways To Attract The Right Career Or Business.*'

For example, I have a policy of not paying for referrals or charging for referrals. However, I ALWAYS thank people for referrals and as I do with every other client, I do my utmost to provide exceptional service to these referees (and I usually provide an extra bonus).

I truly believe that a lot more enterprises could be value and purpose driven if more people had faith in the giving process rather than the taking process. Rather than viewing every other enterprise as a competitor, think about how they could be a collaborator. How can you help each other and your community? After all, in most cases, you will be serving either a different target audience or the same target audience but providing a different product or service.

Our online platforms support this notion. As most platforms rely on algorithms, they respond to like information, not unlike information. If you are linking to websites with similar keywords, similar activity, a similar location or similar transactions, then the algorithms usually view the results as more reliable.

One of my clients owns and operates a luxury property that provides short term accommodation for discerning small groups or families. This property is between two well known holiday locations and is part of a very small community. My client features all of the local attractions, restaurants, affiliated services (wedding photographers, tour companies, markets, festivals, craft makers etc) and even profiles well known community members in her blog. For example, she interviews the local real estate agents and publishes their best tips on her website.

You may think that this is a crazy idea because many of these enterprises could be seen as competitors. But her property is not available to everyone on every day, her guests do not spend their entire vacation inside the boundary fence and they are much more likely to return to the property if they enjoy themselves in the region.

After collecting all of this content and publishing it on her website and through her social media channels over several years, she now receives referrals from 'all over town' and has an excellent occupancy rate. She has benefited by the process of collaborating, both overtly (she provides locally made candles to all visiting guests) and by giving (free publicity) rather than taking (demanding a booking fee for each reservation).

She has also managed to avoid paying exorbitant advertising and booking rates on large accommodation portals!

Action 29: *As you complete research on other enterprises in your location or context range, identify enterprises that may be suitable for a collaborator arrangement. You may be able to share referrals, economies of scale or mutually agreed exchanges. By adopting a giving philosophy, even if there is no direct benefit, you will find that over time, you will receive more*

6. Location Context

The location of your enterprise may be fixed (a shop) or mobile (either moves regularly or is online and available 'anywhere').

As mentioned previously, if you haven't already chosen a location, there are experts who can recommend where to set up shop according to a variety of local quantitative and qualitative data. If your business is not in the optimal position, you may need to work a little harder to attract your target audience - although you may argue that the potentially lower rental or property cost makes it worthwhile!

For now, I will assume that your location is at least average for your local market conditions. If you are aware of any particular challenges (parking availability, sources of traffic, difficult neighbors, demanding landlords etc), then you will need to make some decisions on how to overcome these challenges to get the most out of your marketing efforts.

I will say though that most situations are never completely hopeless. They may be challenging! What I prefer to look for are the opportunities in your present situation. Let's examine these a little more closely.

Action 30: *Rather than worry about the challenges of a particular location - either offline or online, look for quantitative and qualitative data that can help you make better marketing decisions*

6.1 Fixed Address

Let's start by asking the most basic question - do you know your neighbors? Not just right next door, but within the hyper local area? Have you made time to introduce yourself and discuss what you do and how you do it? Have you asked them for their best tips and advice?

I remember when I moved in to where I live now and my neighbor told me not to try and do a right hand turn onto the busy local road. That tip has saved me hours of waiting at the intersection!

However, there are other tips that you can learn from your neighbors that will never be published either offline or online. Like the details of the local lunchtime traffic from the busy offices down the road. Or the children and parents that appear around pick up time. Or more specific information about the average retail tenancy duration and the fact that the crowd pulling supermarket in a shopping mall was offered free rent to set up shop.

Whilst this type of qualitative information can be very helpful at driving context based decisions, quantitative information can also be used to make informed choices.

This information can come from a variety of sources. The local government authorities, regional advisory centres, business associations, unbiased statistical data provided by advertisers and larger enterprises, local newspapers and directories and other general publications.

I have seen many businesses make full scale business decisions based on a 'hunch' or a 'belief' rather than qualitative data. Assumptions are dangerous. Just because X happened, it doesn't mean that Y will occur. Anecdotes are also very dangerous. Just because X happened to someone else or even you doesn't mean that it will always happen.

I would like to encourage you to go looking for some reliable local data. Even the process of sourcing the data will be good for you and your business. It may lead you to the local business association or chamber of commerce. It may encourage you to register for a free training program provided by a local authority. It could lead to a whole new source of your ideal clients.

Please do not assume that your business experience is everyone's business experience or that you cannot access data. Dig a little deeper and you might find some real gold! Ask around - where do other people source their local data? There is an amazing amount of information available offline and online - you just need to find it! You may also be able to source paid data.

Once you do find this information, take a bit more time to evaluate the details. Make sure that it is statistically valid and correct and that any questions that were asked were not leading questions (encouraging a particular answer). Ask yourself why the data was collected. If it was to make a particular advertising proposal appear more attractive, this may not be the best information for your enterprise.

Action 31: *Source reliable local data and information to make informed choices. Do not make decisions based on assumptions or anecdotes. The process of sourcing reliable information can lead to new sources of ideal clients*

6.2 Online Address

Your online address is made up of many different components. The highest priority over the long term is your own website - as this is something that you can control.

If you would like a comprehensive Website Project Briefing Questionnaire to help you select what you would like to do online, please join the 120 Ways Publishing Members Program at http://120ways.com/members as it is one of the free downloads.

Online platforms can be popular one minute and obsolete the next.

An online presence requires a very comprehensive range of decisions. Most importantly, you are trying to attract and convert your target audience. Most algorithms have the 'location' as one of the top priorities.

This is easy to understand when so many people use a mobile device to access information. A mobile/cell phone usually provides an exact location of the user - so if the person is in a suburb and looking for a service in that suburb, it is most likely that their device will show search engine results for businesses in that suburb (or close by).

It naturally follows that if you want to attract people to your location, you need to optimize your location details whenever you publish content online. If a location that is near your location is more popular, you may also wish to include that location name in your online content.

It is a good idea to choose a domain name that is relevant to your business. I personally like to secure .com business names whenever I can, on the off-chance that it may be relevant to be international in the future. This is not always an option and some business owners have already decided to pick a country location domain name (like .co.uk for the United Kingdom).

If your business or domain name can also include your keywords, this can be helpful but it is not essential. NewcomersNetwork.com includes keywords as well as the business name. Of course SueEllson.com only includes my name and not keywords. Dentist.sydney includes both a keyword and a location, but I don't think most people are familiar with this type of website address and Google does not provide any significant increase in search engine results if your keywords are included in your domain name (it did in the past, it doesn't anymore). Fortunately, you can optimize any domain name for specific keywords, even if they are not included in the domain name.

Some people believe that if they register a domain name, they should seriously consider purchasing similar domain names - for example .com firstly then .co.uk, .com.au, co.nz etc.

This is a personal choice based on risk. I have chosen to register my domain names as .com and then also register the .com.au version as the business is based in Australia. I have set it up so that if anyone does type in the .com.au website address into their browser, it automatically redirects to .com.

What I have also noticed is that a lot of people do not type in a website address into their internet browser any more, they simply use a search engine or a voice command to find a particular website. This makes it even more important to search engine optimize your website so that it comes up on the first page of search engine results because so many people are not typing in the exact website address.

An easy to spell and memorable website address can make hyper local marketing a little easier, especially if people hear about it in a way that is easy to remember. It is also important to tie this address into the business in a logical way - it is not a good idea if the domain name cannot be matched logically to the business name - so if you are yet to choose your business name, see if you can choose something that is easy to spell and pronounce and is available with the extension that is most relevant to the nature of your business.

Action 32: *When selecting your business name, see if the domain name with the right extension is also available so that you can attract more relevant traffic to your website. Likewise when you establish a presence on an online platform, see if you can select the same profile name*

6.3 Platform Presence

Most enterprises have realized the benefits of having a presence on an online platform - and platforms like Google+, Facebook, LinkedIn, YouTube, Twitter and Instagram certainly have large numbers of users.

You may have also noticed that for these online platforms to survive, they have had to constantly update their offering and develop new and innovative features to maintain engagement. In fact the online platforms that create the most engagement appear to be able to offer the best advertising opportunities.

For example, Facebook is a social media platform that encourages social interaction and this level of interactivity increases the amount of time that users spend on the platform. It also reveals more about their behaviors and demographics and provides a tailor made audience for advertisers. As the number of hours increase, so too do the number of available advertisement placements. This is why you will constantly see online platforms encouraging engagement.

Have you noticed over time that the online platforms send you emails to remind you of different ways to maximize the value you gain? How they make suggestions about what you could read or who you could follow or how to advertise?

Ultimately though, as an enterprise, you need to think about the following factors before deciding on whether or not to participate in an existing or future online platform:

- Is it used by your target audience?

- Does it provide a way to access your target audience without being annoying?

- Does it provide other benefits related to your enterprise?

- Is it respected, reliable and trustworthy?

- Is there a good general sized audience using the online platform now or in the near future?

- Do you have time to set up the profile and be active on a regular basis?

- Can you measure the benefit of your involvement with any tools or data analysis?

- Will it provide a boost to your brand?

- Will the content you add be dynamic (real time only) or long term (lifetime)?

- Will your content be indexed by Google or online search results and be available in generic search results on an ongoing basis (or will your details be locked behind a login)?

- Are there any potential legal issues associated with your involvement (copyright, distribution etc)?

- Will you have direct access to the audience you create or will you have to pay to play? If you do pay, does it deliver a reward? Do you have to ask people to transfer to your website?

- How easy or difficult is it to migrate your fans, followers, users, viewers etc to your business offerings? Or do they only want to stay on the online platform?

I do not have any issue with 'paying to play' if there is a business outcome that is not annoying. However, I do not like seeing people investing in an online platform for hours on end and then realizing that their hard work only reaches 2% of their audience because the online platform algorithms have changed.

Whilst I encourage people to be open and aware of new opportunities, I also suggest that enterprises consider slightly more established online platforms rather than new ones in the first instance. It can take a reasonable amount of time to set up a quality profile and a lot longer to maintain it - and at the end of the day, your business needs to focus on your main tasks, not online platforms!

In the recent past, a range of social media strategists have tried to implement automatic systems for distributing content and generating leads. I would like to make the point that most users can see through these automation tools (including the online platforms and Google), so I do not believe that they are the most effective strategy moving forward.

Establishing and maintaining an online platform requires a strategic and consistent approach. The online platforms measure a range of behaviors, including how long it takes you to respond to comments and questions. Less established platforms usually lack either a significant database of users or a simple user interface. However, if they provide direct access to a very specific niche (like a professional association portal for your industry), then there may still be merit in getting involved. In some cases, you need to consider both the tangible and non-tangible benefits.

You also need to keep an accurate record of all of your online profiles, your usernames, email addresses and passwords. This will make it a lot easier to outsource the work if you decide to have some support but also to close ineffective profiles if they are not providing a useful benefit.

I have personally tried a lot of different platforms and I 'battle test' their effectiveness by monitoring their in-house statistics and my Google Analytics results, usually over a period of six months. I have deleted several profiles that simply do not perform. I have also expanded others (LinkedIn in particular).

Regardless of which online platforms you have selected, I encourage you to review the content and the performance of the online platform at least every six months and keep it consistent with the rest of your enterprise brand. Remember to tailor the content for the style of the online platform too - for example, hashtags are popular on Twitter and Instagram but they are not popular on Facebook.

As the business owner, it is up to you to take responsibility for your online platform presence. You can choose to do all of the work in-house or work with a digital agency. However, you do need to set very clear guidelines.

For example, I met a branding expert from the United States who hired a young hipster style person and she gave him access to her Twitter account. He sent out tweets that were unfortunately so unaligned to her message that she had to delete the tweets and send new tweets. For all of the people who saw the 'bad' tweets, this was obviously very damaging to her brand - and that was what her whole business was about! Until your delegate understands your voice and prepares approved content for some time, they should not be allowed to post on your behalf unsupervised. Your 'voice' needs to remain consistent.

Action 33: *Select the best online platforms for your target audience and business objectives, ensuring that you have the time and resources to keep your profile current and effective and keep a close eye on the results - both tangible and non-tangible*

6.4 Collective Marketplace Address

When you have a presence offline, online and via platforms, the collective presence creates what I like to call your 'marketplace' address.

This is something that can quite easily be ruined. We all know that the 'grapevine' can be extremely damaging. When negative words travel around on a regular basis, it can easily create a bad reputation - both for you personally and for your brand.

That doesn't mean that you need to be perfect to be in business. We are all human and we all make mistakes and some of my biggest mistakes have led to my biggest opportunities.

There are several reasons why. Firstly, if I make a mistake, the very first thing that I do is apologize - even if I am not entirely in the wrong. I am not going to argue the point because I am 'more right' than the other person. If something has gone wrong, I am willing to accept some responsibility towards fixing the problem.

It can be very easy at this point, especially when you are only partly wrong, to take the issue personally and react emotionally (I know, I have done so on several occasions). So this is when I take a few moments to gather my thoughts and analyze the situation carefully to make sure that I respond effectively rather than emotionally.

I also try and investigate the matter as thoroughly as possible - to understand what went wrong and why it went wrong. I try and gather all of the facts and calculate the best way forward given the circumstances.

If necessary, at this point I also check and confirm details with the person who has complained to make sure that I have not missed anything and together, I like to try and work out a solution.

For example, I was working on a client's website and something went terribly wrong. I told her immediately and said that I would stop charging her until it was fixed. I do not expect my client to pay for the time it takes to fix one of my mistakes. On this particular occasion, I also had to liaise with her website developer and in the end, they had to fix the problem because it was related to there not being enough server space to host the website.

I fully realize that I cannot know everything or predict what might happen whilst carrying out my normal duties, but my client is paying for my expertise, not my training! To solve this problem, I had to provide details of everything I had done over the previous few hours and to be honest, it was a bit scary because I really did feel as if I must have been at fault somehow. As I have said above, I did apologize and I did investigate everything thoroughly. I lost about three hours of my time. What I gained was a continuously happy client, more work and we successfully migrated the website to a new host without issue a short time later.

Once the solution has been finalized, I like to remind the person about how we have resolved the issue and I thank them for their assistance, feedback and involvement. Again, it can be hard to be humble, especially if I am not technically wrong, but I would rather 'lose face' and obtain a resolution rather than 'be right' and gain a bad reputation.

By accepting full responsibility and even a loss of income in the short term, I can assure you that it has always worked out favorably for me in the long term. On some occasions, the business relationship has ended, but it has not ended badly. More importantly, I do not have someone in the marketplace spreading a negative message and damaging my reputation. On some occasions, I have referred clients to someone more qualified in that niche and both the client and the referral recipient have been very grateful - so again, not only have I saved myself from further marketplace damage, I have also provided an opportunity to someone else.

A final comment I would like to make is in relation to standing your ground at the appropriate time. For example, I spent many hours with a client who was in her own creative business and at the time, she had a poorly functioning website, a bad relationship with her website designer and hosting company and very few computer skills. I made it very clear to her that I could do several things towards her goal of setting up a new website, but I did not have the ability to add the shopping cart and as soon as we got to that part, I would stop charging, give it a go, but if I couldn't do it, I would pass the job on to someone else. I also spent a lot of time helping her understand the components of a website, fixing up her emails and records, creating backups and sharing general marketing knowledge.

She agreed to all of this and paid her various invoices for several sessions. More than six months later, when her website was still not online after going to another website developer, she sent me an email saying that the website hosting I had selected was not suitable for the new website that was being developed and that she could not get a refund of the website hosting and she wanted a full refund of the entire amount she had paid me returned to her within seven days.

She also raised a couple of other issues that were outside of the scope of our project. After I got over the initial shock of her demands, I responded as quickly as possible explaining exactly what she had paid for and on that basis, I would not be refunding her payments. I also reminded her that I had answered several emails and phone calls free of charge since the end of her invoice period and I provided answers to her other concerns in the demand email. I did not hear from her again. I suspect that she was probably very frustrated that after six months with the other company, she still did not have a website - but that wasn't my fault! I had not charged her for what she claimed.

From a marketplace perspective, if I had backed down from this situation, I could have easily gained a reputation for being easy to be manipulated or a rip off merchant if I didn't remind her about what she had actually paid for. I also responded as quickly as possible to ensure that the situation did not escalate any further. If I had taken an aggressive approach, I imagine this could have easily led to a legal battle.

If you have a product based business, it can be very difficult dealing with the unrealistic demands of clients and customers. My daughter works at a large retail store and despite it being clearly stated that returns must be made within 14 days for a refund, several customers not only expect a refund after this date but they often return the item after it has been used! She has often told the customer that it is not possible to provide a refund and then the customer asks to speak to the manager and the manager approves the refund. As you can imagine, this only exacerbates the problem, but the retailer obviously chooses to do this, perhaps assuming that they will still spend more in the store over time.

As you can imagine, my daughter is regularly infuriated! In her mind it sets a bad precedent and I agree. That said, ultimately you will need to decide what you will do in your business and you can base your decision on a range of risk factors:

- the dollar value of the item
- the potential loss of future revenue
- the possible damage to your reputation
- the precedent you are setting (a bad precedent could create a bigger problem)
- the goodwill you can create by being perceived as reasonable (if the situation is reasonable or close to reasonable)
- special circumstances outside of anyone's control
- the long term value of the client or customer (a small loss is worth accepting to maintain the relationship - pettiness based on principle can be far more damaging)

If you are clear about the values of your business and you understand the local market conditions and you are willing to accept full responsibility along the way, it can be quick and easy to resolve any challenges, even if you have to wear a small loss. On some occasions, you will need to politely stand your ground. However, if you continually provide fair and reasonable exchanges and strive for productive outcomes, you can create a positive reputation within your marketplace.

Action 34: *Your collective marketplace presence can be challenged by clients and customers and you need to have a clear strategy for resolving issues quickly, respectfully and fairly based on multiple factors. Be willing to apologize, find out the facts and deliver a solution without reacting emotionally and fairly assessing the risk*

7. Market Presence

I have just discussed your location context - the general presence for your business - your fixed address, online address, platform presence and your collective marketplace address.

I would now like to look at the actual real estate that is at that address. If you can visualize for a moment that you are a real estate agent and you need to sell the property where you are currently living. You automatically realize that to secure interested buyers and the best price, you need to present your home attractively. You need to clear away the clutter, clean everything (including the windows) and have nice photos taken for the advertisements.

The same applies to your business. Your clients and customers want to have a nice experience when they visit your business 'home.' Most will not want your business to be messy, disorganized or confusing. You will need to be easily found so that you can generate enough interested purchasers. You will need to be presented credibly so that you can generate trust. You will need to establish a connection with people so that you can generate results.

I refer to this process as 'setting up quality real estate.' I see this as an essential component of your business strategy. As I mentioned earlier, I have worked in real estate for a while and my boss told me, "Homes sell themselves. The only reason they don't sell is the price."

If you extend this concept to your business, if the market does not see any value in your products and services, the price you can attract could be as low as zero (or be a cost if you have to pay to get rid of stock).

Many years ago, the sister of a friend of mine politely pointed out to me that I would often describe how much something cost in my general conversations. She made it clear that I did not have to explain the price of everything all the time. I had never noticed this habit and I am extremely grateful that she mentioned it to me. It changed my life - for the better!

I have now realized that I am no longer impressed when someone tells me how much something is 'worth.' I can also see how some people have fallen into the trap of knowing the price of everything and the value of nothing! We all have things that are priceless to us - like our best friend or some of our most treasured possessions filled with special memories.

In business, we need to showcase our value, not just our price. When a real estate agent showcases a home, they will describe how wonderful it would be to live there thanks to the local amenities, lifestyle and unique property features (like the north facing living area). They usually avoid any discussion about price until they have convinced you that you want to live there.

So if you want to showcase your products or services, you need to think about the value they provide and how that is appealing to your target audience. You need to sell the benefits not the features - the first lesson you will ever learn in any sales training. If you want to secure the sale and make sure the client or customer doesn't go elsewhere, they need to feel as if they are getting a better or different experience through you that is more rewarding.

Action 35: *Setting up quality real estate is an essential component of your marketing strategy. It is a way to showcase the value and benefits rather than the price and features of your products and services*

7.1 Business Premises Look And Feel

I am the first to admit that I am not an expert in retail layouts, merchandising, business fit outs, design or commercial real estate. What I do know is that it is well worthwhile making sure that you understand these principles if you have clients and customers visiting your business premises (and to gain the maximum productivity from your workspace).

What I would like to share are a couple of examples to emphasize this point. A small retail outlet in a busy strip of local shops could not entice passing pedestrian traffic to walk into her store. A store layout expert immediately identified the problem. There was too much open space at the doorway which made it intimidating for people to enter. The staff were also 'occupied' rather than open and attentive when people did enter the store so this meant that they did not attract any referrals either.

A large government department hired an expert in workplace activity based office design and reconfigured the entire layout of the office based on the workflow, staffing and outcome requirements of the government department. He was able to reduce the floor space by two thirds (which significantly dropped the rental amount), increase productivity and create a new and fresh environment for employees.

For many years, a home based business was considered very unprofessional. Nowadays, more and more people are choosing to combine lifestyle and work from a home location (or a co-working space) and these mini-work spaces still need to be carefully designed. As the business owner, you need to make sure that your own health and safety is maintained, that you complete tasks without putting stress or strain on your body and that visitors to your premises are also comfortable. Make sure that your working area is ergonomically optimized. If you are sitting for lengthy periods, please make sure that you can complete your tasks without bending your neck or over straining your arms.

If you cannot assist clients at your home location and you choose to meet your clients or customers at another location or their location, again, please make sure that everything you do is occupationally healthy and safe. Ideally, all of your fitouts wherever you go will be in alignment with your values and your ideal target audience. For example, if you are dealing with senior executives and discussing private personal details, it would be inappropriate to meet in a noisy and busy fast food restaurant!

As this book is about hyper local marketing, I would also like to encourage you to think about spaces that you can use in your local area. Startup food manufacturers often lease commercial kitchens from restaurants when they are not in use (for example early in the morning if the restaurant only opens for lunch and dinner). This saves the startup the full cost of setting up their own commercial kitchen.

Likewise, there are now websites and enterprises that offer various forms of sharing. Car sharing, home sharing, desk sharing, space sharing etc. Think about your real needs and you may find that by asking around your local area, a space that meets your requirements could be walking distance away from you.

This sharing approach also opens up other opportunities to connect with new audiences and can significantly reduce your ongoing costs and travel times. One colleague I met recently said she only visits the city on a Tuesday so if you want to meet her in the city, it has to be on a Tuesday, otherwise you need to visit her in the suburbs. This allows her to maintain the hyper local lifestyle that matches her values and helps reduce her time and money commuting.

Action 36: *If you are going to start implementing a hyper local marketing approach in your business, don't just think about ways to attract people to your products and services, think about ways that your premises can be acquired hyper locally and seek professional advice to optimize the space into an effective tool for your business*

7.2 Business Website Development

My first website went online in 2001 and I have seen a LOT of changes in website layouts since then. If you would like your website to be an effective marketing tool for your business, I believe that there are many essential components you need to consider.

As previously discussed in Section 6.2, you need to choose an appropriate domain name (unique resource locator - URL) and I would also add appropriate website hosting. I have chosen Bluehost (affiliate link https://bluehost.com/track/sueellson) as they offer unlimited websites and uploads and downloads. Most business owners usually end up with at least two websites, one for their business name and one for their own name (see Section 7.3).

Some website designers are now insisting that before they will even consider helping you create a website, you must provide the content up front. A website is similar to a brochure or a proposal or any other documentation prepared by the business - it is a publication. Like every other publication, it needs to be regularly updated, it is not 'set and forget.' In fact most businesses are finding that they need to do fairly significant work on their website at least every two years as well as regular updates, content additions and maintenance every month.

A lot of the significant updating is related to the layout, look, feel and functionality of the website - but interestingly, a lot of your content has the potential to be maintained or archived to provide ongoing value. That is why I encourage you to start with a great foundation that can be added to in the future so that your 'old' content can support your 'new' content.

This is not always possible, especially if you have a predominantly product based business, but it can make a huge difference in terms of online presence and building your digital assets.

One of the biggest priorities for you to come up in online search results is your location. Everyone who accesses the internet is giving away their current location (via the IP address of their internet service provider or the geolocation of their mobile device). So if you are standing in the main street of a city and you search for a hairdresser, it is likely to find a hairdresser close to where you are standing, even if you do not mention the city name in your search query.

So in terms of hyper local marketing, I encourage you to mention your location in your website content and in your metadata. It is also a good idea to include nearby locations as well. You also need to use the keywords in your content that match the most relevant search queries for your target audience.

Google has clearly stated that they expect every website to have an 'About' page and a 'Contact' page. I currently use WordPress.org as the Content Management System (CMS) for my websites and I encourage you to consider the following as minimum requirements for your business website:

- About page and Contact page

- relevant details of your products and services (include everything that your target audience needs to know)

- a publicly available Site Map so that visitors can access any page or post on your website

- plugins that enable you to maintain your website security, backup your website automatically, search engine optimize your website and cache your website so that it loads quickly

- a blog section so that you can regularly add new content that can remain indefinitely - where possible, publish a mix of content that has both a dynamic (real time) and evergreen (lifetime) aspect

- resized and labelled images that you own and preferably original (with both a Title tag and an Alt tag)

- keyword optimized content (but still think of the person viewing the content, not just the search engine robots)

- a key understanding of the business process that you want visitors to complete - what do you want them to do when they visit your website? (See Section 7.3)

- consistent layout and regular use of an individual Style Guide aligned to your business and your target audience

- similarly formatted and branded content on your other business online and offline real estate (logos, colors, fonts, styles, look and feel)

- additional bells and whistles according to your business - videos, memberships, email newsletter subscriptions, media kit, frequently asked questions (FAQ), associated apps, social media or event integrations etc

It is important for you to have a good understanding of the use and value of your business website. Although a lot of business is done by referral - also known as word of mouth (around 85%), if the referred person chooses to visit your website before doing business and they don't like your website, then you run the risk of losing that referral.

I have been teaching people how to create a simple WordPress website for several years now and I always remind them that done is better than perfect. I would rather see someone start with a basic website and grow rather than wait longer and have an almost perfect website.

I say almost perfect because it is virtually impossible to start with a perfect website. As soon as it goes live, you will come up with other ideas (or other people will give you other ideas). So in my view, you are better to get your Minimum Viable Product up and running and then just do updates and revisions as time goes on. Realize that to grow a business, you have to start somewhere. Your website will always be a version number rather than finished.

One of my clients managed her own website entirely on her own for four years before calling me back for an update. As a sole trader, I was very impressed to see that she had maintained 5,000 unique visits a month for most of that time (and all she does is add some fresh, personally crafted content every month).

Anyway, I found a new layout (theme) that was a good 'quick fix' but it had a red colored font and she said "But red is difficult for people to read." I said, "Yes, but let's just get the website up and then we can change the font color later." If we had stopped to change the font color at that point and then decided to look for another theme, we could have wasted hours and not progressed at all. She ended up being very happy to have a new website layout done in less than two hours of consulting time!

Action 37: *Make sure that your website meets minimum Google requirements and has the essential components to stand up to the rigour of judgment from people who have either found your website on their own or been referred to your website by someone else. Understand that your website will constantly evolve over time and it is a good idea to start with a Minimum Viable Product and improve with revisions later*

7.3 Personal Authority Website Development

When I first started my Newcomers Network enterprise and I was contacted by journalists, I was always surprised when they wanted to know my story rather than the story of the business. I wanted to share the concept of the enterprise, not my personal details!

Whilst you might have a great idea for a business or even a great business, you may not be someone who wants to 'put your name in lights' and tell everyone your story. This could be related to your cultural background or your personality preference or as a result of a negative experience in the past.

What I have realized is that, like it or not, clients, customers, the media, other businesses, stakeholders etc all want to know your story and reasons why you decided to be an entrepreneur or business owner.

If you feel a little uneasy about this concept, I would like you to take a moment and think about a website you visited where there was no 'About' page, their Contact page did not include a street address or phone number (only a Contact form) and a general Google search only revealed their own website and no other references. How would you feel about buying products or services from this business? Would you feel confident that the business was even legitimate?

The way I see it, if you want to be in business, you need to be the face of your business, at least to some extent. There are very few CEO's who can get by without ever being interviewed, photographed or asked to represent the enterprise at formal occasions. That doesn't mean that you have to be a perfect diplomat and ambassador and have your name and face in lights at all times, it just means that you have to have a presence that people can verify.

As you already know, my first book was *'120 Ways To Achieve Your Purpose With LinkedIn'* so as a minimum, I would encourage you to fully develop a LinkedIn Profile as this will help you appear in Google Search Results when someone looks for you by name. It is also a good idea to have a page on your website that is exclusively about you - for example http://yourbusiness.com/about/your-name.

The next level is a personal Authority Website. This website usually has your name as the domain name (URL) - for example http://yourname.com. This is where you can showcase your background in a way that feels comfortable for you.

As a minimum, your Authority Website needs to include:

- your name, qualifications and membership details

- a biography that can be used to introduce you with the details of your business

- a high resolution photo that can be downloaded for print publications

- a contact form or contact details or the details of your agent

If you would like to go to the next level with an Authority Website, where you actually use it as a tool to generate interest, referrals and opportunity for your business, you could:

- have a blog where you regularly (at least three times per year), add new content. You could also include an archive of all of your 'past' content

- provide a media kit in preparation for journalist enquiries

- showcase your background in more detail - publications, presentations, career and business journey

- include a portfolio of your work and/or picture gallery

- publish testimonials and reviews (you may have to ask for them)

- provide tools and resources that people can access immediately as well as a shop for more value added items

- offer bonuses and discounts for your resources that are not available through other channels or use it as a tool for connecting with affiliate programs

- your social media feeds - Facebook, Twitter etc as well as any other resources hosted elsewhere - podcasts, ebooks, videos etc

- appropriate calls to action depending on what you would like to secure - free publicity or media coverage, speaking engagements, profiling in relevant publications, joint venture partners, affiliates etc

- visually appealing instant credibility images - well known logos for where you have been featured or profiled (make sure that the logos have been uniformly resized and are good quality)

- subscribe options - newsletter, blog notifications, podcasts, video channel, special offers list etc

- list of past clients or collaborators, particularly if they are well known or recognized - this could include keynote presentations at large conferences and key stakeholders, suppliers or distributors associated with your business. These mentions give you 'borrowed' authority

- easy to find popular content, recent content and specific content depending on the visitor's interest. Profiling the popular content can be very effective

- separate your content into how people like to consume the content - visual (videos and pictures), audio (podcasts and recordings) and written (text, posts and publications)

- additional engagement tools - upcoming events, webinars and expos, online tools (like quizzes and relevant assessments), free valuable downloads, social media feeds etc

I encourage you to make sure that your personal Authority Website is easy to navigate and that you keep like information together so that everything is easy to find. You will need to think carefully about the categories you are going to use both now and in the future so that you can add content in a logical manner.

Remember that even if your past experience was in a different field, there are still many transferable skills and most people are usually curious about understanding the 'story' behind a person. I have also purchased the domain names of my children and I often joke that they will have to pay me a lot of money if they want to own them in the future! I have even heard of some parents and godparents purchasing domain names for children when they are born and one man has created an email address for his daughter and he sends her an email every year on her birthday so that when she is older, she will be able to look back and see her birthday greetings. I liked that idea!

If the concept of all of this content is completely overwhelming to you, particularly if you are someone who likes to remain private, remember that for the most part, this content is all historical - it is not about what you are doing right now or the future (although it can be used to attract those opportunities).

Also, you could choose to write your content in such a way that you are perceived to be a 'guru' or 'expert' or you can simply describe what you have done and infer the guru or expert status. I prefer the second option to be honest. That said, I also have to be careful that I can live up to the perception that I create! Rest assured, I do think very carefully about what I publish online before I publish it and in some cases, I stop broadcasting information even though I have it available as I do not want to saturate my marketplace at any point, but I do want to retain my currency and relevancy within the marketplace.

You also need to think about your ultimate goal. Are you wanting to profile yourself as an individual or do you want to help people understand why you do what you do and transfer them to your business website? Perhaps you would like to generate additional sales through your own identity? All of these goals can be achieved through an effectively designed, updated and maintained personal Authority Website.

Action 38: *A personal Authority Website in your own name can provide additional interest, referrals and opportunities for you and your business. It can be very brief and just provide a basic outline of your background or it can showcase you as an authority within your industry and/or profession. Select your goal and go for it*

7.4 Real World Marketing And Advertising

Whether you are a franchise business in a particular location or a small business in just one location (or anything in between), you will need to have a range of fixed and moving messages in the marketplace.

Fixed messages can include outdoor or indoor signage, billboards, car decals that remain visible and moving messages can include merchandise, brochures, business cards, proposals etc.

If you would like to include a hyper local approach to real world marketing and advertising, including your location or context information is vital.

You will also need to think about your target audience and what will appeal to them.

There is a famous quote by John Wannamaker - "Half the money I spend on advertising is wasted; the trouble is, I don't know which half." I would like to suggest that whether you choose to invest time or money into marketing or advertising, it is important for you to make a calculated investment.

I usually encourage startup businesses to choose all of the free options first. That doesn't necessarily mean that they are the best, but they are a good place to start when there is a zero or limited budget for marketing and advertising.

I can honestly say that I always consider a range of factors before I spend any money on marketing and advertising and for most of my business life, I have not spent any direct money on marketing and advertising - but I have spent a lot of money on my education about how to market and advertise my business.

You will learn a lot about these techniques throughout this book. More recently, I have spent money to attend and present at major conferences and expos. If you look at the actual dollar spend and the directly attributable return, I would calculate that I am running at a loss - but my business is running at a profit!

Why you may ask? Well it is because the exposure and branding generated by these big ticket items increases my presence in my location and within my context vertical. It makes me stand out and it increases the value perception of my business. I have always worked with the idea of a long term vision rather than a short term quick win and I look for multiple ways to re-purpose any of the content generated from these marketing and advertising activities so that I can continue to source a benefit beyond the initial spend.

What marketing ideas do you usually use? Would you like to assess the viability of your marketing ideas? If so, I would like you to rate from 0 to 10 the following items. A zero reflects either not applicable or not possible and 10 says absolutely and positively verifiable and correct.

Marketing Idea Viability Test

Describe the Marketing Idea _____

Aligned with your values	0_1_2_3_4_5_6_7_8_9_10
Reaches your specific target audience with good distribution options	0_1_2_3_4_5_6_7_8_9_10
Reaches a wider audience that knows your target audience well	0_1_2_3_4_5_6_7_8_9_10
Is personalized for the person receiving the message	0_1_2_3_4_5_6_7_8_9_10
Can be automated	0_1_2_3_4_5_6_7_8_9_10
Can be replicated	0_1_2_3_4_5_6_7_8_9_10
Can be up scaled	0_1_2_3_4_5_6_7_8_9_10
Is affordable (cost per customer acquisition)	0_1_2_3_4_5_6_7_8_9_10
Is good for the local community	0_1_2_3_4_5_6_7_8_9_10

Is not harmful to the environment (and may be beneficial for the environment)	0_1_2_3_4_5_6_7_8_9_10
Allows for collaboration with another non-competing businesses	0_1_2_3_4_5_6_7_8_9_10
Builds your brand in the local area or context	0_1_2_3_4_5_6_7_8_9_10
Can be re-purposed	0_1_2_3_4_5_6_7_8_9_10
Is evergreen (relevant today and tomorrow)	0_1_2_3_4_5_6_7_8_9_10
You can maintain publication or business rights	0_1_2_3_4_5_6_7_8_9_10
Can be archived and kept online on your website	0_1_2_3_4_5_6_7_8_9_10
Provides specific data and measurable results	0_1_2_3_4_5_6_7_8_9_10
Provides new qualitative information	0_1_2_3_4_5_6_7_8_9_10
The follow up can be completed quickly	0_1_2_3_4_5_6_7_8_9_10
The idea can be improved and updated	0_1_2_3_4_5_6_7_8_9_10

Was there anything else you thought of when you asked yourself these questions? If so, write down your ideas or concerns now:

_____

_____

_____

Your total score ____

The maximum score is 200 points.

If your idea is in the 0-50 points range, unless it is free and you have the time to do it, I would suggest that you ignore the marketing idea as it really could be more trouble than it is worth.

If the score is between 50-100, I would suggest that you need to think very carefully about proceeding and really assess whether or not you will be committed to making the marketing idea work for your business.

Once you move into the 100-150 category, you are getting much closer to a viable idea. However, you need to carefully evaluate the strengths and weaknesses and make a business decision on whether any additional time or money you need to spend will generate a reasonable return (branding or cash flow).

If the marketing idea scores 150-200 points, you are well on the way to a successful marketing idea. It is important not to be complacent at this point because there is never one single silver bullet that solves every challenge. I would also like to reiterate that you must take responsibility for the whole marketing idea. There is no point in paying a huge amount for a particular marketing idea and then not following up on the leads or opportunities that have been generated. You don't just pay money and then not analyze the results and look at ways to improve outcomes the next time you consider the opportunity.

It is also important to re-evaluate your ideas over time. The value from certain activities can change - circulation or attendance can decline, the number of inclusions can change and even the commitment of the individual or enterprise offering the opportunity can change, sometimes without notice.

For example, I was involved in an expo and the previous year, the exhibition company had spent a lot of money on television advertising. I falsely assumed that the same would occur the next year, but instead, they only had radio advertising in the final week. I was very disappointed. Fortunately, they changed the ticket price to free and that attracted a lot more visitors to the expo, so I ended up with an alternative benefit - however, I may have gained a lot more recognition for my business if the television advertising had proceeded. I will never know.

You also need to think about some new factors that are coming in with technology. Some online platforms are becoming:

- noisy (too many posts or contributors)

- highly competitive (only the good quality content gets attention)

- expensive (requiring you to pay to play)

- complex (requiring you to master a new set of rules, skills, sharing abilities)

- unpredictable (regularly changing - what worked yesterday may not work today)

- overwhelming (too much to do, see, watch etc)

- demanding (require a lot of work, technical competency, production quality, personal input not automation etc)

You may like to factor in these issues on top of your Marketing Idea Viability Test.

What I do know is that regardless of the outcome of any marketing idea, tomorrow there will be another day and as a business owner, I need to let go of any disappointment and simply move on! I need to accept the good and the bad and make a more informed decision the next time when a similar opportunity becomes available.

Action 39: *Before selecting a marketing idea, consider assessing the idea via a marketing idea viability test and measure the concept against a range of criteria. Once selected, even if the idea is not 100% perfect, be committed to making it a success but also be willing to let go and move on if it doesn't go according to plan*

7.5 Currency, Recency And Relevancy

At any given point in time, certain marketing ideas have different levels of currency, recency and relevancy.

Currency refers to how valuable they are within the current context or location. Do they perform well in the current marketplace? They may be old ideas or new ideas, but either way, they still work well at this point in time.

Recency refers to how recently they were created. Sometimes it takes an entirely new approach to keep up with the times.

I was involved in a small community group that wanted to sell tickets to three concerts via a cash collection at their meeting each week - but they also wanted to sell the tickets to people in the community who did not attend the meetings - so obviously this method simply would not work for their current goals. They implemented an online ticket purchase option but unfortunately they didn't sell very many tickets that way as they didn't use the system themselves and they didn't promote it actively - but if they had done so, this recent innovation could have made a huge difference to their ticket sales. Sadly, the following year they went back to their old system and they had dismal sales and the year after that, they had one concert instead of three. This year, it appears to have been cancelled altogether.

Relevancy refers to how relevant the idea is in relation to the values of the business and the target audience. There is no point adopting a marketing idea that would be irrelevant to your target audience. It is a bit like trying to sell your service via an app that only works on iPhones when most of your target clients have an Android phone.

I am always amazed at how often people choose ideas that are not relevant to their target audience. They save pennies in valuable areas and waste pounds in useless areas. They often waste a lot of time too. Just because something has been done a particular way for a long time doesn't mean that it is still relevant - the proverbial goal posts may have changed, so it is important to change and adapt.

I have previously mentioned the 'shiny object syndrome.' Unfortunately I have met a lot of people who have attended what I call 'ra-ra' seminars where they learn the 'latest marketing ideas' and they appear to be instantly sold on the latest system, they rush to the back of the room, they buy up big and then they never implement the system.

Or alternatively, they try and implement the system but they realize later that the idea will only work in a city with a huge population and a high level of discretionary income.

So, as a further expansion on the marketing idea viability test, I encourage you to think about the currency, recency and relevancy of any initiative you implement in your business. If you are spending time with other business owners within your location or context, you may be able to ask around and see what works in their business.

Action 40: *Every marketing idea or business initiative that you implement in your business needs to be valuable within your current context (currency), recently created if a new challenge has appeared (recency) and relevant in relation to your business values and target audience (relevancy). Avoid wasting time or money on ideas that ultimately are not aligned with your business goals*

8. Online And Digital Marketing

The ways to market your business online have changed significantly over the last 10 years. I suspect they will change in many different ways in the years to come.

At present, we are mainly relying on text information to source answers to our questions. The search engine robots index online text based on a variety of algorithms (complex mathematical equations), to generate the best and fastest results.

These algorithms are constantly updated to make sure that the best results are featured, not the 'spam' results. When the idea of search engine optimizing online content first appeared, search engine optimization specialists would recommend all sorts of techniques to help a business appear at the top of online search results.

Unfortunately, a lot of these 'sneaky' techniques have eventually been black listed as black hat techniques. Some of them include:

- sourcing backlinks from other websites (sometimes in other countries)
- re-posting the same content on multiple websites
- trying to add keywords in a font color that is the same as the background color so they do not appear to the user but they may be added to the index
- buying fans or followers on social media platforms
- promoting a website design company on the bottom of every page of a website

Suffice to say that the problem with these or any other black hat online digital marketing techniques is that they are eventually incorporated into the search engine algorithms criteria checks so if your website or online presence has used any of these techniques, you will find that you have paid to have them added and you will need to pay again to have them removed (preferably before you are black listed or penalized and removed from search results).

Action 41: *Do not be tempted to implement shortcut search engine optimization techniques that have the potential to be black listed in the future. If you do, you will usually pay to have them added and have to pay again to have them removed as well as recover from any penalty that may occur*

8.1 White Hat Search Engine Optimization (SEO) Techniques

The good news is that there will always be 'white hat' techniques that will stand the test of time and search engine algorithms and updates to help you appear on the first page of organic search results.

These principles are not guaranteed either right now or in the future, but so far, they have stood the test of time:

- including your location name in your content (and an interactive map)
- including keyword specific content that is user friendly
- regularly updating and adding new content
- including interlinks (within your website), external links (especially to high authority and high ranking websites), genuine backlinks (to your website) and reciprocal links (where you link to a website and they link to you) - but not too many in relation to the amount of text on your website
- content that is marked up appropriately (headings, snippets, meta descriptions, titles, alt tags for images etc)
- content that is shared on high ranking and high authority websites

As you can see, all of these suggestions are based on the written word with the goal of providing the viewer (customer) with a great user experience.

More search engine queries are now being spoken rather than typed, so a key element of future search engine optimized content will be making sure that your content answers spoken questions (called conversational queries) rather than typed word based queries.

At present, the word or identification content within images, audio files and videos is not fully indexed in search engines, but I believe that all of this content will be indexed in the very near future (at present, the descriptions for these objects are used but they are usually very brief).

Once this type of comprehensive search is enabled, the internet will be able to use machine learning, artificial intelligence and advanced insight based predictions to deliver even better automatic and natural style search results.

Essentially, your content needs to be search engine friendly and compliant - authentic, relevant, valuable to the viewer and for the benefit of your business, actionable.

Action 42: *Make sure that any content you publish on behalf of your business is search engine friendly and enables people to have a good user experience. Good quality content can ultimately lead to actionable behavior that leads to opportunities for your business. Wherever you have an opportunity to provide details, tags or descriptions with your content, do so*

8.2 Search Engine Ranking Factors

Google, Bing and other search engines will never tell you exactly how their algorithms assess website search engine results (or even whether or not your site will be indexed and available in search results).

As most searches are currently completed with Google, I encourage you to visit https://www.google.com.au/insidesearch/howsearchworks/algorithms.html for a more comprehensive outline of some of the current criteria being considered when ranking your website.

You may also like to think about:

- the popularity of your website (compared to others in your niche - revisit your competitor analysis information)

- how long people stay on your website when they click a link to your website from a search engine results page (SERP)

- the credibility of your website (this assumes that people will spend at least 30 seconds or more on your website)

- the actions your website inspires (do visitors dig deeper and complete transactions?)

- how well your website converts (if people go to the shop page, do they buy?)

- how quickly they go through to a completed transaction (if instructions are simple and easy to understand, if buttons say 'Call, Buy, Register or Subscribe' rather than 'Submit')

- making it quick and easy to complete processes (by pre-ticking relevant boxes)

- choosing a relevant domain name (register as early as possible, even if you don't plan to publish immediately, but do not worry about an exact keyword match domain name as these do not guarantee selection - which also means you do not necessarily need to register every other variation of a domain name - but do a risk assessment before making a final decision)

- nominating the country where you are trying to attract the most search results (this can be done via the country code in the domain name (for example .co.uk for the United Kingdom) or by nominating the target country in the Google Search Console / Google Webmaster Tools at https://www.google.com/webmasters

- making sure your website loads quickly (in less than two seconds - for every second after two seconds there is a significant drop off in the amount of time the person stays on the website)

- ensuring your website is optimized for mobile devices (check out the Accelerated Mobile Pages Project at https://www.ampproject.org)

- securing some initial traffic by either paying for advertisements or utilizing other influencers, publications or networks to visit your website

Some of these items will be discussed again in different sections of the book. The reason they are mentioned here is just to set the scene for you to think about these factors when creating or updating your online presence. Your goal is not just to create loads of visits to your website or clicks on your website, your ultimate goal with your online marketing is to generate conversions.

Action 43: *Search engine algorithms assess multiple criteria to assess the relevance of your website for the search engine index and search engine results. Understand these principles when creating and updating your website to help your enterprise attract additional traffic and ultimately, conversions*

8.3 Content Marketing Strategies That Work

Can you see how all of the above Search Engine Optimization suggestions are based on Content? Consistently adding, revising and optimizing content?

I have personally found that my 'old' content regularly resurfaces to the top of search engine results because the search engines have identified that the content has:

- generated engagement (click throughs, shares etc)

- been viewed for a specific duration (multiple seconds or minutes)

- been helpful (and not made the viewer bounce back to other search engine results)

- loaded quickly (because images were re-sized and the on-page formatting was appropriate)

- been re-visited as well as viewed just once
- been featured on other websites and online platforms, newsletters etc
- been found via a direct link from somewhere else like forums, groups etc
- been constantly added to (or updated) over time
- been formatted appropriately so that it is scan-friendly, broken up into useful sections with headings, bullets, numbering, images, videos etc.

This re-purposing of content hasn't happened automatically. The content has been featured on my own websites but also on other high profile websites and from time to time, I send out a reminder about the content being 'popular' so it gets a renewed boost.

What I like about a content marketing strategy for a well designed website is that with a good content road map and a consistent approach to providing value to users (visitors) over time, you can help search engines deliver great results.

I encourage you to think of multiple factors when creating your content:

- dynamic content (relevant right now and perhaps aligned with a current topic)
- evergreen content (relevant on an ongoing or lifetime basis and always topical)
- indexable content (published now but sorted or archived logically so it remains accessible over time but remains historically useful)

As a business, you need to work out what sort of content is going to be added on an ongoing basis. At the most basic level, this includes text, images (including infographics), audio and video.

Over time, I believe that other technologies will also be part of the multimedia content mix - presentations, animations, virtual reality, games, apps, simulations - in fact any form of digital media or interactive technology.

Action 44: *Creating and publishing search engine optimized content allows you to attract good quality search engine results. Ideally, your business should create a mix of dynamic, evergreen and historically useful content that has been enhanced with additional digital media*

8.4 Amplifying The Value And Conversions From Your Content

Regardless of what type of content you produce and publish, responding to a current issue allows you to generate dynamic content - it is relevant and current right now. If it is extremely topical or clever, it may also go viral.

Producing evergreen content allows you to get value from your content today, tomorrow, next week, next year etc. - essentially over a lifetime.

By having a logical system for adding your content so that it can be easily sorted, indexed and found over time allows your older content to continue to perform well long after it has been published.

It is also a good idea to think about how you can optimize your content on both your website and anywhere else that you publish information. If you want to maximize the opportunities for your business, you need to identify what has worked well and then amplify its impact.

For example, one of my longest clients has one particular post on her website that performs better than any other page or post - even better than her Home, About and Contact pages combined. After discovering this fact, we reviewed the content on this post and updated the post to help convert visitors to paying clients.

We discovered that the reason the post wasn't converting visitors to leads was because the entire visitor question was answered in the post. To convert the post to a lead generation tool, we adjusted the content to think about other ways we could help the visitor who had discovered this post. We did not remove the valuable and useful content, we just increased the included value, created a much more relevant call to action and provided more effective actionable suggestions.

Now that we know how valuable this post is, we can extend its value by trying to re-share it through online platforms and make the post even more relevant for the high performing search result and similar search queries.

If you are just starting out in business, I encourage you to start with adding content to your website on a regular basis and broadcasting the details of that new content through various channels - social media, email newsletters, online platforms (especially Google+) etc and also share it with key individuals who are willing to pass it on to their networks.

Generating engagement and community discussion takes time so this may not happen immediately after posting if you are just starting out. But you need to build up a great back catalogue of good quality and well distributed content. If you can encourage people you know to Like, Comment or Share the content soon after you have posted it on online platforms, that will help.

Likewise, if your content does hit a nerve and performs well, consider redistributing it with a different introduction or message. You do not need to respond to every 'Like' but if you can respond to every Comment or Share, this will be viewed favorably by online platform algorithms.

This particular technique has been proven by another man I met who had amassed over one million Facebook Page Likes for his Korean Pop Music enterprise. To maintain the level of community conversation, conversions and responsiveness to comments and shares on his Facebook Page, he had 80 people across the world dedicated to the task of responding to Comments and Replies as quickly as possible.

He would always encourage his highly engaged community to visit his website where he had special offers, a shop and various techniques to add visitors to his business database. He generated a very healthy income with this methodology - but as I have mentioned, it took 80 people to maintain this lead generation funnel.

The risk of this particular strategy is that if the Facebook algorithms change, his strategy could become redundant overnight - or he may be required to 'pay to play' to maintain the momentum. If his payments continued to generate an income, you could argue that he could just continue - but I like to manage risk and not be at the mercy of any platform or process that is susceptible to significant change. The principle of creating regular content and distributing it effectively is the essential lesson here. If it performs well, do what you can to amplify its effect.

Action 45: *When you identify content that has performed well for your business, make an effort to amplify its impact by adding even more value, updating your call to action and providing more effective actionable suggestions. If people respond with a Comment or a Share, make an effort to respond personally.*

8.5 Developing Viral Content And Conversions

Have you ever noticed that the most popular content that gets shared around online platforms is usually a positive message that evokes a strong emotional reaction? You may have also noticed that it is:

- witty, funny or a little bit unusual

- visually appealing (usually includes an image or an image with text or video)

- it appears very genuine (perhaps including numbers, facts, statistics or a quote from someone with authority)

- it could be something ground-breaking, particularly innovative, controversial or distinct in a unique way

- it triggers off a reaction with your target audience and then they instantly react or respond by commenting or sharing

- it responds to hard data and facts as to what people are genuinely interested in (there is a joke that the internet will always be about 'cats' - and of course who can resist a baby or a cute animal doing something funny?)

- it is easy to view, share and re-distribute (and this process is usually very quick too and strategically located for ease of use)

- it provides value in the form of information, education or entertainment

- it is memorable and persuasive in its own right and the viewer feels compelled to share the experience with others, especially if it triggers a surprise

- there is an element of story (relatable) or interactivity (participation) that helps engage the viewer

It would be easy to think that generating something that goes viral is the key to business success - however, that is like being a musician who is just a one-hit-wonder. If you want to drive conversions rather than just traffic, you need to consistently provide content that has the potential to be viral but also actionable. At the end of the day, making something popular is good for your vanity, but it is not necessarily good for your business.

Viral content needs to provide value and the call to action that accompanies the content needs to be congruent and aligned. If you create a great video and then say - "buy this product right now," it may not necessarily work. But if you trigger an emotion that makes the person want to buy the product, all you need to do is provide the call to action that will facilitate the person's choice with the transaction - "choose your favorite color now."

To test out ideas on what could go viral, look at what has gone viral in the past. Again, there is no need to reinvent the wheel - borrow concepts and ideas from others (but don't imitate exactly as you will look like a cheapskate and a copy cat). Experiment and see what works depending on the nature of the content, the time of day that you share it, the locations where you share it and so on.

Also consider the language that you use. Try incorporating hypnotic and persuasive words that can encourage a person to take action. You can also add a level of credibility by associating with a brand or person that is well known and respected - and if you want a hyper local flavor, personalize it to focus on your context or location.

To really assess the virality of your content, you may like to use additional testing and measuring tools. You can track how many click throughs have been generated via traditional Google Analytics but there are also many other online tools that can:

- track your links

- track the profile of other viral links

- reveal trending topics

- provide keyword suggestions

- measure click engagement and bounce rates

- provide details of backlinks to content

- export analytics data

- operate as an internet browser extension and provide on-screen information

If you have a 'mid way' option before the final conversion, you could track how many people engage with the first stage (pop up subscribes, notifications, survey results, engagement with incentives etc).

Viral content can also be manufactured with a helping 'paid' hand. You may like to sponsor a post and have it re-distributed automatically more than once to your defined target audience. A post that was missed on the first view may generate engagement if it is seen several times.

For example, I regularly find that a previously popular quote or video regularly re-appears in my news feed from different friends days, weeks or even months after I saw it for the first time. I may not share it the first time I see it, but I am sometimes tempted to share it after I have seen it three times.

When sponsored content first appeared in news feeds, it was often automatically dismissed - but now that sponsored content is often targeted at people who are genuinely interested in the topic, the rate of conversion is increasing.

To sum up, viral content aims to automatically encourage the viewer to share it amongst their network and it has the potential to significantly increase the overall reach of your content - with or without your involvement.

Action 46: *If you can generate content that encourages viewers to share it through their networks, you can significantly increase content views, engagement and conversions and amplify its impact. There are many different ways to create content that has the potential to go viral - so think carefully about your target audience and what sort of behavior you would like to trigger before publication and use different tools to test and measure what has the greatest potential to go viral*

8.6 Sending The Right Signals

In the past, a great deal of marketing was based on demographic information which grouped people into certain categories based on specific sections of the population.

With the explosion in data that is now collected through so many different sources, more and more marketing is based on data analysis which is used to predict a person's behavior (or possible interests).

There are many examples in our everyday online activity. Have you noticed how:

- advertisements appear on your screen related to previous searches or websites you have previously visited

- your search results often include details of locations or websites you have previously visited

- items or topics appear in your news feed based on the background of your most common denominator connections

- you do not automatically receive notifications unless you choose 'Follow'

- 'people you may know' suggestions automatically appear via online platforms and you often do know the people listed

- automatic play selections are closely aligned to your personal preferences (music, videos etc)

- if you have engaged with content from a particular person, you are more likely to receive notifications about content from that person in the future

These examples are just a small sample of an analysis of the data that is collected every single day from your online activity. As a business owner, you need to think about the behavior signals you are sending out and how to reach your target audience.

Cookies, tracking pixels and platform algorithms are constantly collecting and assessing data to help generate relevant user experiences. Search engines are constantly assessing whether or not what you find works for you, if it is true editorial content rather than advertorial content, what your overall intent is with a search and how popular certain results perform over time.

So as a business, you need to be aware of how your behavior is affecting your results and how you can use these tools to attract your target audience.

For example, if you want to see how your website is performing in search results for your keywords, you really need to be able to complete a search from your 'target audience' person's device. Your search results could easily be skewed by your past online behavior.

If you want to add cookies, tracking pixels and measurement tools that can track behavior on your online real estate for your business, you can then make decisions about what to do in the future in direct correlation to your target audience's behavior.

For example, if you have a Facebook pixel on your website that calculates that a certain person has visited your website, you can then create an advertisement that will appear in that person's news feed (without you ever knowing the details of the actual person who visited your website). This is a great way to reinforce an experience the person received when they visited your website, particularly if it is related to a particular page of your website (for example, a special upcoming event).

Naturally the type of signals that are being monitored and the types of activities that can be generated from these signals will constantly change over time. For now, I just want to encourage you to think about your own online behavior and the behavior of your target audience and assess how being able to understand the concept of signals can be used to tailor your hyper local marketing activities.

Once you understand the signals concept, it may be necessary for you to consult an expert to install these tools and make appropriate recommendations on how to best utilize the data you collect and optimize your conversion ability. You may also like to re-assess how you behave online as it is also affecting your online experience.

You may decide to regularly clear your browsing history and cookies, sign out of your online accounts when searching online and view content in your internet browser in incognito mode. Alternatively, you may like to leave everything turned on so that the content you see is more automatically tailored to your interests based on your previously transmitted signals.

Action 47: *Be aware that you and your target audience are generating signals based on your measured behavior. There are various tools you can use in your business to track and connect with your target audience including cookies, tracking pixels and other measurement tools*

8.7 Sourcing Hyper Local Website Links

In Section 8.1 I discussed having links as part of your hyper local marketing strategy and on your own website, you will want to have interlinks, external links, backlinks and reciprocal links.

However, the last thing you want to do is have an ad hoc strategy where you just aim to collect as many links as possible. With a hyper local marketing strategy, you need to collect links from your context and location sources.

I have found that a lot of websites will often mention a name of a person or business but not link to their online presence. This is a wasted opportunity - for both websites!

For example, a lot of professional associations offer a membership program. Unfortunately, a lot of them do not list the members on their website, or if they do, they do not provide a link to the member's website. If they did and the member linked to the professional association, both websites would benefit from this reciprocal link.

Likewise, a lot of members of professional associations fail to link to the professional association on their website - another wasted opportunity.

Online platforms like LinkedIn allow you to link to more than one website, so again, there is another opportunity to link your own website as well as your professional association/s to your LinkedIn Profile. This also helps the algorithms measure your interests - if you are linking to a context vertical, that has the same keywords, then you MUST be interested in that topic.

So, let's look at a range of ways to maximize links as part of your hyper local marketing:

- always complete your online platform profiles and make sure that you are linking to your business website

- add the details of any other links you have online to your website, to your Google+ profile and anywhere you can list multiple websites

- keep your other online platform profiles up to date (for example your professional membership profile). As a member, you are usually reminded to pay your membership fee but you may forget to fill out your online profile. If your professional membership does not currently offer a website link, ask them to make one available

- source local websites where you can add a link to your website - in particular local online directories, business listings and local government records

- look for local industry groups, trader associations, regional networks etc and see if you can participate and establish a link on their website

- consider aggregator or portal websites (for location and context), especially if they are good quality websites and/or offer a free listing. These are particularly relevant for certain industries, in particular accommodation, tourism, hospitality etc

- consider local business networks or community groups that offer an online presence as well as events and activities

- look for local media - radio, newspapers, television, online magazines, podcast programs etc and see if they offer either a free or paid listing

- see if local classified advertisement resources offer links as well as advertisements

- if you enter any awards and are a finalist, link to this notification

You may find that there are many other locations for securing links in your local area. The above list is focusing on 'open to all' offerings within a context or location, however I will examine a variety of other specific relationships you can develop throughout this book.

Your priority should be to constantly look for linking opportunities, particularly reciprocal links that are related to your business purpose and values (not just links for the sake of links). Links will be particularly valuable if they are located on a website that is:

- closely related to your context or location (even more value if the keywords are similar)

- a high authority website

- a highly ranked website

- a highly search engine optimized website

- influential in its own right

- part of a diverse group of websites with relevant links

- well established with a good performance track record
- well indexed in search engines
- popular, reliable and regularly appears in search results
- able to generate conversions - for their own enterprise and yours
- regularly updated

Likewise, you can offer a similar value to other enterprises if your website meets these criteria as well.

Action 48: *To market your website hyper locally via website links, look for websites that offer a range of search engine benefits based on the concepts of relevance, authority, ranking, search engine optimization, influence, performance, indexing, popularity, reliability, conversions and currency (updated regularly)*

If you have decided to ask another enterprise to link to your website, you need to think about the most appropriate way to ask for the link.

A lot of people do not like to be 'sold' to. The idea of telling the person that this will be great for you if you link to me via email is probably not the best way to get started.

You need to really assess the situation and make sure that you understand the nature of their enterprise, their target audience and their values. Once you have this understanding, you need to personalize your request and clearly explain the benefits and value to their enterprise of providing the link. It also needs to be their decision in the end and you need to be polite throughout the process, even if they say no.

There are also special circumstances. If you have been featured in the media or a publication, the journalist may not automatically want to end the editorial commentary with a plug for your business. In this case, try and provide the journalist or interviewer with a specific value-add so that they may be more inclined to provide your details.

For example, if your business has been profiled in a publication that is talking about an upcoming local festival, you may be able to provide a specific link to information about your involvement in the festival (http://yourbusiness.com/local-festival-name-year). This type of link provides genuine value to the reader and links to specific information on your website. It is also better than a direct link to the festival website. Naturally, on this page or post on your website you would also link to the local festival website.

If you have asked for a link, make an effort to also link to that enterprise on your website - that way you can both benefit from a reciprocal link. Even if the other person or enterprise decides not to link to you, you can still link to them because there is still search engine value from a link to another relevant website.

Action 49: *When asking for a link to your website, make sure you do your research and personalize your request, clearly outlining how some value can be exchanged. Remain polite, even if the answer is 'no.' Remember that you can still link to them even if they do not link to you*

8.8 Improving Overall Online Performance

The ability to remain in natural organic search results takes some effort. Likewise, if you pay for traffic to come to your website, it still takes some effort to convert the visitors into clients and customers.

You may be motivated to perform in both of these areas either internally (your own motivation) or externally (in relation to other enterprises). The source of the motivation is not so important - but the results are.

As a minimum, it needs to be extremely clear when a person visits your online presence (website, online platform, app etc), what they need to do and of course it has to be matched with what they need or want.

If you are just starting out in business, it is very tempting to have your needs met on the first draft minimum viable product. You usually know the topic quite well and you have a base level of knowledge and understanding that your potential client or customer does not have.

You may want to tell them everything before they consider a purchase or you may forget to tell them what they need to know to make a purchase because you incorrectly assume that they have a base level of knowledge.

Obviously neither end of this spectrum is suitable for a sustainable business. Most sales experts will agree that you need to showcase the benefits (how it will add value, help them, meet their needs etc) rather than the features (describing all of the specific details of the products or services). That said, if you do not provide the specific details they need to make a final decision, they will go elsewhere.

For example, if you need to buy a new refrigerator and you may have made some choices about the specific benefits you would like - French opening doors for the refrigerator section for easy display, drawers in the freezer for easy access and a stainless steel finish to complement your industrial style kitchen.

These benefits can easily be showcased in a photograph and a brief product description. However, one feature that you will definitely need to have described if you are planning to put the new refrigerator in a specific spot in the kitchen near a pantry doorway, is the dimensions of the refrigerator. If the refrigerator dimensions are not included in the product description, you are likely to look for another supplier that does provide this information.

So please, focus on enough benefits to convince your client or customer, but ultimately, provide enough detail so that they can make a final decision.

Action 50: *Your online performance can be improved if you focus on benefits rather than features, but remember to meet the needs of your target audience and provide them with the specific details they need to finalize a transaction*

Secondly, try to focus on specific outcomes for your target audience. You cannot be everything to everyone.

There is a website that I regularly showcase when I am teaching people how to Create a Simple WordPress Website. It is for a local plumber. The home page of his website is actually quite old fashioned and it has not adapted to the current trends in website design.

However, it is extremely clear, wherever you look on the screen, that what you should do when you look at this website is call the plumber on the telephone to make a time for the plumber to visit your property and fix your plumbing problem.

The website clearly shows how you can pay for your consultation (various credit card and payment options are clearly visible) and there is a huge amount of information about all of the different types of problems the plumber can fix - all neatly sorted into categories but also accessible via helpful icon pictures and menu buttons across the screen and on the left hand side. There is also a nice photo of a smiling and clean plumber fixing a tap right in the centre of the page.

Although there is a lot of information on this home page, it is extremely clear that you are only required to do one thing - call the plumber. Most online marketers will tell you not to give a person too many choices, because if you do, the person will often choose not to do anything.

To learn more about how people make choices, have a look at Sheena Iyengar's research and findings about choice. This will be particularly informative if you have a target audience that has a natural preference for a certain style of decision making.

There are many successful enterprises that offer low cost, medium cost and high cost options and different people within your target audience will choose different options (or they may travel on a sequence, starting with low cost and moving up to high cost over time).

For now, I just want to reiterate, if you want to perform well in business, it needs to be completely obvious what your target client or customer needs to do to complete the action you want them to complete.

Action 51: *Your online conversion rate can be increased if you provide the appropriate amount of choice for your selected target audience. If your enterprise can do this well, there is a very good chance that your website will also perform well in online search results for that target audience*

So if you have clearly described the benefits, provided the appropriate amount of choice, the final part is to make it easy to complete the transaction. Unfortunately, I have found that a lot of websites and online platforms make this process very difficult.

The first time I chose to purchase some paper carry bags online, I conducted a range of online searches to find out what would be a reasonable price to pay for various quantities based on various bag dimensions. I was staggered by the range of prices I found but also by the quality of the websites that I visited.

I started with an online marketplace where I could easily compare multiple sellers. The variation in the quality of their presence was unbelievable. Most listings did not provide adequate information to make useful comparisons. I also found that they were also quite expensive (they obviously had to cover the online marketplace fees and they tried to remain similar in price to other retailers).

Secondly I tried online searches and I visited some of the paid advertisements websites to gain a clearer picture of what was on offer. These websites were quite easy to navigate although they were still quite expensive, but they were less expensive than the online marketplace.

Thirdly, I looked at organic search result websites. The initial websites performed quite well, but the further down the search results I went, the worse the online experience became. The latter websites were clunky, several options were out of stock and believe it or not, some did not even offer online ordering through a secure e-commerce solution.

I ended up choosing a local store that offered a fair price (not the cheapest) and a good experience. They came up in organic search results, they had a Google My Business page and excellent online reviews.

Although they did not have the bags in the color I originally wanted (white), they did have them in red and I decided that it would actually be more interesting to have a red bag than a white bag so I ordered them and everything happened exactly as they promised. They even invited me to their mailing list.

This is an example of a business that has clearly created a service that meets the needs of its target audience. I was specifically seeking a timely and convenient solution and their website provided this experience.

So what should you be aiming for on your website? Here are some basic goals according to David Jenyns:

- website speed (the time it takes to load) - less than four seconds

- bounce rate (the percentage amount before they leave) - less than 55%

- time on your website - greater than two minutes

- pages per visit to your website - more than two pages

If your website is not currently achieving these results, don't panic. However, now that you understand these metrics, you can consider ways to achieve these results in the future.

I would also suggest that your website should be:

- maintaining or increasing the number of visits all of the time

- converting a reasonable (and increasing) percentage of visitors into clients / customers

- seeking feedback from visitors as to how to improve their user experience (UX)

- kept fresh and interesting over time (reviewed at least every two years)

- building and earning a consistent reputation over time (where your content is referenced in multiple quality locations)

Action 52: *Make it easy for your clients and customers to complete their transaction online. You need to have a website that works well and provides the person with the safe and reliable experience they expect. The benefit to you and the customer is that if you provide this experience, your website is also likely to perform well in organic search results*

8.9 Website Ranking Threats

If you are competing in an area where there is a high level of competition and a high number of searches for your specific products and services, naturally it will be a little more difficult to attract an audience via organic search results. In this case, you will need to provide an A Grade experience at all times and constantly improve your offering to rank well.

If you are in a more specific niche (ideally with a high frequency of searches but a low level of competition), there are still some other threats to your success:

- if you are paying for advertisements and your target audience is using ad-blocking software to prevent ads appearing in their search results

- if you are relying on generic keyword searches only and sophisticated target audience viewers are using Boolean search operators (", AND, OR, NOT etc)

- if you are not incorporating voice activated searches (sent through an internet browser or directly into a mobile or desktop device where the search results can be found either within the device or somewhere on the internet, in an app etc)

- if your statistics do not improve over time. For example, you do not make any effort to increase your traffic, lower your bounce rate, add new content regularly etc

- you do not have a significant and regularly used external presence on online platforms, social media or other websites

- your content remains static and does not go viral at any time

- a significant competitor comes in with a more effective approach

- future game changers in the online world (nothing stays the same forever)

If you would like to generate independent results directly from search engines (not associated with any other hyper local or referral marketing techniques), you need to remember that most click throughs will go to the top two or three results on the first page of search engine results.

There has been a bit of a joke circulating from an anonymous contributor, "Where do you hide a dead body? On the second page of search results because nobody looks there." Statistically, this is very true! As a business, you cannot possibly know everything that is changing in the online world, but if significant shifts do occur, you need to be willing to respond and adjust your presence accordingly.

If you would like to receive a list of our Currently Most Popular Search Engine Optimization Techniques, please join the 120 Ways Publishing Members Program at http://120ways.com/members as it is one of the free downloads.

Action 53: *Be vigilant and aware about the most significant changes that are occurring online and be ready to adjust your online presence accordingly. Whilst hyper local marketing relies more on referral techniques, if you would like to independently attract search engine results, you will need to be far more strategic, particularly if you are competing in a high frequency or high volume marketplace*

9. Paid Marketing

So far, most of the suggestions I have made for marketing your business online have only required time, development or membership costs, not costs per click.

For most businesses just starting out, this reduces the overall risk - because paying for every click can quickly churn through a lot of money or business capital and not necessarily generate sales, particularly if you are still going through iterations from your original minimum viable product website or working on more clearly defining your target audience and the most viable business model for the long term.

I personally believe that a 'startup' or 'organic' growth model is the best way to establish a business. If you start with what you know will work, even if there is a lower profit margin, you can move forward over time (and be less likely to fail).

Many new business owners who start with a cash payout from their previous employment make the unfortunate mistake of spending all of their cash on setup costs without testing the viability of the concept first. If possible, start your idea out on a part time basis first and then when it gains momentum and profitability, go full time.

Once the business builds, you can strategically inject those funds back into the business when you have a greater chance of moving to the second stage of your development.

For example, in previous years, I have saved money so that when it came time to write three books, I had enough cash in reserve to continue paying for my living expenses when I wasn't consulting. It also gave me the capital to invest in additional branding and promotion for the books as well as all of the setup costs for adding a new component to my business model.

I encourage most new business owners to start off with what has been proven to work well for centuries - word of mouth referrals from people you already know.

Interestingly, I still do quite a lot of consulting and teaching at a discounted rate for my longest clients because I value my relationship with those clients and they have kept my business going through the tough times.

This commitment has also generated ongoing referrals, so even though my charge out rate is quite low for the time I spend with those selected clients, I continue to make a profit thanks to the full price referrals I constantly receive in return. This process works well for both of us!

I also classify this approach as a form of 'paid marketing.' In this case, I am paid whilst I am marketing. It is an excellent model for service based businesses because you are still earning money whilst you are marketing. Product based businesses can also use this strategy with various types of discounting.

There are also many other types of paid marketing - where you pay up front for the marketing services provided. However, please remember that you still need to assess these paid marketing ideas according to the Marketing Idea Viability Test in Section 7.4 to make sure that they will be a good choice for your products and services.

Action 54: *Before embarking on a paid marketing initiative, start out with what you know will work, even if there is a lower profit margin because if you are paying per click, you can quickly churn through a lot of cash. Adopting a startup or organic growth model can help you develop a viable business. Future paid marketing ideas need to pass the Marketing Idea Viability Test*

9.1 Search Engine Marketing (SEM)

Search Engine Marketing (SEM) involves paying for advertisements that will appear in search engine results. So if your target audience is using Google, it will most likely be Google Advertisements as part of a Google AdWords campaign.

Over time, the cost per click (CPC) has increased because the competition for advertising has increased and the amount of traffic on the internet has increased. My major concern with this type of marketing is the fact that it is a 'digital expense' and most of us are fully aware that expenses usually go up, not down.

That said, there are ways to reduce your spend. If your advertisements are particularly successful and generate good results for users, Google may offer you a discounted CPC rate.

For example, if the top four advertisements were $4 per click for the number one listing on the first page of search engine results, $3 per click for number two, $2 per click for number three and $1 per click for number four, you may wonder how the first advertisement could possibly be available for less than the other three listings.

However, if most people choose the first advertisement on a regular basis (because the link performs well, the copy (text) in the advertisement is enticing or it is part of a much larger AdWords campaign etc), there is the potential for additional bonuses to be offered to keep you paying for your clicks - for example, a lower CPC, bonus advertisements or features etc. These benefits could change in the future.

Personally, I have never had to use paid search engine marketing because my other hyper local marketing techniques have created a digital and real life asset that regularly generates referrals and those referrals have kept me in business for years.

However, if you would like to consider SEM as part of your hyper local marketing strategy, I recommend that you:

- create a campaign with a certified advertisement partner who fully understands the search engine platform, even if there is a premium for their service (even if you get this person to start you off and train you on how to use the system - you do not want a novice spending your hard earned money). This person may be able to make other general suggestions about your business operations before starting the advertising campaign to ensure that the SEM campaign is successful (like check to make sure that when they land on your website, it converts visitors to clients or customers)

- make sure that all of your digital assets are operating effectively - your website, your online platforms, your social media, your business premises etc so that you can actually deliver the product or service in line with the advertised promise

- confirm that all of your resources are converting effectively so that you have a greater chance of converting the paid traffic to sales

- have a system in place to measure the results from your paid marketing so that you can assess whether or not it is viable to continue, whether or not you are attracting the right target audience and whether or not there is a genuine return on your investment

Some people falsely believe that if there is a problem with website traffic, paying for traffic will solve the problem. Unfortunately, it doesn't.

For example, if you have a shop and suddenly two bus loads of people arrive at the door, it doesn't mean that every one of those people will buy something immediately. If it was two bus loads of tennis players and you have a golf shop, you may find that they are just happy to browse rather than buy.

In my view, you need to be genuinely confident that your website will convert traffic to sales before you even consider SEM as a marketing or hyper local marketing strategy.

My different websites generate far move views than conversions and that is okay. My websites also qualify my clients so that the people who contact me are ready to pay for my services.

You need to make sure that if you are implementing an SEM campaign, your SEM attracts exactly the right type of target audience who is willing to pay for your products and services. If you get this right, SEM can work extremely well and lead to genuine sales.

Unfortunately, most of the business owners I have spoken to have tried to do this either all on their own or they have used an advertising partner who doesn't fully understand their business process or the traffic conversion process and they have ultimately wasted a lot of money.

I encourage you to put every effective business strategy in place before you start spending a significant amount of money on SEM.

Action 55: *Search Engine Marketing (SEM) should only be considered as a hyper local marketing or general marketing strategy if your website successfully converts traffic to sales. Your SEM certified partner needs to work with you to maximize your ability to reach your specific target audience for the best cost per click (CPC) rate. All SEM needs to be carefully measured to ensure that there is a return on your investment*

9.2 Social Media Marketing (SMM)

Similar to SEM, paid Social Media Marketing is best implemented with the help of an expert, especially in the setup and training stage. The nature of social media platforms is constantly changing and the variables allowed on different campaigns are constantly being upgraded, especially on platforms like Facebook.

The key to effective SMM is again, making sure you can directly reach your well defined target audience.

As mentioned in Section 9.1, all of your business operations need to be working effectively and you need to ensure that the SMM campaign leads to conversions, not just extra traffic.

In my view, the best paid SMM campaigns include:

- direct access to very specific people

- excellent tracking and measurement analytics

- the ability to move people from the social media platform to your database

- additional branding and awareness - be careful about the Cost Per Thousand Impressions (CPM) amount as it may appear 1,000 times in a news feed but never be clicked or really 'seen' by a person because there are other ads appearing at the same time

- the ability to eliminate false views or clicks generated by robots, competitors or repeat clicks by the same person

Advertisements and sponsored messages can be viewed negatively on certain social media platforms or have very little engagement if placed in the wrong screen location. If you are considering SMM, you need to look very carefully at the different options.

For example, you may gain more value out of paying someone to write informative approved posts that you share through your personal network and then ask them to respond appropriately to comments and shares rather than pay for a sponsored post that goes into a business name news feed.

Sometimes there are options for very low cost campaigns that are useful for brand awareness. You may also choose to pay a premium to send a personalized direct message to a key decision maker. A premium subscription to the social media platform may also come under the expense classification of SMM.

In my personal view, there are a range of potential opportunities in this space, but unless the social media platform has a good sized audience and an opportunity to reach a clearly defined target audience that matches your needs, this hyper local marketing strategy has the potential to be another money waster.

For example, I have experimented with small spends on Facebook, but to be perfectly honest, I would realistically need to learn a lot more before being able to take full advantage of all of the choices available.

In the early days of Facebook, there were a lot more ways to directly access your Facebook Friends, the people in your Groups and the people who had Liked your business Page. Now, a new notification reach rate could be as low as two percent of your total audience (if they even login to Facebook).

Nowadays, a lot of social media platforms with an active and engaged audience require a 'pay to play' approach. Unfortunately, they often keep the contact details of these people in their records - so even if you spend money, you still cannot directly reach these people through your paid or unpaid activity on the social media platform. That said, if your message goes viral, it may still be worth it.

Once again, I encourage you to put every effective business strategy in place before you start spending a significant amount of money on SMM. If you decide to spend money, make sure you source some quality advice first - from someone who has a proven track record of success.

Action 56: *Social Media Marketing (SMM) should only be considered as a hyper local marketing or general marketing strategy if your spend successfully increases your brand awareness and/or sales. Your SMM qualified and successful advisor needs to work with you to determine the most effective techniques for your purpose (content marketing may be more helpful than sponsored advertisements). All SMM needs to be carefully measured to ensure that there is a return on your investment*

9.3 Online Advertisements

In the early days of the internet, banner ads were quite popular, although they didn't generate very much revenue for the people offering the advertisements because the conversion rate was extremely low and advertisers generated more opportunities from other marketing activities.

Soon after, online classified advertisements started appearing on niche websites, particularly in the big money making classified advertisement categories of real estate, cars and jobs.

Consumers loved this change because it meant that they could see all of the related information for their chosen topic in one place and newspapers and publications hated it because the revenue from those classified advertisements had been subsidizing journalist salaries for years and now it was disappearing fast!

Over time, the niche portals that have generated the most traffic and engagement have secured most of the advertising dollars in their vertical and this has knocked out a lot of competition and increased the advertising card rate for the big players.

However, not even this trend could last. In the jobs category, the game changer platform is LinkedIn - they have provided an alternative solution for job seekers and employers and the classified jobs websites have suffered enormously. Now, as few as 10% of vacant jobs are advertised.

What has also happened is that a range of go-between comparison services have emerged. If you contact XYZ company, they will compare 'all' of the products or services in a particular niche and 'help' you source the best deal.

I believe that these comparison services should be honor bound to fully disclose how they make these comparisons. They often collect a commission for every 'sale' and the consumer doesn't receive a true comparison service because the companies listed with these aggregators usually have to pay to be a part of the comparison service and have to add in this cost to their offering. I tend to avoid using these services at all as I feel as if they are double dipping under the guise of offering a 'service.'

As a business decision maker, you therefore need to decide which online advertisements are most likely to be effective at attracting your target audience to your products and services.

For advertising to really be effective, it needs to be seen in a similar location on many occasions (this is why advertising sales staff normally encourage you to run a longer term campaign rather than a once off advertisement - and it is also why the relative cost drops significantly with a longer term arrangement).

In a hyper local marketing context, I would like you to consider the most local opportunities available (by location or context).

For example, a local garden nursery that sold garden products, plants and associated supplies decided that they would like their online advertising to reach members of the local community gardening groups. One of these gardening groups hosted a Meetup Group and a lot of free events and they were also responsible for maintaining a local community garden.

So, the garden nursery contacted the Meetup Group Owner and offered to provide mulch and potting mix on a regular basis for use in the community garden. In return, the Meetup Group provided an advertising spot on the Meetup Group's online profile.

This type of online advertisement is clearly seen every time one of the group members looks at the Meetup Group as well as every time a new potential member visits the Meetup Group. This advertisement is paid for in donated goods (rather than cash) and naturally every time the donated goods are received, the local community gardening group members are reminded of the local garden nursery.

The online advertisement does not need to be renewed or replaced because it is an ongoing, fixed arrangement. This type of online advertisement could also be classified as social media marketing or even 'sponsorship.' However, the principal of having an ongoing presence in front of their exact target audience in the form of an online advertisement has been achieved and all of the benefits of the exchange have remained within the local community.

If you think creatively, you may find that there are many other types of local enterprises that have the ability to provide online advertising that will reach your target audience.

There are also online media agency planning services that allow you to buy online advertisements through digital integration services. You may also be able to list your business on these portals so that other enterprises can advertise on your website.

In days gone by, heavy traffic websites would often have Google AdSense advertisements on their website. Personally, I have removed these types of advertisements from my websites as they do not generate a reliable income and they detract from my main message.

Personally, the only types of online advertisements I would consider from a hyper local marketing context are advertisements that:

- are on non-competing and complementary local enterprise websites

- directly reach my target audience

- are well located on the screen and are easy to read

- remain present on a continual basis (minimum of three months)

- enhance the relationship I have with the enterprise (and potentially help generate referrals)

- are affordable and don't blow out in cost per acquisition without a significant increase in revenue (as a general rule, I prefer to pay a fixed cost for the presence rather than a CPC or CPM, especially at the beginning of the advertising relationship)

- are located on a website that performs well in its own right and is search engine optimized for my location and/or context

- enable me to track their performance (even if it is just via a tracking link or a review of my website analytics)

As you can see, as soon as a dollar spend is involved with any form of marketing, I like to make sure that there is a direct correlation between the amount spent and the results.

That said, the time I spend on my business is at least as valuable as my earnings, but as a general rule, I prefer to take the long term approach and create a digital asset that automatically generates leads rather than take the short term approach of a digital expense that has the potential to quickly increase in cost.

That said, I would definitely consider online advertisement exchanges with local enterprises. The Meetup Group example above is a case in point. Absolutely everyone in the community benefits from this type of online advertisement - both online and offline.

Action 57: *The best hyper local online advertisement opportunities have the potential to support the local enterprises and the local community. These online advertisements are likely to be more effective it they can be maintained on an ongoing basis and if they can enhance business relationships and encourage referrals. Larger scale online advertisement opportunities need to be examined much more carefully to ensure that there is a fair exchange and a reasonable cost per client or customer acquisition*

9.4 Aggregator Websites

I am not a big fan of aggregator websites as I believe that most are set up with the intention of just skimming from an existing transaction rather than providing any real value to a client or customer. That said, in certain industries, you almost have to have a presence on an aggregator website to be considered a legitimate operator and some aggregators have really helped some smaller enterprises enter the bigger market.

So, let me put my personal preferences aside and share some tips on how to optimize your presence on a paid aggregator listing, especially if you have looked at the pros and cons and can see legitimate value

Firstly, you absolutely must complete your profile in full, accurately and with as much information as possible to help you stand out. Your images and visual content needs to be sensational (not happy snaps from your mobile phone). Your logo needs to be sized appropriately, links need to be checked to make sure that they work and you must re-confirm your details at least every six months as new sections are often added to the platforms and the listers who keep their profile up to date are much more likely to appear first in search results.

If the aggregator website offers reviews, you need to respond to these reviews quickly and appropriately. You also need to respond to any referrals or enquiries immediately. To optimize your profile for your location or context, remember to:

- include your location name (and if possible, the names of other well known locations close by)

- try and secure a unique URL for your listing so that you can set up a reciprocal link on your own website (preferably publicly available rather than behind a membership login)

- showcase your involvement with the aggregator on your website if it provides additional branding or recognition power (for example, as seen on Trip Advisor etc)

- add in any feed services or embed code to your website that provides a value add to your target audience

- showcase any special promotions that you have secured on your website or in your email correspondence or online platforms

- have a look at any of the other features and benefits that they offer on top of your aggregator listing and see how these can be incorporated in your business

You also need to be very vigilant when selecting an aggregator service. You need to fully understand the 'costs' of the service, even if it is 'free.' Perhaps a condition of listing is that you must provide a referral fee and this may cut into any profit on the transaction (which you may accept if you can carry the cost and it generates future business).

Ideally, it is a good idea to chat to other enterprises that are listed on the platform rather than listening to the sales spiel from the aggregator company. Unfortunately I have seen so many aggregator services come and go, all offering so much but delivering so little.

You really need to make sure that the aggregator has a good sized database of happy clients and that the aggregator website is generating a lot of traffic. They may have the most amazing visual or technical platform in the world, but if they do not have a successful way to drive your target audience to you, it is best for you to wait until they reach 'critical mass' before getting involved.

What I have found is that a lot of these aggregator websites request a lot of information up front and this puts a lot of people off getting started. They assume that because everything is automated, it is just a case of filling in boxes and the system will make money in its own right.

The most effective aggregator websites have started with people physically working with individual enterprises and helping them to create an online profile (for example, this is how Airbnb got started). Once critical mass was achieved, other people were more than happy to fill in all of the details because it led to results.

If you are having difficulty filling in the details or making the best use of the platform, ask for assistance, especially if you are paying for the listing.

Finally, I encourage you to do your homework and find out how other listers are using their listing to their advantage. Check out their profiles and ask yourself, "Why are they attracting business?" Test and see whether or not your listing is appearing in search results within the platform but also in general online search results.

Also compare the various aggregator sites in your industry - not just locally but internationally. I have often found that international sites rarely have a comprehensive listing in every location, so see if you can negotiate a special rate because of your uniqueness. Watch out for the updates from the aggregator and make sure that you constantly monitor the performance of your listing, through your own channels, not just through the reports that the aggregator provides.

Action 58: *Good quality aggregator websites with a large database and high traffic volumes have the potential to lead your target audience directly to you, provided you do your homework first and optimize your profile and any of the other features they offer as part of the aggregator service. Consider both local and international aggregator websites but make sure that you can still independently measure your results before subscribing to either a free or paid service*

9.5 Professional Body, Industry Group And Association Memberships

Thanks to the internet and the concept of freely accessing information via an online search, many professional groups, industry bodies and associations have started to find it difficult to maintain or increase their number of financial members.

I am a firm believer in the intrinsic and extrinsic value of group memberships.

I have found that a lot of membership groups are often run by hard working individuals (mostly volunteers) who feel passionate about developing their profession or industry and yet a lot of people adopt a 'free loader' approach and don't contribute because they cannot see a direct return on their investment.

This goes completely against the hyper local marketing philosophy. A great deal more can be achieved if everyone does a little bit - it should not be up to a few people to do a lot!

Membership has a lot of advantages and one of the most useful benefits is that it gives you direct access to your target audience vertical. Most memberships also include regular news, events, directory listings, mentoring and professional development opportunities etc.

Unfortunately, I have found that there are a lot of people and organizations who pay their annual membership fee but then they do not follow up in any meaningful way. They are simply missing out on a range of opportunities for their professional life and their business.

To gain the most value from your paid memberships, I encourage you to plan what you will do each year and:

- thoroughly complete your membership application with all of your details

- check your details (via your online login but also via the membership group website) and PLEASE make sure that you keep these details up to date (diary to check your listing every six months)

- provide a reciprocal link (possibly include their logo too) from your website and/or online platforms to the Membership Group

- include the logo and website link on any relevant online or offline enterprise information (provided you have permission to do so)

- read their newsletters and correspondence so that you can stay up to date

- offer some form of voluntary assistance at least once a year (help out at an event, write an article for their blog or social media, participate in a project) - it is fantastic networking opportunity and as I have said before, if everyone does a little

- find out who else is a member and connect with at least one member you have not met before at least once a year (even if you just go to one event and meet a new person there)

- support the membership group in your own unique way - follow or like their profile on online platforms, share their content, advocate on behalf of members in everyday negotiations

- consider working collaboratively with another member, particularly if they are located nearby. Sometimes individual members and smaller enterprises can support larger enterprises by being available on an as-needs basis

- give referrals to other financial members, especially if you are busy and cannot accept an opportunity

- consider participating in a mentoring program (either as a mentor or a mentee) so that you can share your unique value

- encourage other individuals and enterprises to join the membership group

- consider upgrading your level of membership and/or becoming a certified or accredited member to demonstrate your commitment to the industry

- recognize and celebrate other member achievements - congratulate award winners

- make the most of any additional membership benefits - printed directories, event sponsorships, discounts, merchandise etc

- share the good news around your community - don't assume that because other people are not a member that they are not interested in the topic and what is happening in your industry

- consider becoming involved in a more tangible way through a committee position, a project or even a part time paid role

I have personally been involved in a wide range of membership groups in a voluntary capacity for as long as I can remember. I have learnt so many new skills, formed some fantastic business and networking relationships and received excellent quality referrals.

More importantly, in exchange for my time and service, I have been instrumental in delivering several tangible and rewarding initiatives that have benefited both members and the wider community. I encourage you to get involved (if you are not already)!

Action 59: *Membership of a professional body, industry group or association has many intrinsic and extrinsic benefits - provided you get involved and make use of the opportunities on offer. Remember to update your details every six months and plan what you will do each year in advance*

9.6 Gifts

The popularity of giving gifts to clients and customers has fluctuated over the years. On big ticket transactions (like a property sale), it is almost considered mandatory to provide a 'congratulations' style gift.

There are now a plethora of personally labelled merchandise products available for distribution - pens, electronic gadgets, clothing, household items and so much more. Whatever you choose to use in your business, it needs to be aligned with your target audience and provided at an appropriate time in the sales cycle.

For example, a local training college specializing in bachelor degree programs in natural therapy printed their promotional flyer on a piece of firm paper that had been infused with seeds to a local native plant. It also had a printed QR code on the front so that the person could scan the card, collect the information electronically and then place the card in a pot and grow a plant. Whilst not a formal 'gift' as such, I thought it was a fantastic way to give a 'gift' when sharing their marketing information - even before a sale occurred!

So to adopt the hyper local approach to gift giving, I encourage you to source the gifts you provide from a local supplier, or from within your own business.

If the gifts are aligned and complementary to your product or service, even better! I have a personal preference for nicely wrapped plants from a local nursery as these last a little longer than cut flowers. I tend to avoid alcohol or anything that might be against someone's personal beliefs.

Other alternatives include:

- local crafts - handmade close by
- local produce - sourced via farmer's markets or local specialty shops

- complementary product or service samples - for example, a beauty treatment sample from a local business for a hairdressing client

You may also like to consider providing additional products or services from within your own business after a certain milestone has been achieved or for a special occasion. Personally, I give my new consulting clients a copy of one or more of my books!

Other options will be discussed in Section 11.4.

If you are the receiver of a gift, I encourage you to make a special effort to personally say thank you. This will be discussed in Section 16.5

Action 60: *Consider sourcing some locally created products and services to share as gifts with your clients and customers. You can choose different options for each part of the sales cycle and you can also provide products or services from your own business*

9.7 Donations

Some cultures and countries encourage philanthropic donations to education, community or sporting groups and welfare organizations. Some governments encourage donations to worthy causes by providing tax deduction incentives. Some people refuse to donate anything to anyone!

For now, I would like to encourage you to think of the different types of donations you could make within your hyper local context or location. There are many ways that you can 'give back' to your community and it doesn't necessarily need to be in the form of a cash donation. You could:

- volunteer your time and expertise (or the time and expertise of your team)

- provide free or low cost products and services

- provide access to opportunities - for example, allow a disadvantaged job seeker an opportunity to gain work experience in your business

- share your resources when they are not in use - for example, host a startup enterprise at your premises when you are not working there

To come up with creative ways to make a donation, just look around you and look for any level of excess capacity that you have available. Do you have an oversupply of old stock? Perhaps it is time to find a local enterprise that could benefit from this resource and at the same time, you can re-stock with saleable more profitable items.

A number of businesses have started to align projects or events with a values aligned cause or charity. For example, $1 from every sale goes to XYZ cause or all profits go to a particular charity for a gala dinner. If the beneficiary is based hyper locally, fantastic! You may be able to work in conjunction and help each other achieve your individual objectives.

Corporate Social Responsibility (CSR) initiatives have also appeared over recent years and larger organizations have encouraged employees to offer their services to the local community on a pro bono (free) basis.

This means that your business may qualify to receive assistance or a donation and if you are just starting out, don't be too proud to take up this option! Various economic development groups often have low cost or free small business mentoring and assistance services. If you do receive this benefit at the beginning of your business, you can simply say thank you and return the favor in a few years time!

Action 61: *There are many ways that your business can provide a donation to your local community and there are also programs that may allow you to receive a donation. Be creative in the way you give back to your community by examining any areas of your business where you have excess capacity and by looking at local causes or charities that share common values where you can both benefit from working together*

10. Database Marketing

For as long as I can remember, I have heard the expression, "The money is in the list."

A database is simply a tool to keep a record of information. To make sure that a database works for you and your business, you need to understand some of the basic principles of databases.

Firstly, it is best if you can have one source of truth - not multiple records in different formats. Secondly, every field in your database should only have one piece of information - for example, a first name would go in one field and a last name would go in a separate field. Thirdly, all of the information should be added in the same format for each record. Finally, if you create a good structure for your database in the beginning, it will save you a lot of time in the future (categories, groups, sort tools etc).

Unfortunately, a lot of businesses end up with different sources of truth. They may have an email mailing list in the Cloud, a Customer Relationship Management System (CRM) for sales and then a different accounting system for accounts payable and receivable.

Probably the worst option is three different spreadsheets on three unconnected computers!

To make the concept of databases even more complicated, you also have limited basic records in online platforms and on social media (like names of connections but not email addresses that can provide direct access to your clients and customers).

Perhaps the first step when thinking about hyper local marketing and databases is to think about how you need to access the information for your multiple purposes and to make sure, as much as possible, that you are not duplicating any of your effort. If you do need to transfer information over to another system on a regular basis, try and make sure that you have an efficient system for collecting all of the information you need from the beginning.

A well designed database and good business processes will help you effectively market your business, complete transactions, follow up where necessary and report on results.

If you are a very small business, you may think that you can manage a lot of the information in a simple system that relies to some extent on your memory. I would like to encourage you to think about systemizing your record keeping as soon as possible - preferably in a way that allows your system to cope with a bigger demand in the future as you grow (or at least be exportable so that you can import it into a new system). Just remember that at some point in the future, you will need to be able to give other people controlled access to your records.

A good database allows you to record all aspects of the sales cycle. Prospecting, relationship building, sales, feedback, follow up and referrals. It also needs to be kept up to date. It is an essential asset that is usually the backbone of most businesses and it usually has a significant influence on the value of your business at the time of sale, acquisition, transfer or IPO listing.

The way I have used my own databases has changed over time. In the beginning, I collected a lot of information from people before adding their details to my records. Now, I find that most people are very reluctant to give you detailed information and I usually start with a first and last name, personal email address and a mobile phone number.

I have also found that over time, the way I reach out to people has had to change to generate results. I am finding that fewer people are responding to emails and more are responding to SMS messages on their mobile phones or notifications they recognize in a news feed.

A lot more people are unsubscribing from email mailing lists but they are willing to connect on online platforms. Some online platforms work very well for some activities (like event specific portals) and other platforms only provide dynamic value rather than lifetime value (but the dynamic value is still useful so I continue to distribute dynamic content).

So rather than thinking that your business database is one system that you manage from within the business, you may need to expand your view and think about all of the databases that you are interacting with over time - because it is a combination of all of these databases that leads to a range of hyper local marketing opportunities.

You also have a range of data sources, analytics and reports that you can collect from multiple locations - your own records, social media, online platforms, website visitors, internet browser add-ons etc. A successful business needs to monitor the most important results from each of these locations. A hyper local business needs to drill down to the information related to the specific context or location and then make calculated and well informed business and marketing decisions.

Action 62: *To market your business hyper locally, you will need to manage multiple databases and implement business processes that capture the details and attention of your clients and customers as effectively as possible. Ultimately, you will need to reach out to people in a variety of ways, so do what you can to make the collection and management of data as efficient as possible. When reviewing the results, look for the most relevant information related to your location and context and make well informed decisions*

10.1 Email Newsletter Marketing

The trends in email marketing have also changed over time. In the early days, emails were new, novel and a great deal cheaper than sending information in the post.

Like a lot of new ideas, the concept went from a new innovation and a fantastic tool to a huge nuisance! Unfortunately, there will always be people who will abuse the privilege of new opportunities and ultimately ruin the new innovation for the public majority (with email they do this by spamming people with unsolicited and unwanted content including computer viruses).

As email marketing has matured, so too has the level of sophistication of email marketing systems. Email marketers can find out who opened an email, what they clicked on and even track their behavior after the click. This is one form of content driven marketing (like your website) that you can control and you own (unlike online platforms where you are at the mercy of their systems and their algorithms).

If your business has access to a large number of people via email, you may be tempted at some point to send out too many emails and suffer some 'collateral damage' and run the risk of losing subscribers because in the end, you still make enough sales to justify the process.

However, I would never adopt this approach, regardless of the sales potential. Not because I have a holier than though attitude to business, I simply believe that everyone should be treated with respect and that if you want to succeed in business, you can't do a bad thing here and expect a good thing there. You need to have a long term vision, not a short term mentality.

You also need to be congruent across all of your business and marketing activities. In a hyper local context, you run the very real risk of alienating everyone very quickly and ruining your reputation.

So here are my best tips for email marketing:

- always provide some form of value in every email you send out to your list. Include useful information, a valuable offer or something entertaining and make it as accessible as possible (suitable for HTML and plain text email systems)

- avoid using too many images - a lot of email systems, mobile phones etc do not show images and if the person cannot quickly see what your email is about, they are more likely to avoid reading the message and move on to the next email

- carefully choose the time of day to send your email - I find that more people are likely to unsubscribe if you send it first thing in the morning and almost no-one reads it if you send it in the middle of the night. Most email systems allow you to schedule the time of delivery

- as a hyper local business, think about what you are trying to achieve with your email marketing. Personally, I like to send one email, once a month at a similar day and time. This gently reminds the recipient about my business without being intrusive. I don't worry about whether or not they read it (but I still aim for 20% or more opens), I simply want to remind them that I exist and not annoy them in the process

- think about your goals with the email content. Some email marketers will encourage you to only include one story and one action. I prefer to use email marketing as a way to maintain and build my relationship with my clients and customers so that they can either come back for additional purchases or refer me to people they know. This approach ensures that I regularly receive referral business

- consider tying your email marketing to a regular in person or live activity. The Camberwell Network email newsletter that I send out once a month reminds readers that the following day, I will be hosting a free and open to everyone networking event at a local venue. The reader then has a chance to reconnect with me and other hyper local businesses all at the same time, so we all benefit

- be as consistent as possible in the formatting of your email marketing. Make sure the branding and styling is aligned with your website and other digital content. Include links to your social media profiles and website. Include your contact information (phone number, address, instant messaging etc) and your tag line to reinforce your business motto. If your layout follows a similar structure each month, people will learn how to find the information that is most relevant to their needs

- consider including the main menu links from your website in your email newsletter so that readers are reminded of what they can expect to see if they visit your website (Home, About, Products, Services, Contact etc)

- make sure that when you add people to your mailing list, you always add in the information to your email sending program in a consistent format (like their mobile phone number in exportable automatic international SMS sending format rather than the local region version)

- allow subscribers to unsubscribe (but don't make it too obvious!)

- consider providing some hyperlinks in URL format, especially if you think the person will print the email or they can only receive plain text emails - for example use http://camberwellnetwork.com instead of Camberwell Network. I often use this format right at the top of my newsletters so that readers can quickly look at all past editions online - for example http://camberwellnetwork.com/newsletters (rather than using 'View this email in your browser' which may not be a clickable link in plain text email programs)

- publish your email newsletters on your website (a great way to add fresh content on a regular basis)

- label your images and provide hyperlinks with images (opening in a new page) to maximize engagement and click through opportunities. Remember that the text that appears in an image cannot be seen by someone with a plain text email program - so if you have text on an image, make sure that you still have enough text in your email so that they can read the content if they cannot download the pictures

- think carefully about how you will end your emails (either your everyday emails or your newsletters). There are various viewpoints on the length of email signatures, the formatting and content of the signature and whether or not to include the previous conversation in a reply email. Make conscious choices about these options. As a minimum, personalize your email signature from your phone (much better than 'Sent from my iPhone' which looks as though you don't know how to set your email signature)

- monitor what happens each time you send out an email campaign and work out ways to improve future editions. A few years ago, I was a member of the Victorian Writers' Centre and they used to send out their email newsletter with an offer of free tickets to an upcoming movie and the first people who replied had the best chance of winning tickets. I actually did this a few times and won free tickets, so as you can imagine, I would always watch out for their email newsletters and engage immediately!

- consider linking to a video. More and more people enjoy this type of content. At present, email programs do now allow videos to play whilst looking at the email, but if you have an image of the video, you can put this in your email and hyperlink the image to the video URL (just take a screen shot of the video on YouTube or Vimeo and add this as an image). In the future, you will probably be able to use some embed code in the email

- don't be afraid to promote other hyper local enterprises! Share the love, people will respect you for sharing good and useful information, particularly if it is a little bit quirky and has a bit of personality

- distribute consistently. Don't start by writing an email newsletter once a week and then go to once a year! In the early days, I encourage you to distribute an email newsletter once a month and if that becomes too difficult, go to once every two or three months. But don't stop! Quality is definitely better than quantity for hyper local marketing. Brief and to the point probably works better than long and detailed, but remember that some people are 'click resistant' so the main message needs to be in the email

Action 63: *Email newsletters can be very effective for maintaining and building relationships with your hyper local contacts, clients and customers. Make mindful choices about the purpose, setup, frequency, format and content and be consistent with your distribution schedule. Make allowances for plain text viewers, incorporate video links and consider aligning your cycle with a live activity*

10.2 Joint Ventures And Strategic Alliances

Many hyper local businesses can find it difficult to compete against larger enterprises and corporate organizations. However, there is a way to access these types of opportunities - through joint ventures and strategic alliances.

These can be fairly loose and informal arrangements where you simply help out with an overflow of work from time to time (provided you have already developed a business relationship). This is a very good starting point as you can both assess whether or not you could work together in the future on an ongoing basis.

Alternatively, you may offer yourself as a 'white label' associate. In this case, you go in wearing their 'brand' (or even their clothing) and for the duration of the transaction, you are representing their business. This is a good second stage option - but be careful, do not go in and spruik your own business, you will lose the opportunity of any further work very quickly - and it is unethical!

A third option is to strategically associate yourself with the larger enterprise. You may work on joint projects, be part of a joint bid or tender or simply work together by sharing resources or talent. For example, you may be able to work together and enjoy discounted logistics, greater purchasing power, discounted products from the same supplier, provide more comprehensive consulting services etc.

To access these opportunities, you really need to get to know how the hyper local businesses around you operate. Where do they go for their products and services and can you join forces in some way so that you can both benefit?

It is a slightly more advanced form of referral business.

A word of warning though. You need to partner with people and enterprises with a similar value system. To manage your risk, I encourage you to maintain your independence and autonomy in the startup phase so that if something goes wrong, either one of you can walk away without contractual obligations. You need to trial and test how it will work first. Once your relationship has been proven to work over time, then you can consider a more formal ongoing commitment. Stick to this rule even if it means a slightly lower profit margin.

As an independent consultant, I am 'on the books' of a range of organizations (including an international company based on the other side of the world). These relationships do not always lead to a regular supply of business, but they definitely add a good level of credibility to my hyper local business. In fact, being a hyper local representative for an international business works well for a variety of reasons. You can normally access advanced systems and procedures, comprehensive free marketing, qualified referrals and the associated brand power.

The international company also gains a great benefit because you can tailor their product or service offering to the local context as you have all of the local skills, knowledge and networks. This work may not pay as well as work sourced locally, but in many cases, you don't need to 'do' a lot of work to keep receiving the referrals (provided you continue to deliver good quality products and services and keep them in the feedback loop).

This partnership approach can also help your business grow. If you are at the stage where you need to expand but you can't quite afford to hire additional staff on a regular basis, you may be able to outsource a component of your business function to another hyper local business or person. Wherever possible, I always encourage businesses to find staff that live locally. It is a great hyper local strategy and it saves everyone a lot of time, energy and resources!

If you are hiring people on a regular or outsourcing basis, focus on making sure that they have the right attitude (you can always train them in the skills they need). As the saying goes, hire for attitude, not aptitude.

If you are going to use your business database for joint ventures or strategic alliances (like affiliate marketing initiatives or joint promotions), once again, be very careful about how your relationship with your clients and customers could be affected by the brand or performance of the other business. As a general rule, I will offer a general marketing opportunity rather than a direct access opportunity.

For example, I have a relationship with some of my clients and customers on social media, so I may be happy to share the details of another business in this forum, but in most cases, I am not prepared to send out a personalized promotion to everyone on my database. Once again, your reputation is at risk by sharing this information, so make sure you feel completely comfortable with the arrangement before agreeing to a real or implied joint venture or strategic alliance.

Action 64: *To find suitable joint venture and strategic alliance opportunities hyper locally, you will need to find out how other hyper local businesses around you operate. Always start with a trial and test approach where either party can leave the arrangement before making an ongoing commitment. Consider representing international organizations at the local level and also using this approach to expand your business in the future*

10.3 Partnerships

To be brutally honest, I am not a big fan of ongoing business partnerships. I have heard of so many falling outs, unfortunate consequences and expensive court cases. In a hyper local community, it can also have a ripple effect and community members may feel as if they have to 'choose a side' which makes it even more uncomfortable for everyone involved.

Although most partnerships start out with two or more people believing that they are contributing equally, expectations are usually generated without direct communication and when one person makes an observation and evaluation about another person's commitment, everything can start to go pear shaped very quickly.

Sometimes these situations happen by extraordinary circumstances (sudden illness, family crisis or significant market change). In most cases, I have seen lots of small issues just build up over time and resentment gradually increases. I prefer to develop relationships where each person is fully responsible for their performance and ongoing involvement and can leave at any time.

For example, a lot of business coaches and advisors will encourage consultants to establish a retainer relationship with clients. I believe this model is inherently flawed - because there is no formal obligation for the person to provide outstanding value - there is room for the consultant to coast along and not be fully committed.

I also do not believe in the 'hourly rate only' model either. In this situation, there is a potential conflict of interest. If a consultant takes longer to complete a task, they get paid more! Likewise, the client can squeeze extra value from one hour and gain a benefit that is worth significantly more in dollar terms.

So to take this concept a step further, I like to build in a performance metric to every business exchange.

Yes, I charge my clients on an hourly basis, but I either work directly with them for that hour (so they know full well that they have received an hour's worth of assistance) or I predict that a certain task will cost a certain price and they either agree to pay that price or not.

This model is completely transparent for both people on either side of the transaction. Studies have shown that most people perform better when they are paid per hour than for overall time. As a business owner, even if you know a task may only take the expert 10 minutes, you realize that their expertise is worth the amount they have quoted for the job if they give you a fixed price up front. If the task happens to take them longer than expected, you do not have to wear that cost.

If your business is based on products, you simply need to make sure that the value of your products is at least as much as the person is willing to pay.

So for effective partnerships and business exchanges, I believe you need to factor in the principles of accountability, performance and dedication and avoid any conflicts of interest. This is not always easy to maintain over time.

So in the beginning, if you can operate on a direct exchange basis, you can again trial and test the arrangement before making an ongoing commitment.

If it is worked out on a per hour or per transaction basis only, either person can walk away at any time - this helps create accountability, encourage good performance and ultimately lead to ongoing dedication.

If something sounds too good to be true, it probably is! If you are not sure about whether or not to establish a partnership or not, test the people involved over time before forming an ongoing partnership. If you do decide to make an ongoing commitment, make sure that you all understand exactly what you are agreeing to do to maintain the partnership, regardless of external circumstances.

My personal preference is to work in parallel on a transaction basis rather than in partnership on an ongoing basis. That way, I can absolutely encourage my hyper local counterpart but I am also free to go elsewhere at any time, without lingering resentment. If we are meant to keep working together, we will.

On some occasions, I have ceased business dealings because the other partners are simply not keeping up their end of the bargain. I always remain polite and respectful, but if it is clear to me that our values are not aligned or they are not doing what they promised, I will not hesitate to stop working together. I would rather end a business relationship early and stop wasting my time trying to make something work if the other people are simply not as committed as I am.

This happened when I tried to set up a not for profit initiative to encourage younger entrepreneurs to come together and network hyper locally. I gathered a small group of people who told me that they were committed to the concept and they would help out between events and at events and that they would encourage people to attend, invite guest speakers etc.

Alas, within 12 months, I was the only person doing any of the work and the excuse I always received was that they were all 'too busy.' I can guarantee you that I am busier than any one of them! They were happy to attend the events and gain a benefit, but they were not willing to contribute. I gave them all fair warning, but nothing changed. So I wound it all up. I still host a networking event that is open to all ages, but I have it set up in a way that is easy for me to manage on my own.

Some larger scale transaction based partnerships have worked particularly well for me. By aligning my business and services with a larger scale hyper local festival or event, I have generated some fantastic opportunities. However, I don't just 'pay my fee' to participate, I look at other ways to add extra value to the organizers or enterprise. So if you do decide to consider any form of partnership arrangement, consider ways that you can add even more value to the business relationship, even if it is just a few shout outs on social media!

If you decide to form an ongoing business partnership, make sure you go in with your eyes wide open and make sure that it is a fair agreement that all parties are willing to maintain.

Action 65: *To form a successful partnership, you need to make sure that you and the other person or business can maintain your accountability, performance and dedication, despite changes in circumstances. Always start with a trial and test approach first and before making an ongoing commitment, make sure that you both understand exactly what you are agreeing to. Alternatively, consider working in parallel or on a transaction basis*

10.4 If / Then Scenarios

As you grow your business and become accustomed to managing multiple relationships, databases, reports, platforms, stakeholders and expectations, you will need to make some more complex decisions about what to do right now and what to do in the future.

If you source any professional expertise, you need to carefully examine whether or not the person providing the advice has a personal preference for recommending their solution or the best solution for your business. I encourage you to understand your business well enough to be able to ask the right questions!

The more comprehensive CRM systems will allow you to market your business based on if / then scenarios. So if a client or customer does this, then the system will do that. For example, if they sign up for your email newsletter, a week later, you could send them a special offer. If they click on the offer, they can move forward on the sequence A path, if they don't click on the offer, they can move forward on the sequence B path.

In some people's ideal world, every customer would follow a linear trajectory and every aspect of your business would be automated. If profit was your only motive, I guess this would be a perfect business model.

However, most people are not 'linear.' Our world is becoming less and less chronological and more and more relational. Different aspects of life are becoming connected - either by circumstance or data!

So if you have the ability to take your clients and customers on an if / then journey, remember that your best laid plans may not perform optimally in every case. You will still need to constantly assess and review how your iterations are working and modify them accordingly.

From a hyper local marketing perspective, I encourage you to constantly factor in your knowledge of your hyper local location or context. There will be unique variables that you will need to incorporate into your scenarios. If you are going to automate some of your business processes, consider how these will have the potential to affect other aspects of your business

That said, most businesses will not be ready to implement complex if / then scenarios until they have been established for some time (and worked out the most reliable sequences) or they have a large enough number of people on their database that can go on the if / then journey.

However, the principle can still be applied even with a small database of clients or customers. For example, if your customer spends more than $1,000, perhaps they will then qualify for a special offer. Alternatively, if you receive a referral, then you can automatically contact the referer and personally thank them for the referral.

Hyper local strategies can include a location or context component. You can decide that once a hyper local criteria has been met, you will move on to the next hyper local level. For example, if you establish a hyper local marketing referral program through one business and you iron out all of the glitches over time, you can then source a new hyper local marketing program from another business.

The essential component of the if / then philosophy is automating some of your business processes and it is never too early to think about ways to simplify your business processes.

Before you go too crazy with the if / then idea, make sure that you are using statistically valid information for creating your sequences. Be respectful towards your clients and customers and if in doubt about a particular technique, try it on a small sample size basis first.

In a hyper local context, you also need to be aware that if a person feels as if they are just on an automatic marketing sequence, they may simply opt out and tell other people that your business treats people as 'just a number.'

Action 66: *If / then scenarios can be applied in a hyper local context or location, but you need to make sure that you base your sequences on reliable information that considers the nature of your clients and customers and how they may feel if they are put on an automatic marketing sequence. That said, it is never too early to think about business processes you can automate in your business*

10.5 Follow Up And Feedback

My favorite marketing strategy is to follow up with existing clients and customers. Even if they do not buy directly again, I like keeping in touch and building my network of good business relationships.

It is very easy if you do not have an automatic process to forget to follow up with past clients and customers (and in some businesses, you will never have any details about your clients and customers - for example, a retail store where they pay for their products in cash).

Sales 101 will always teach you that it is so much easier to sell an additional product or service to an existing client than it is to create a new client from scratch. So why is this marketing strategy so often forgotten?

I could be very cynical and suggest that very few consultants would make any money on selling you a brand new customer acquisition product if all you needed to do was re-sell to your existing customers!

You may also be thinking that once your customer has purchased your main product or service, they won't necessarily need to buy anything from you ever again - I disagree!

If you are able to maintain an ongoing and helpful relationship, these individuals could be your hidden sales team, proudly spruiking your services all over town! Perhaps this is the time when you could refer them on to another hyper local business? For example, if you helped them build a new outdoor entertainment area, perhaps someone else could be referred in to do some landscaping?

You might think to yourself, "Why would I promote the landscape designer? I am not going to make any money out of that transaction!" I would argue that by providing extra special service, which will be remembered, you may find that not only does the customer promote your outdoor entertainment area skills but that the landscape designer promotes you as well!

You simply cannot be all things to all people, so be willing to share opportunities around your local context or location. Other ways you can follow up include:

- sending a thank you for your purchase message after the final invoice payment

- putting your VIP clients on an automatic personal contact schedule (at least three times a year to maintain the relationship)

- sorting your inhouse database and following up directly with anyone who has not made a purchase within the last six months

- sending a special greeting, gift or offer on a special occasion (anniversary of service, birthday, festive holiday time etc)

- inviting your clients and customers to an exclusive function where you provide some form or education or entertainment and refreshments (fun, food and free usually works well with most people)

- automatically sending all of your clients special offers on a periodic basis or as a result of a special event (for example, a novelty gift with your new address details if you are moving to new premises)

- offering a complimentary gift or service as a surprise after any form of good behavior (for example, an online review, a social media share etc)

- a competition, survey or quiz that you send to everyone to find out more information about your performance to date and to also find out what they would like to see in the future

Naturally, there are many other ideas in this book that could be used as a follow up technique.

Feedback is also a really useful tool for improving your business. If you receive a bad review, a complaint or have some form of difficulty, it could be a red flag warning you about what you need to address. View this feedback as a wake up call to upgrade your business processes, products or services.

If you respond appropriately to feedback, especially if it is negative feedback, you can actually strengthen your relationship with the person or business and potentially gain even more business. If you handle it badly and behave defensively, this can have a negative impact.

Regardless of how well you complete your tasks, there will be some people who are simply never satisfied. So be careful not to change your entire operations thanks to the anecdotal complaint from someone who was simply having a bad day and was extra grumpy!!

Action 67: *Following up with existing clients and customers can often be a more effective marketing technique than constantly trying to find brand new clients and customers. Consider implementing some automatic follow up processes into your business and respond to useful feedback with appropriate improvements*

11. Program Marketing

There have been countless marketing programs developed over time. I guess the ones that most of us try and avoid are 'network marketing' and 'pyramid schemes.'

A lot of programs require some form of effort or commitment to really be effective, so if you are considering any sort of marketing program, just be aware that most of them require some level of input and work to be truly effective, at least in the beginning.

What I like about some programs is the fact that they push you into lifting your game. The sheer process of implementation gives you an opportunity to reflect on your achievements and acknowledge your good works. They can also prompt you to consider new ways of working and they are often the catalyst for good ideas for you to try out in the future.

Good programs also offer ongoing benefits. After implementation, you can continue to capitalize on their value and perhaps even improve the quality of your marketing channels, brand presence and business reputation.

As I have discussed previously in Section 7.4, you should check to see if they pass the Marketing Idea Viability Test. If they don't, remember that you are taking on a certain level of risk. That doesn't mean that the idea will fail - sometimes even the worst ideas can succeed because of the sheer will and determination of the person involved!

However, I would like you to seriously look at how much time and expense is involved before implementing a formal marketing program. Some programs can offer some quick wins, but fail miserably over time.

Be very careful about implementing an idea that runs the risk of alienating your clients and customers (either intentionally or unintentionally). If you are trying something out that is radically different, consider a small trial group run through first.

If it is a new idea, don't take the seller's word about its potential success. Speak to other businesses who have implemented the program and find out whether or not it has helped their business. A very senior bank manager once told me that if anyone wants you to rush through a lending application approval, say no! If someone demands a fast decision, there is a very real chance that the deal is dodgy. It was great advice and his philosophy has proven correct many times throughout my business journey!!

Action 68: *Marketing programs usually require some level of effort and commitment to implement. However, they can help improve your business processes and lead to ongoing benefits to your marketing channels, brand presence and business reputation. Carefully evaluate the program with independent research before purchasing a marketing program*

11.1 Award Programs

The first time I completed an awards application, I found it quite difficult. I had to provide details of my business in a different format to how I saw the business myself. It gave me a tool to personally examine what I was doing and how I was doing it and the process made me think more laterally about my business processes and also what I could do in the future. To my complete surprise, I received a Highly Commended Award! I seriously couldn't believe it! I really did not think that my brand new business was worthy of any form of recognition.

However, I did appreciate the formal recognition I received and I have continued to promote that recognition over many years. If you are in your own business, it can feel a lot lonelier than going to work and being part of a team. The regular feedback that you receive in a workplace just doesn't exist when you are running the show. Even if you do not reach the award 'finalist' stage, entering an award gives you an opportunity to pause and reflect on your achievements.

Many years later, I started working with one of my clients who had been entering a particular award for several years and for the previous three years, she had been a finalist. I looked at her applications and although she had told a fantastic story, it didn't really give an accurate picture of all of her achievements.

So we sat down and collected the current year's full details, looked at the word count for each question on the application form and really tried to focus on the highest priority items for each question first. We provided more specific results, we grouped like information together and we also flavored it with a few memorable examples.

That year, she won the award. However, we could not rest on our laurels, we had to make sure that the following year, she had an even better application. So we mapped out what we would do for the following year by combining the best activities from the last few years but we also chose some new initiatives to implement so that we would have a better story for the next application.

She won again. But this time, she started questioning whether or not the award was really providing any value to her business. It took a lot of emotional energy to prepare the application each year and a huge commitment in a small business to constantly implement new initiatives. I explained that what we needed to do was capitalize on the winning of the award.

So apart from maintaining the best activities and incorporating new initiatives, during this particular year, we started spruiking the award win. We included the details on her marketing materials, her website, her email signature, on the front of her office etc.

True to form, she continued to maintain her best activities and her new initiatives, but this time, she took an even bigger leap - she decided to add in a whole new department to her business. This new initiative was going to increase her business asset value, provide a direct source of ongoing referrals and generate a regular guaranteed income.

As you can imagine, that year she won the Award for the third year in a row. This time, she also organized a video to be taken at the Award ceremony and she marketed the award win with the video as well as the award logo in her most relevant business collateral. Her business continues to grow and develop, as does her commitment to her clients and her industry. I am really proud of her achievements.

I truly believe that she would not have taken this big leap in her business without the subtle influence of the awards process. To her credit, she has not only entered the award for her industry, she has also entered several other awards - for Customer Service Excellence (rated by direct contact by the awards company with her clients), Retail Business Awards (with a category for her industry) and national awards. I really admire her commitment to continuous improvement.

In summary, entering awards will encourage you and your business to:

- analyze and reflect on your performance

- provide a marketing tool for you and your business, locally, nationally and internationally

- improve your credibility, brand awareness and recognition within your industry, profession and community

- encourage you to keep taking the next leap in your own growth

- provide you with a framework for measuring results and assessing yourself against industry benchmarks

- give you a great day out when you attend the awards ceremony

- enable you to reach the judges and other competitors in a more direct and informed manner

- have specific information that you can showcase in all of your marketing and give you direct access to media opportunities that either you generate or the awards company generates

- provide you with a framework for a 'performance review' of your business

- receive a nice certificate of participation or trophy to display at your premises

Don't ever underestimate the power of formal recognition. It may not provide a direct measurable benefit to your bottom line, but for many clients and customers, it provides an extra level of trust and confidence in your ability to deliver quality products and services.

When you start on the awards journey, consider entering awards that are relatively easy to enter first. Quite often hyper local awards are much easier to win than national or international awards, but once you have a few smaller awards under your belt, you can aim for the bigger awards as the process familiarizes you with what is considered award-worthy.

When you go to the awards ceremonies, listen carefully to the stories of the winners to find out what they are doing that is unique and inspiring so that you can create your own unique and inspiring initiatives. Always make an effort to promote the awards to your databases as that will also help the awards companies make their efforts worthwhile (and raise the profile of the awards in the broader community so everyone wins).

Even if you do not receive any formal recognition as a finalist or award winner, you can still mention that you are an 'entrant' in the awards. That way, you can still gain value from the process of entering.

Don't forget, it is not just about you nominating yourself for an award, you may choose to nominate someone you know or another local enterprise for an award (especially if you are not eligible to enter). You may even choose to nominate them anonymously.

If you win an award where someone else nominated you and it comes as a complete surprise, don't waste the opportunity - make sure you at least get some happy snaps on your mobile phone and share the good news far and wide as soon as possible!

I do understand that the time it takes to prepare an award application and also the cost of entering an awards program may be hard to justify because you cannot measure your return on investment. However, I genuinely believe that there are so many benefits and ways you can gain mileage from the process - even if you don't win! Remember, there is always next year!!

To begin the awards journey, do some research to find out what awards you could enter either hyper locally, locally, nationally or internationally. Look at their criteria and enter the 'easiest' awards first (but make sure that the award is a legitimate award assessed by a suitably qualified judging panel, not just an expensive advertising tool promoted as an 'award').

Start collecting information that you can use in various awards. Over time, develop an awards strategy as part of your overall marketing strategy and use it as a tool to continuously improve your business. Make sure that you always re-purpose the awards content across all of your marketing and business channels.

Action 69: *Identify hyper local, local, national and international awards that your business can enter either now or in the future. Collect information, maintain your best activities and continuously develop unique and inspiring initiatives that help your customers, clients and the industry. After entering the awards, promote your involvement across all of your marketing and business channels*

11.2 Affiliate Programs

The only affiliate programs I really like are membership affiliate programs - where you support a professional membership group as an affiliate member because you do not qualify to be a full member.

Unfortunately, most of the people that I have met that have signed up for affiliate marketing programs have found that they have 'burnt' their mailing list or website with promotion for another business and they have received very little in return.

That is not to say that affiliate marketing does not work. There are plenty of 'experts' who will tell you that affiliate marketing allows you to simply promote other people's products and you can just skim a percentage off the top. Money for nothing essentially.

Once again, this goes against my principles of business being about a fair exchange. What I do know is that done well, an affiliate marketing program can actually help both parties.

I will start by saying that as a general rule, I have a policy of 'no affiliates' unless I already have a relationship with the company offering the affiliate program. That makes it very easy when I am approached by a person trying to sell me the latest internet marketing craze, I can simply say 'I have a no affiliates without a relationship policy.' It saves me a lot of time.

They will often try and tell me that their system allows me to track and measure everything (fair enough) and allows for false clicks to be removed etc (again fair enough) but the reality is, they usually damage my online brand, they usually do not generate any income and I feel as if I am being used.

In these cases, I am usually not a user of their products or services either, they simply want direct access to my clients and customers. Do you really want to give away direct access to your hard earned clients and customers?

Anyway, I don't want to focus on the negatives. I want to focus on what will help you make a decision about whether or not to participate in an affiliate program.

I currently participate in two affiliate programs, one with Crazy Domains for people I know who want to register a domain name http://bit.ly/crazydomainssueellson and one with Bluehost for people who would like to purchase website hosting https://www.bluehost.com/track/sueellson.

I have chosen these companies because I have been a customer for many years and I have received the products and services I have expected to receive and both companies have been most helpful and responsive when an issue has occurred.

Crazy Domains offers a very miniscule affiliate remuneration program and before I can withdraw 'cash' I have to sell a lot of domain name registrations, although they will allow my earnings to be offset against my own Crazy Domains account!

Bluehost is slightly better affiliate program with a set fee per referral that is automatically paid on a set date after the initial transaction occurs (no minimum total before payment). Both companies provide basic online reports.

However, whilst I currently participate in these programs, if at any point in the future their products and services deteriorate, I would immediately withdraw from the affiliate program.

So let's examine the essential components of a good hyper local affiliate marketing program:

- it is with a business that is complementary to your business and that you may already have a tried and tested relationship with

- it provides a product or service that you do not provide but would be helpful to your clients and customers

- it does not detract in any way from your brand presence, message or business processes

- it is not forced on any of your customers, it still allows them to choose whether or not to accept the opportunity

- it is fully transparent that you have an affiliate arrangement (you may also need to mention that you do not pass on their details directly)

- you can honestly say (preferably through direct experience of your own over time) that they can deliver the products and services on offer as described

- you have the option of explaining why you recommend that business (particularly relevant in a hyper local context when the local service may be more expensive than a large company)

- it allows both businesses to capitalize on location based online searches, reciprocal links, complementary keywords and marketing etc

- it can generate new opportunities for both businesses (you scratch my back and I'll scratch yours)

- it is measurable in some way (even if that is not quantitative)

- you regularly provide feedback to each other and look at ways the offering could be improved in the future (even if it is not a directly dollar for dollar exchange)

Affiliate programs can come in all shapes and sizes. Not just online website links, email newsletter mail outs and social media shout outs.

My local electrical store has an affiliate program where a percentage of every sale is automatically donated to a local charity that I select from their list (and yet I don't pay an extra cent for this opportunity). I really like how they offer a part of their profit to the local community and it gives me a great feeling to know that my local spend is generating a real benefit to a local charity.

I also have a loose affiliate (or referral) arrangement with some of the people I know in my business circle. I refer people I meet to them, even if I don't work directly with the person I have just met. I don't expect or require a payment for this arrangement, but in return, they offer me free and direct access to their services at any time and they often recommend my services to their clients or keep me in mind for other opportunities aligned with my expertise.

So to wrap up, just remember that like all marketing ideas, ideally, an affiliate program should pass the Marketing Idea Viability Test. If you decide to operate outside of this framework, it could still work, but what you must always preserve is your relationship with your clients and customers. Please do not abuse that hard earned connection with a 'quick win' idea that can easily ruin your brand or business. It is just not worth it.

Action 70: *Affiliate programs need to be carefully assessed before implementation and ideally should offer a complementary product or service. At all times, you need to preserve your* *relationship with your clients and customers. Good quality affiliate programs have the potential to help both businesses and the local community both directly and indirectly*

11.3 Formal Recognition Programs

There are a variety of different types of recognition programs.

You may be recognized individually by a formal qualification, certification, accreditation, official order, community status award etc. Declaring these recognitions in a post nominal (letters after your name) or on your marketing material can provide your clients and customers with some level of assurance that you are formally recognized by an external body.

Alternatively, another person or business may nominate you for formal recognition without you knowing about it until you receive the formal recognition. This is again, like an award you receive, something to celebrate and share. It always surprises me to find so many business owners who do not provide this information in an easily accessible or visible location.

However, in a hyper local marketing context, when I think of a recognition marketing program, I think about recognizing my clients and customers.

There are various ways to recognize your clients and customers for their part in your business success. You could:

- provide selected discounts or special offers after a certain criteria has been met (dollar value sales, duration of relationship, random selection etc)

- if your business is a business to business (B2B) enterprise rather than business to customer (B2C), you could think about ways you could support their enterprise that is aligned with their target audience (for example, if they have a huge Facebook following, perhaps you could support some of their Facebook initiatives)

- nominate a person or a business for some external recognition

- with their permission, showcase their story through your network to recognize their achievements

- refer them to someone you know who can help them in some way (for a business, this could be to a journalist for some free publicity or for a customer, you might organize a free service and pay for it on their behalf)

I am sure that you can think of many different ways to recognize the people and businesses that have helped you in your business. I believe it is important to recognize these influencers on a regular basis, even if it is just a simple thank you card in the post (which they are much more likely to keep than an SMS or email).

Think about how good you feel when someone recognizes your efforts. Think back to when you were at school and a teacher or classmate positively acknowledged one of your achievements. How did you feel? Pretty good eh?

The only thing that you need to be careful about is causing the person or business you would like to recognize any form of embarrassment. If you think that they could feel uncomfortable about receiving recognition (particularly if it is public recognition), it may be a good idea to start off with something less elaborate and more private first. If you are still not sure after you have tried the simple option, it may be a good idea to personally check with them before going ahead. Some people are extremely shy. If they ask you not to go forward, please respect their request. In most cases, they are likely to be very honored that you were willing to recognize their value and that will be recognition enough.

There are other very simple ways you can recognize people on a daily basis. You can use their name and make an effort to remember their story and make further enquiries at a later date. For example, if they told you it was their birthday on the weekend, the next week you could ask "How was your birthday?"

Old fashioned insurance agents used to personally contact everyone on their birthday. Some major hotels go to great lengths to remember regular guests' personal preferences and then make sure that there is a special item waiting in their room when they arrive. Credit card companies and loyalty programs do all sorts of things to keep their customers engaged by tracking spending patterns and making suggestions.

These are all programs that focus on recognizing the individual person in some way. Marketing overall, as mentioned earlier, is much more driven by behavior than demographics, and the way I see it, recognition marketing is a concept that acts on this behavior.

Action 71: *Formally or informally recognizing your customers, clients or other businesses can be a very effective strategy for acknowledging their contribution to your business success. You can incorporate recognition in your everyday business processes or participate in more formal recognition programs. Recognition marketing is a tool for acting on past behaviors*

11.4 Rewards Programs

The ability to collect data has enabled a huge variety of rewards programs to get off the ground. It seems that virtually every large organization either offers a rewards program or is listed on someone else's rewards program.

However, I believe that there is a huge range of opportunity for hyper local businesses to participate in rewards programs, particularly if they cooperate and collaborate with other local businesses.

More of these ideas will be discussed in Section 15. But for now, I would like to discuss the basic principles of a rewards program:

- it is usually incentive based and is used to recognize and reward a particular behavior or sequence of behaviors

- it provides the person or the business with something extra that they may or may not be able to obtain in another way

- it encourages the person to repeat a behavior (it is best if the reward is actually something the person or business would like rather than a token that is useless to them)

- it gives the person or the business an opportunity to provide additional value either based on behavior or as a special and unexpected benefit

- ideally, it gives your business access to new clients and customers and can potentially go viral (like bring a friend offers or rewards for new introductions etc)

- it can be either exclusive or shareable, depending on the nature of the reward

- it can be provided via your own products and services or through another business

- it can be improved or repeated over time

From a hyper local context, I encourage you to shop around and really think about how you can incorporate the products and services of other local businesses in your rewards programs. Do not be afraid to ask if they can also personalize the reward in some way. For example, "This product has been exclusively designed for clients of XYZ business." If the product provides the details of your business and the other business, it is a double win for brand recognition! If the service dovetails perfectly into what you offer, it is a wonderful value add.

Action 72: *A well designed rewards program can encourage repeat behavior, access new clients and customers and potentially go viral. Make sure that the rewards you offer will be well received by your ideal clients and customers. Wherever possible, source the rewards from within your own range of products and services of from a hyper local context or location*

11.5 Surveys, Quizzes And Research Programs

The first research project I conducted in 1999 for my first business involved printing out a three page questionnaire, distributing them via the post to selected businesses with the target audience I needed for the research with reply paid envelopes included and hoping that enough people associated with that business would then complete the survey and they would individually return their completed questionnaire. I chose to personally telephone all of these businesses first before sending them the questionnaires. It worked. Most of the surveys I sent out were completed and I received 96 valid replies.

Five years later in 2004, I used the internet to reach people via email, Yahoo Groups, mailing lists, online forums etc and I asked them 20 questions. I have no idea how many people saw the survey or the questions, but on this occasion, 541 people completed the survey.

In 2016, I sent a quick three question online anonymous survey out via a well established email mailing list, via social media with reminders and I received 12 responses.

I realize that this is only one little sample anecdote, but I would like you to think carefully about what you would like to achieve before using a survey, quiz or research program to achieve it.

As it turns out, the first research project was part of my final year subject as part of my University degree and it was very clear that it was a valid research project. The second project was sponsored by a very well known international bank (HSBC) and I was given expert assistance by an academic from a prestigious local university. The third one was just a 'quickie' for my local Camberwell Network mailing list.

So you can see that the quality of the purpose encouraged more people to get involved. Most people are savvy enough nowadays to realize when you are only sending out a survey to try and get more sales and it is a lot less likely to generate a good result.

My first research project helped develop my first enterprise, Newcomers Network. The second research project helped create a Newcomers Kit that was downloaded thousands of times all over the world - from the US Consul General in Dakar to the Head of Human Resources at the World Bank. I also hosted three very successful events with the second project and these enabled a lot of people to network and share information. The funding I received from HSBC Bank made it all possible - so everybody benefited (it was also an excellent branding activity for the bank).

I also believe that any research you complete should lead to something of value, not just an excuse to do more research! That is why I have always re-purposed the findings for a constructive outcome.

In a hyper local context or location, with some collaboration and some like minded partners (both business and academic), you have the unique opportunity to create information that can be shared worldwide.

I also worked for a dating agency and they wanted to encourage more men to register for their services. In this case, we used surveys as way for the men to anonymously learn more about the service without providing their personal details. The surveys helped them understand ways that they could achieve success in the dating world and it was a good 'warm up' for their first no-obligation appointment.

The process worked so well that we then had to create a similar survey for women! In this case, we used it more for a selection process rather than an attraction process as they wanted to attract women who were well educated and financially secure.

Surveys, quizzes and research programs can help you secure both qualitative and quantitative information that can be useful to your business and the wider community. It can help you gather and define your thoughts in a constructive and structured way (a bit like the awards process can as mentioned in Section 11.1) and also help you clarify opportunities for the future. If you can share your wisdom to the wider community, it also enables others to benefit and it is an excellent branding exercise that puts you at the forefront of thought leadership.

In my case, I have used it to both start a business and also to develop a business, so the process can be used in a variety of ways. However, I have also found that working with academia made the entire process much more valuable.

Action 73: *Surveys, quizzes and research programs can help your business and the community collect a range of useful qualitative and quantitative information that can be used either to start or develop a business. I also recommend working with academia and sharing your findings internationally so that you can improve your business brand*

11.6 Accreditation And Certification

In some industries and professions, you are required to obtain and maintain a formal accreditation or certification to be able to carry out your business. If this is a formal requirement, as a minimum, I encourage you to publish this information on your business website.

There are some industries and professions where securing an accreditation or certification is a relatively new initiative. Some allow a grandfathering period where members who were classified as certified members can retain or upgrade their membership before a certain date and not be required to complete a formal accreditation process.

Other professional bodies will insist that a formal academic or industry qualification must be obtained and in some cases, a certain level of industry experience be obtained as well before they will allow an individual or a business to secure the accreditation or certification.

Overall, I agree with the concept of accreditation and certification. I am fully aware that some of these programs do not fully address the needs of clients, customers and other businesses, but that is not the point. If a certain requirement is declared (or legislation exists), then it helps maintain a higher standard for the profession or industry overall.

There will always be businesses that are at the 'top' of a sliding scale and businesses that are at the 'bottom' of a sliding scale of performance, but the process of accreditation and certification helps provide a framework for a base level of consistency and reliability.

So how can a hyper local business take advantage of the accreditation and certification process? You can:

- showcase your accreditation and certification both online and offline

- aim to secure a higher accreditation or certification

- meet the requirements to maintain the accreditation or certification

- consider other affiliated types of development, improvement or advancement

- find out how other businesses are maximizing their accreditation or certification

- reassure your clients and customers that you are maintaining your accreditation and certification (a quick message in an email newsletter once a year would be worthwhile)

- consider being involved in suggestions for improvements of the accreditation or certification process (or get it started if it doesn't currently exist in your industry)

- make sure that any online or offline listing you have for your accreditation or certification is maintained accurately and linked to your online and offline content

- consider finding out about international accreditation or certification as this can potentially give you more credibility (provided it is a genuine assessment body)

If your business is accredited or certified and someone else's isn't, it is not a guarantee that you will get the business. I am well aware that there are many businesses that are very successful financially and yet the individuals within are not formally accredited or certified.

For example, I would have thought that anyone who provides rigorous body massage should be formally trained in anatomy, however, there are plenty of massage therapists who do not have any formal qualifications receiving regular work - because their clients have benefited from the experience and shared that information by word of mouth.

At the end of the day, accreditation and certification is only one piece of the business puzzle. However, I believe it is an important piece because I am all for encouraging ongoing professional and business development, for maintaining and improving standards within a business and the industry and for encouraging everyone in the industry to have a minimum criteria to reach so that clients and customers can receive good quality products and services.

You may also like to extend this concept to your own business. What ways could you accredit and certify your own performance? What would it take for you to maintain and improve your business offering year on year? What ideas could you implement in your hyper local context or location to improve business effectiveness? What systems would you put in place to increase your knowledge?

For example, perhaps you could set up a local accreditation program. You could collaborate with several other complementary businesses and encourage each other to streamline your business processes, your recruitment and even your sourcing and logistics.

By joining forces, you could all help each other raise your individual standards as each person in the group would have a unique range of skills to help you grow. I would suggest that in the initial phase, you brainstorm some ideas, then test and evaluate these with a designated 'test case' business and then consider implementing the accreditation program across the business group.

This model would be ideal for a local retail precinct. You could establish standards for store presentation and layout, customer service, online and offline marketing, new initiative implementation etc and each year, review each business's performance against the criteria. A little bit of healthy competition could see a quieter precinct become vibrant again.

In a service context, you could establish a different set of criteria focusing on expertise, responsiveness, results, online and offline marketing and new initiative implementation etc. By creating a process that requires a business to document their achievements, you are much more likely to see improvement. As the saying goes, "What gets measured gets done" (anonymous source).

Action 74: *Formal accreditation and certification programs are worth securing and showcasing, maintaining and improving and potentially developing in your hyper local context or location. They are not a guarantee of business success, but they are an important piece of the business puzzle that can be a catalyst for continuous improvement for your business and for clients and customers*

12. Public Marketing

There are many ways to market your business in a public manner. Some of this happens intentionally, some unintentionally! What you do need to be aware of is what is happening and respond accordingly.

As a child, as I have mentioned, I spent quite a lot of time on Kangaroo Island - Australia's third largest island. My paternal grandparents owned a guest house and motel very close to the main street. I would often walk down the street with my grandmother and as a young child and it seemed to take a very long time. That is because on the way, my grandmother would stop and chat with nearly everyone who walked past! The good news is, I would be rewarded when we got to a certain shop with a small bag of mixed lollies (candies).

Conversely, I never walked down the main street with my grandfather. He was always on a mission, to the post office box, to the bank, to the grocery store, no time to meander and chat. Everyone knew that he would leave at 3pm for his daily trip to the shops and as a child, I knew not to interrupt!

Now as you can imagine, my grandmother was a much loved and admired member of her local community. Years later, I met a couple and I they told me that they had stayed at my grandparents guest house about 15 years ago when my grandmother was alive. Sure enough, they remembered her!

Apparently they had said that they liked the jam they had for breakfast. So that night when they got back to their room after being a 'tourist' for the day, there was a pot of jam waiting for them. I asked them if they could remember anything about my grandfather and they couldn't.

This is old fashioned, hyper local marketing. Not only did my grandmother have a presence in her local community, she also created a permanent memory with her guests. She secured both location and context hyper local marketing. My grandfather didn't – although he did have other skills and kept the business running through some tough times and lived until he was 90!

Nowadays, public marketing is not just done in the offline world, it is also done in the online world. For the most part, I will focus on the online world as this is where you, as a business owner, can respond to and potentially influence what happens.

Just a quick reminder though that bad news can travel fast. If something bad happens, people are generally much more likely to share the news with others. But I don't want you to panic. Most public crises tend to die off within the media lifecycle – daily for a daily newspaper, weekly for a weekly news and current affairs program etc – because let's face it, there will be a new edition published with more 'bad news' and that will take precedence. Unfortunately some journalists like to pick on certain individuals or organizations and this takes a little more effort to counteract. More about this in Section 14.3.

Like all marketing ideas, you need to select the public marketing techniques that will work best for you and your business and be ready to manage the issues associated with public marketing techniques that occur without your instigation.

Action 75: *Public marketing can be intentional and unintentional, online and offline and can be shared within a hyper local context or location. Bad news can also travel fast, but it usually only lasts for the duration of the media life cycle. Your business needs to be prepared to manage the issues associated with public marketing techniques*

12.1 Generating Content

As you can imagine, after writing three books and countless articles, courses, emails, faxes, letters etc over many years, I find it relatively easy to write content – but most people do not find it easy to write. More people feel comfortable speaking and some people only feel comfortable completing tasks.

So if creating content is not really your thing, you have some other options.

You could curate content by collecting content from other locations and sharing it through your channels (including your own website, social media and online platforms, provided it is attributed or referenced appropriately).

You could compose content with a ghost writer by recording your voice, transcribing the recording and editing or sharing ideas with the ghost writer and letting them prepare the first draft.

You could make a contribution towards other people's content. For example, a blogger might interview three people and include your content around the issue in the final piece.

Once this content has been published and/or shared, it has the potential to go viral and provide public marketing about your business.

However, if you are going to use this technique, I would encourage you to only share content that educates, informs or entertains – I would not encourage you to share a sales or advertorial message (loosely disguised sales information in an editorial setting).

Good quality content published in a location where your target audience can see it, is a very effective form of public marketing. If it is published on a reputable website, please encourage the publisher to include a link to your website (if possible).

Action 76: *Public Marketing can be obtained by curating, composing or contributing content to online and offline publications (including your own website). Aim to have good quality informative, educational or entertaining content published where your target audience will see it*

12.2 Reviews

In the early days of reviews, consumers relied on the honesty of the business to share the details of reviews they had received from satisfied clients and customers. Businesses could easily edit out the bad reviews too!

Now, with online reviews, anyone can say what they think, even if they lie or exaggerate the truth. In some cases, the business owner can report the review and ask for it to be deleted, but not always.

A number of my clients have become very fearful of online reviews and will often consider not creating online content because they fear getting bad reviews. I see it as a part of business nowadays. The good news is that as a business owner, you do have some protections and also some strategies for overcoming bad reviews.

For example, Google reviews are particularly well managed. Firstly, every review is checked before it is published. If it contains sales or contact information, it will not be published. If multiple negative reviews are received from the same IP address (computer internet location), they are likely to be removed (potentially being added by a competitor). If you receive a review and it is published, you have the ability to respond to the review (and naturally I would suggest that you respond to every review appropriately and as soon as possible).

If you do receive a bad review and you are able to respond, please remember to:

- thank the person for their feedback

- acknowledge the person's concern (I am sorry to hear that you were disappointed with our products or services)

- personally address every item in their review (referencing every item in your response)

- be solution focused rather than reactive or defensive (you can explain details appropriately but you can also invite them to return the product for a replacement or make another appointment for one hour at no cost)

- again, thank the person for their feedback and explain how they can reach you directly

If the issue is resolved, you may like to go back to the response and provide an update (thank you for returning your product, we trust that you will enjoy using it in the future).

You may be reluctant to adopt this approach if the client or customer was 'in the wrong' but how you respond to negative reviews will be assessed by other potential or existing clients and customers. There are multiple benefits to this approach (which I have personally experienced with my own enterprises and for my clients' businesses):

- other clients and customers will spring to your defence (this happened after a response I provided on LinkedIn)

- you will increase your overall search results because you responded to the review (and you will receive extra brownie points if you respond as soon as possible after the review has been posted). They are also more likely to appear in search results for your business name

- people reading your reviews will know that they are genuine reviews from real people (not just false five star reviews posted by your friends on different computers over a one week period when you started out)

- customer and client reviews are perceived as more genuine than advertising and are more 'credible' – so the more reviews you receive, the better

- it will increase your performance in online search results (particularly with Google reviews as these require a login to be entered and if a friend writes a review about a business and you are connected to that friend, the business that has been reviewed is more likely to appear in your online search results)

- negative reviews can give you clues on how to improve your business (although it would be nice if the person just contacted you directly!)

- you can reflect on the nature of your business in response to the reviews

- you can re-use the reviews on your other online and offline content

- you can look at other reviews and look for ideas on how to improve your own business

I see reviews as one of the best hyper local marketing strategies around, particularly if you can secure good quality reviews on the most relevant review sites for your business or industry (as well as on large generic review sites).

As an overall strategy, I encourage you to:

- identify the best places to create a business profile on generic and industry specific review websites (like Yelp etc)

- invite your clients and customers to add a review to the website (you may need to encourage them to do so by providing specific details on how to do it)

- turn on notifications so that you can be advised when a new review is added

- respond to reviews as soon as they are added (but politely, please don't be emotional - just wait a day if you become furious!)

Action 77: *Identify the best review websites and add your business details so that you can receive reviews. Encourage your clients and customers to add reviews and respond appropriately to reviews as soon as possible*

12.3 Recommendations

Recommendations are usually received either directly from clients and customers or via online platforms. For example, on LinkedIn, they are specific details you can add to a person's performance in a particular job (a bit like an online written reference).

A lot of businesses, particularly with high value transactions, will ask clients to provide a written recommendation at the end of the sale. These can be received in writing on paper or a card or via email or sometimes, directly on the business website.

In most cases, a recommendation is likely to be a positive statement about the products or services received from the business. I have often found a whole pile of past recommendations in a file somewhere in my clients' offices – where they do not provide any value to the business at all!

So my first suggestion to you is to find all of your recommendations and decide how you are going to showcase them to your potential and existing clients and customers.

There are a variety of ways:

- display them at your business premises

- scan them and put them on your website

- re-type them and put them on your website

- add them to your marketing collateral – proposals, tenders, advertising package etc

- put different recommendations in your email signature

- ask the client or customer to add them to a review website

- add a recommendations tool or plugin to your website and have them rotating independently

- add them to social media or online platforms

If you choose to place them on a public place, it is important to ask for the author's permission before adding their name to the review.

Action 78: *Recommendations need to be adequately showcased in a public way to provide maximum value but make sure you have the author's permission to list them publicly first*

12.4 Referrals

Some businesses operate on a formal referral basis (determined by a signed agreement with agreed conditions) or informally with or without any verbally agreed details. Other businesses are required by law to clearly state the details of any referrals and the specifics of any commissions or payments made to secure the business.

In a local context or location, referrals can be extremely valuable. Referrals can be initiated by:

- networking and events

- direct contact

- portal or comparison services

- directories

- word of mouth

- complementary businesses

- like minded professionals

- members of an association or group

- chatting in a public place - in fact anywhere really!

I am fortunate to have had many happy clients who have then referred people they know to me. It is very interesting because so often they tell me that they have made referrals, but the person does not always contact me.

However, I do not worry because I have designed my business funnel to qualify my referrals so that I attract people who are ready to contact me to make an appointment (I don't want to spend hours on the phone or send multiple emails when it may not lead to business - I simply don't have the time). That said, I do have one particular referer who has sent many suitable clients to me so I make an extra special effort to look after him.

There are many reasons why you might be receiving referrals but not actually securing business. So what can you do to maximize your chance of receiving referrals but also qualifying your referrals so that they lead directly to business opportunities?

- you absolutely must have a good quality website that appears in search results when the person looks for your name, your business name and hopefully your primary keywords as well

- your business profile on social media and online platforms must also be good quality but also consistent with your business brand (same message everywhere) and also tailored for the location where it is published (your Facebook strategy will be different to your LinkedIn strategy)

- you must make it very clear with whatever information the person receives about you or your business (your business card, brochures, online and offline content) that they know exactly what they should do next (and provide instructions)

- you need to be consistent in your business approach at all times

- be willing to overcome disappointment and keep going even when referrals don't lead to business

- you must be very responsive to enquiries and feedback

- you must follow up with the referrer to personally say thank you for the referral - EVERY time

- you can encourage the referer or the referee to make additional referrals in the future

- you can encourage the client or customer to provide a review (because these provide more credibility when another referee completes their due diligence)

With the wealth of information that is now available online, paradoxically, many people are asking other people, "Who do you recommend?" This means that referrals are probably one of the most important business strategies of our modern times.

In a hyper local context or location, the more that other people and businesses know and understand about your business, the more likely they are to be able to make referrals. So don't be too shy. You might think that something you do is bleeding obvious, but to someone without your knowledge and experience, it could be something, new, exciting and very relevant.

So the other technique I would encourage you to develop is your curiosity. Be willing to share details about what you do and how you do it, but also be willing to find out what other people do and how they do it. By listening to their story, they are more likely to be interested in hearing your story - and you will most likely learn something new too!

In my view, referrals are very much a two way street. You cannot expect to receive referrals if you do not give any referrals. You may not be able to give the person who gave you a referral a referral back, but you might be able to give a referral to someone else. If you find that you are always receiving referrals from one particular person, please let them know you appreciate it and acknowledge it in some way - you may also like to let them know about the referrals you give to other people so that they know that you too are 'paying it forward.'

Personally, I get a real thrill out of being able to share a good referral. I do it without expecting payment or a gift in return (but I do expect a thank you). If I make a referral and the person has a bad experience and tells me, I do try and find out what went wrong and see if I can assist in any way. If the issue cannot be resolved, I usually do not refer to that person or business again as a bad referral can be a bad reflection on me - I have to be confident that the person or business I am referring will be able to provide good quality products and services.

As I have said, with more and more business being completed by referral, I really encourage you to develop this skill in your business.

Action 79: *Good quality referrals that lead directly to business require you to make sure that your online and offline content meets the due diligence requirements of your prospective client or customer. Be curious and always look for ways to provide referrals to others and make sure that you always say thank you for referrals you receive*

12.5 Reputation

Your overall reputation, as a business or a person, can be influenced by many different factors, but the foundation underlying your reputation is your values.

You could 'pretend' to appear a particular way, but it usually does not last. It is not because you are not a fantastic actor, you may be able to get away with it for a period of time, but ultimately, your true values will shine through.

I often talk about this when I am working with a client who has been unemployed for a long time. Although they may say everything they should say in a job interview, they will usually miss out if they have lost confidence in themselves - people can sense this feeling, particularly if they meet you in person.

So it is with business. You may be very successful in business, but if you have a high turnover of staff, you need to ask yourself, why? How are you being perceived? If potential repeat customers never come back, again, ask yourself why? You can follow all of the perfect business techniques but not be successful and you can be very imperfect and be very successful in business.

This is why you hear so many stories about successful entrepreneurs who left school and failed university but they went on to amazing business or philanthropic success. That doesn't mean that people with a good education cannot be good in business, I just think that it is popular culture that likes to say that even if you were down once, you can get back up again.

My view is that there are a number of common denominators with successful business owners. I find that they:

- have a very clear reason for being in business and they tell people about their vision (I am a true artist and I love bringing beauty into people's homes)

- don't pretend or apologize for who they are (they behave authentically all the time and don't mind if some people don't like them)

- are willing to be vulnerable and admit their mistakes (they don't say that they have the answer for everything but they do apologize immediately and sincerely if they have made a mistake)

- are prepared to live outside of their comfort zone (and take calculated risks, make tough decisions and carry out their planned actions, even if they don't 'feel' like doing it on a particular day)

- collaborate with others and ask for help (they realize that they can't do everything on their own)

- regularly encourage, praise and thank others and are not intimidated by someone who can do something better than they can (in fact they regularly seek people who are more capable than they are to work with them)

- are proactive about moving forward and often rely on their intuition (they learn from what they have done and keep moving forward)

- accept full responsibility for what they do and how they do it, fully understanding that there may be consequences that they will need to recover from (and they are also prepared to make a firm stand if required)

As you can imagine, if a person follows through with these types of behaviors, they are much more likely to create a good quality reputation in their own business, context and location. I want to emphasize here that you absolutely do not need to be perfect - news flash, none of us are!

However, at the end of the day, if you don't follow these general principles, if your behavior is inconsistent, if people do not know what to expect or you do not respond appropriately when a crisis occurs, you will find that your reputation can suffer.

That said, even if the worst happens and you are vilified, either fairly or unfairly, you can still recover. You simply need to continue practicing good behaviors on an ongoing basis. It is never too late to be ethical and authentic. The only difference is, it may take a bit longer to build a reliable reputation - but it can be achieved.

I have personally worked with a very high profile corporate advisor who was jailed for white collar crime. He had built a range of very successful enterprises and then, unfortunately, made a few mistakes. He was prosecuted and when he was in jail, he learnt how to cook and he also learnt how to be ethical. He was punished for his wrong doings and he has redeemed himself, even though the media continually hounds him and his family.

It is never impossible to recover, but he did tell me that he always tells people up front about his past so that they don't discover it by surprise later. He is a true survivor and he has grown and developed along the way and is back working as a very successful corporate advisor and he even lectures on the topic of governance!

So in his case, despite having a bad reputation in the past, he is living proof that you can get back up again. But as he also admits, it takes regular, consistent effort over time to rebuild trust.

He has a little test that he likes to share with people - "How would you feel going home and discussing your idea with your wife and children?" I think it is a good start for assessing the business and life decisions you make.

I have always been taught to be honest, regardless of how difficult it is at the time to admit a mistake (or even announce a mistake that nobody knows about at that time). In fact on a few occasions, my parents rewarded me for telling the truth even though I did the wrong thing!

I guess the main thing that I have learnt is that it is best to deal with one small wrong doing at the beginning than it is to do one small wrong thing and then keep trying to cover it up. I was told at youth group that telling a lie is like dropping a stone into a pond of water, the ripples just keep going and going and going. To be honest, I didn't want to suffer through all of those ripples - or try and remember what lies I had told and to whom to keep it all covered up over time. That sounded way too complicated. I figured it was a lot easier to just fess up in the beginning and so far it has worked a treat for me.

In business, I have had a few difficult customers from time to time, but I have always been able to resolve issues within 24 hours and it is so liberating to be able to wake up every day with a clear conscience.

Unfortunately, I do suffer when something goes wrong because I know full well that it was never my intention to cause any issue or discomfort with anyone else at anytime. I may have been perceived as having done the wrong thing, I may have even done the wrong thing, but it was never my intention to do the wrong thing.

It is not always easy to convince someone that the intention wasn't there. So what I have learnt to do is realize that on some occasions, it is not my issue, it is actually their issue and no matter what I did, they were going to be disappointed.

Once again, the first thing I do in this situation is apologize, even if I am not at fault The other person has still suffered and I simply do not want anyone else to suffer (even if they have caused me suffering). If necessary, I allow myself to take some time to emotionally recover from the impact of their complaint as I do not want to respond in the heat of the moment.

I then calmly sit down and work out how best to resolve the matter. In most cases, I try and gather my thoughts, write them down and then personally speak to the person. If that is not possible, I will providea response in writing. Sometimes, I speak personally and then confirm in writing.

Interestingly, by adopting this approach, where I do not try and criticize the other person or blame them for misinterpreting the situation, I often find that we both end up growing and developing in a positive way. Even though the process can be painful, the outcome can be extraordinary.

So for now, I would like to give you good courage to admit your known (or unknown) mistakes and apologize and work out ways to improve the situation in the future. It may not be easy, but it is definitely worthwhile. I am sure that most people will respect you for your courage and this will help you build or rebuild your reputation. It is never too late.

Action 80: *Your reputation will ultimately be revealed by your values. Successful business owners are prepared to be authentic, vulnerable, proactive, apologetic and responsible. Even if your reputation has been damaged, it is possible to recover, so I encourage you to live courageously*

12.6 Testimonials

The big trend in testimonials is not just a reproduction in text of a previously provided testimonial, it is a testimonial with:

- a photo

- a link to the person's website/LinkedIn profile (for verification if needed)

- a video

- a star rating that will appear in search results (thanks to a website plugin/snippet feature).

There are a variety of ways to secure testimonials. You could:

- have it as part of your business process where you directly ask each client or customer to provide a testimonial (works well with a quick paper evaluation form at the time of the transaction or at an event)

- have a recording area set up at an event (where you have a video camera and a descriptive visual background, usually with your business name or logo included)

- contact past clients and ask them for a testimonial and give them clues as to what you would like them to discuss in the testimonial (great if you have some samples or past testimonials with your keywords included that they can adjust and put into their own words)

- provide a quick three question online survey so that you can say 95% of our customers say .... with an additional section for a specific comment - "What I most liked about XYZ business's products or services was...." You may also be courageous enough to ask "What could XYZ business do to improve their products or services...."

- you could find what people have written about your business in online reviews and reproduce the content in an appropriate online or offline location

Like general reviews and recommendations, testimonials are even more personalized and directly attributable to a specific person. Some people are still skeptical of the authenticity of a testimonial, but it is pretty difficult to 'fake' a video testimonial.

I believe that testimonials are simply another form of reviews and recommendations. What really helps is the overall quantity, but also the perceived quality of the person providing the testimonial and don't forget to put them on your website and where appropriate, on your online profiles.

One of my clients conducts media spokesperson training. He has probably 150 testimonials on the testimonials page of his website. But even more interesting is the job titles and the organizations represented on this list - all of the major corporate, educational and government organizations across the country.

I usually include dates to give some context (reviews over time), but it is probably better to leave the content as 'evergreen' without the dates so that if you forget to update the website page every few months they won't look old!

Action 81: *Make an effort to secure a range of quality testimonials from well recognized individuals. If authorized, include a link to their online profile so that people can verify the testimonial and/or take a video. Publish the testimonials on your website and where appropriate, on your online profiles*

12.7 Feedback

What systems do you have in place to receive feedback from your clients and customers? Do you ever ask them about how they found out about you? Or how well your products and services met their needs? Do you ask what was most valuable but also, what you could improve?

Feedback is extremely helpful - because it can give you clues on what to change and improve. That doesn't mean that you need to jump every time someone makes a comment, some people will never be happy regardless of what you do!

Some feedback simply needs to be heard and received with a thank you. You do not need to snap back and justify why you do things a certain way, particularly if the feedback feels uncomfortable or even unreasonable.

There are a variety of ways to collect feedback. Naturally, you could simply ask at the time the transaction occurs, but it is probably better if it occurs slightly after the transaction as it is a way to follow up and keep the connection going after the transaction has occurred.

Have you noticed how accommodation providers will often send an online survey after your visit asking for your feedback and offering you the chance to win a special prize if you complete their form? In principle, I don't mind receiving these requests, but when they ask me to answer what feels like 50 questions that is going to take me 15 minutes or more to complete, I refuse!

So please don't fall into the trap of demanding too much from your feedback. I also encourage you to help the person remember what they liked the most (this leaves them with a positive thought about your business).

As always, thank them for providing feedback. If it is negative and not anonymous, make an effort to follow up with them personally and let them know what you have done to remedy the situation for the future.

You may also like to keep a 'change' register. A list of the things that you have done to upgrade and improve your products and services to remind yourself that you are an adaptive business. It is a great list to review over time as we often forget what we have done on our journey to the present moment. It is a good way to re-affirm your ongoing commitment to continuous improvement. It is also a good record to show new employees and contractors so that they can understand your business methodology.

Action 82: *Create a reliable system for collecting feedback from your clients and customers and respond with the appropriate actions as required. Do not react emotionally to uncomfortable or unreasonable feedback. Keep a record of changes you have made to re-affirm your commitment to continuous improvement and show this list to new employees and contractors*

12.8 Advocacy

I am someone who simply cannot sit on the sidelines and do nothing when I can see that something really needs to be changed or improved or even just reported to the relevant authority. I am the sort of person who if I see something out of place, I put it back, without even realizing what I have just done. In fact sometimes, I have to stop myself from putting things away - especially when I am visiting a friend's house!!

Anyway, I digress. As a citizen in a local community, I believe all of us have a personal responsibility to add some sort of value to the community in our own way. If we have a skill in a particular area, we should aim to contribute and help others in some way.

One of the ways I help people is through networking. I provide opportunities for people to come together to connect, collaborate and share experiences

A natural consequence of this initiative is that I find ways to share the value and importance of local business in the local media and I help other local initiatives gain further opportunities by promoting their activities at state level. I am not conducting mass rallies or lobbying politicians for legislative changes, but I am empowering more people to connect and by a consistent effort over time, I am advocating on behalf of all local businesses.

There are many ways you can be an advocate in your hyper local context or location. You could:

- take on a leadership role in a group, association or industry body

- make representations on behalf of someone who does not feel comfortable standing up for themselves on their own

- go with someone to a meeting or event because they are not comfortable attending on their own

- provide a work experience or internship opportunity for someone who either needs experience or has been unemployed for a lengthy period

- invite new people to an activity so that they have an opportunity to learn something new about what they can do in the future

- encourage people to join a membership or advocacy group so that they can support an initiative in cash or in kind

- share details of how a person can support a campaign that overcomes an issue (for example, details of what to do on social media, petitions to sign, rallies or meetings to attend etc)

- simply make the time to listen to someone's concerns and ask how you can help

Some people have the impression that an advocate is someone who is on some sort of crazy mission and that they have to be a little bit left of center to pursue their cause. I couldn't disagree more. It is all of the little actions that make a huge difference in the end. If each person did just one little thing, then one person would not have to make such a big song and dance about it!

Tragedy is often the trigger for an advocacy campaign. I know that if I had not suffered when I moved interstate, I probably never would have set up Newcomers Network and spent so many years helping newcomers ever since. I see this as a productive outcome from a personal tragedy. What often happens is that one significant act in a particular direction motivates many more people to also take action. I have been so pleased to see so many other newcomer related initiatives get off the ground since I started my small campaign!

I often wonder though, why does it take a 'disaster' to initiate change - either in our community or in ourselves? That is why my last point in my advocacy options list is about listening. If we simply take a moment to listen to others, we can often find that there is something we can do to help. When we hear the person's story, we don't have to provide a solution, we simply need to ask them, "How can I help?"

If you have decided to take on a cause, I encourage you to always adopt a positive, consistent and long term approach with your negotiations. I have never, at any point, criticized a person or a business or government directly. I try and understand their position and look for ways we can move forward. My initial idea may not work, but over time, because I keep coming back with another idea, then another idea, then another idea, I eventually get heard and change occurs.

If we think carefully about the society in which we live, most of the luxuries we enjoy today are as a result of the collective efforts of so many people who have gone before us. People have fought in wars, gone without, sacrificed themselves or their family for the collective good. I admire these people enormously. Service before self. We must all pause for a moment and thank them for their efforts - we have so much to be grateful for.

I trust this section of the book encourages you to think of one small way you can be an advocate in the future. We all have unique gifts and I encourage you to use yours in a way to help your hyper local context or location. The good news is that when you help someone else, it will make you feel good too!

Action 83: *There are many different ways you can be an advocate in your hyper local context or location. Use your unique gifts to find a way to help another person or group by completing a lot of little positive actions over time. You will benefit and so will your community*

13. Events Marketing

I have lost count of how many events I have attended or run. Wow, what a ride! Over time, I have learnt to be a little bit more selective as my time has become so much more valuable. When I factor in the time to travel to the event, the time at the event and the follow up I need to complete, I really need to assess each event on its merits and how it will develop me or my businesses.

I have also made plenty of mistakes. I have wasted hours trying to get people to attend an event and then up to 80% of the people who have said they were going to come have not shown up.

There are plenty of consultants who will tell you that running events is the key to quick riches. But there are a huge range of expenses and risks. There are also a range of principles that if you apply them to either individual events or series of events, you are much more likely to be able to see a return on your time and investment.

The biggest advantage of an event is that instead of reaching just one or a few people, you can reach a lot more. Statistically, your odds of securing an opportunity are greater when you meet more people, but it also depends on what you are trying to achieve. If you are in the first stages of your business relationship, it is an excellent way to begin your business relationship.

However, over time, you will want to develop a closer connection and this may take a different type of approach - either a personal meeting or a much more tailored event. I have attended a lot of free ra-ra events at large hotels where it is very much a numbers game. Thousands at the first event, then smaller group events, then high priced personal retreats. However, the investment to secure thousands at the first event is probably beyond the budget of most hyper local businesses.

So in this section, I want to share my absolute best tips on how to make events marketing really work for you and your business. These tips are based on a huge amount of experience in a world where people are becoming increasingly fickle and reluctant to commit. Even if they do commit to attending, they often change their mind at the last minute and go somewhere else instead!

Action 84: *Before attending an event, think about the real cost to you and your business including the time to travel to, attend and then follow up after the event. You can potentially reach more people, but the risks can also be higher, especially as more people appear to be fickle and reluctant to commit*

13.1 Free Events

I like hosting free events for a variety of reasons:

- there is no cost barrier to attending

- the people who choose to attend are usually prepared to accept some level of responsibility for a successful outcome (and they are not expecting you to give them everything but they may get a sales message because they didn't pay to attend)

- it saves a lot of hassle collecting payment

- they are less likely to complain if they did not enjoy the event (after all, it was free!)

- you can often negotiate cheaper or free room hire

- you can think of more creative ways to make it work and attract people to the event

- if you provide them with free refreshments or anything of perceived value, they are much more likely to share the details of their experience, even if they do not 'buy' from your business (it generates referrals)

- it creates goodwill because you are not demanding a payment upfront

- you are more likely to secure some free publicity and others may be more willing to share the event through their networks

Some people will say, "But if you charge people to attend, they are much more likely to show up." Overall, yes, I agree. When I help coordinate professional development functions for professional associations, we get a much better response when there is a ticket cost involved.

However, I see free events as offering a different opportunity for your business. I see them as an excellent opportunity to:

- promote your events (and your business) far and wide including on events websites, your website, online platforms (like Meetup), on social media, in the media etc without 'selling' anything

- provide people with a chance to meet you in a non-threatening environment (useful for both products and services businesses)

- improve your brand awareness, particularly if the events are run on a regular basis

- provide regular content for your newsletters, website, social media etc - happy snaps, guest speaker profiles, outcomes etc

- allow you to join forces with other organizations, festivals, groups etc without there being issues over who pays for what and who receives what

- be a good warm-up or segway to a paid activity

So before you rush off to hire an expensive venue with full catering for a single event in one month's time, I would like to share with you my absolute best tips for running free events to really generate value for your participants and for your business:

- make them regular - like 5:30pm on the third Wednesday of every month or second month (there is no day or time that is perfect for everyone, so pick what you believe will work best for you and your target audience but is not in a peak time)

- choose a venue that suits your target audience and try and book it at a time when it is available for free because it is not busy at that time (this helps the venue attract new clientele in an off peak time, but remember to encourage your guests to purchase a refreshment). Ideally, make sure that each person can easily pay for their own refreshments (or be prepared to cover the cost)

- make sure that you provide full instructions on how to find the venue, get there by public transport or car (plus where to park) and any peculiar requirements (like a dress code, age limitations, details of where to find the lift etc)

- whilst I usually host my events in public spaces and other patrons may be in attendance, I try and make it easy for conversations to occur, so as a rule, I choose a venue with carpet and sound proofing so that it is not too noisy and it doesn't echo. It needs to be comfortable for your target audience and not in a location that is too difficult to reach

- make sure that people who are coming on their own know exactly what to do and that they are made to feel welcome when they arrive. I always provide a hand written first name sticker and I immediately introduce each person to someone else when they arrive

- make sure that your event description lets people know what to expect. Will you be having a short presentation? Will there be networking opportunities? Do they need to bring anything (like a business card or device)? Can they invite someone else? What should they wear? What time will it finish? Do they need to arrive by a certain time to be included? Do they need a security code or some other instructions to access the venue? Will they be invited to purchase something and if so, how can they pay for that offering? Will there be an obligation to purchase anything (hopefully not - otherwise it is not really free)?

- what do you encourage the person to do at the event? Mix and mingle? Chat or listen? Share ideas or business? What could they do after the event?

- follow up after the event. Post some photos on social media and/or your website, send them a personal 'thanks for attending' message, provide details of anything you promised to send and consider adding them to your mailing list for future events (but allow them to unsubscribe)

- avoid making the process complicated or expensive in any way. I find that the easier it is to run the event without a lot of work or time, the more value I receive. If you are running free events and it takes a lot of time or money and you don't receive a benefit, you can easily become resentful and your guests will notice

- find some other people who can provide backup if you are not able to attend or organize the event on the odd occasion. These people will usually appreciate the opportunity to assist - I usually pick a person who has attended frequently or offers a similar service and can gain some direct benefit by being listed as the host for that month. However, I do make sure that I fully brief them on the necessary protocols and I usually check to make sure that is what happened before considering them for a second opportunity. After all, my reputation is at stake!

- I always personally thank the venue every time and I do my best to promote the venue around my network. The venues have frequently collected other bookings as a result of this sharing and proactive approach. At the beginning of the relationship, they don't usually offer me anything in return (not even a free drink!), but over time, I have been able to receive a substantial discount on paid events I have hosted at the same venue

Free events are not a quick fix marketing solution. What I have found is that within 12 months, I have a regular patronage every month. That said, I do still send an email reminder a day before the event to the mailing list I have generated and it is automatically promoted on event listings, online platforms and social media.

I also find that I attract people with similar values and they regularly share the details of the event with other like minded people. This marketing occurs without me doing anything!

I don't always receive a converting client or transaction after every event, but I keep attracting enough clients over time that justifies my time and effort. So I always arrive with a willingness to be there.

I also find it to be an excellent source of ideas and inspiration from people I otherwise would not see. This is extremely valuable as I can re-purpose this information in my business. It also enables me to build and maintain business relationships without visiting people individually.

If you are a 'single shingle consultant' working in your own private practice, you may like to host a more intimate small group over breakfast (where you pay) so that your like-minded clients can network directly and you can informally say 'thank you' to your clients. Again, you can host this at a local cafe and feel a little more connected in your community.

Action 85: *Free events work best if they are regular, easy to coordinate and attend and you treat them as a brand awareness and information gathering exercise. They are also very effective at building business relationships in a non threatening environment*

13.2 Hosting Paid Events

There are times when I host paid events. These usually offer a premium opportunity - specific training, special guest speakers, a notable activity etc.

Just because you have a mailing list and you promote the event through all of the right channels, it will not guarantee ticket sales. If your event has a history of being worth attending (an annual gala event that attracts 200 people every year), then it is going to take a bit more work to encourage people to attend.

What I have found works best is directly contacting specific people, by phone or in person, and asking them if they would like to come and if they know someone else who would like to join them. You will eventually sell a few tickets here and a few tickets there - but this takes quite a bit of effort but it gets the momentum happening.

You also need to make sure that you have enough lead time. There is a theory that people need to see the details of an event at least three times before they will make a commitment. So there is every chance that the first time they receive the details of the event, they will not respond.

You can also ask key people (very effective if you are on a committee) to share the invitation to people they have personally chosen that they think would find the event of benefit. But once again, remind them to send the invitation out more than once.

Think very carefully about where your target audience for this event congregates. Is it on social media? Is it on a particular mailing list? Do you need to pay for an advertisement on a particular website or publication? When you receive a booking, do you contact that person and personally ask them to forward the invitation on to other people who may like to attend?

There are some other techniques that can help with ticket sales:

- provide a substantial discount or benefit for immediate action or early registration

- sell the benefits in the event promotion - what will the person gain by attending?

- showcase the value they are receiving and any extra bonuses they may be able to receive by attending

- selling the tickets on a website like Eventbrite that allows people to share the details of the event automatically via Facebook or other distribution channels (even if the fee that Eventbrite collects eats into your profit a little, this listing also makes the event open to a wider audience)

- adding the event to other event platforms for promotion to a wider audience

- offering different price points for particular guests (students, members, etc)

- affiliate programs with like minded and complementary businesses (where a percentage of ticket sales could go to the referring business)

- association with a charity or cause (all profits or $XX from every ticket goes to XYZ enterprise)

- personally re-invite all of the people who have attended a previous similar event or one of your other events - and perhaps give them a special 'pre-release' offer

- make sure that you are 100% committed to selling the tickets. It is very frustrating to all concerned if an event is cancelled

- make sure you check the dates and other potentially competing activities. I once had to organize a first time event after a public holiday and on the first day of the school holidays and it took a Herculean effort to get people there!

- consider giving away a few free tickets in return for some promotion through that person's networks, particularly if they are influential

- make sure every stakeholder also promotes the event through their networks - the speakers, the venue, the sponsors, the exhibitors, the master of ceremonies etc

- do whatever you can to support the stakeholders, speakers, venue, sponsors, exhibitors, the master of ceremonies etc so that they are more likely to provide assistance

- tie the event into another well publicized activity, festival, expo etc (see if your event can be listed in their program, promoted through all of their channels etc)

- have a publicity and media campaign

- make sure the event is listed in local online 'What's On' listings, particularly those that are popular with your target audience or have a lot of traffic

- create a full action plan for the entire process, from start to finish. It is so easy to forget an important component, especially on your first few events

- allow plenty of time to receive all of the printed materials, banners, merchandise etc to arrive before the event date (I have had to run events without this material so be warned!)

- have some backup options in place. Sometimes the worst can happen, so think about what you will do if a speaker cancels, you can't get enough paying guests etc. Have a contingency budget and a time buffer

- make sure that you have all of the necessary licenses or insurances that you need to run the event, again, well in advance

As you can see, this list is a lot longer than the free events list! That said, you can apply all of these ideas to both free and paid events. In a hyper local context or location, you can narrow down your event partners, sponsors etc and really saturate the local target audience.

For example, on special occasions, I have asked all of the local networks to share the details of a particular event, especially when it provides genuine value for the people who are attending. I always work on the basis of sharing useful information (not selling). Most people seem to resist a sales message, but really appreciate the sharing of knowledge and value.

That said, people still need to be given specific instructions on what they can do next, without feeling obligated. But they can be encouraged! If they receive something funny or a little unexpected, this creates a fantastic opportunity to create a longer term memory about you and your business.

In most cases, people like to feel involved and participate, but that does not mean that they want to be singled out in front of others as this can be very uncomfortable and embarrassing. If they receive something that they don't want, this can be difficult to overcome!

Overall, well planned and executed paid events can be a very strategic tool for helping you and your business reach your target audience and their networks.

Action 86: *If you have chosen to run paid events, make sure you understand the commitment and action steps involved. Events can be a tool for opening up opportunities through the event promotion and referral systems you use*

13.3 Speaking At Events

In terms of events, this is probably one of the best ways to utilize your time. Let me explain why. You:

- get promoted to an organization's entire mailing list

- they get the numbers to the event

- they organize the venue, the catering and usually the cost of attending (I do get annoyed when they expect you to pay for the privilege, especially if you are sharing useful information)

- they send the reminders and process the payments

- you are automatically introduced to people

However, it is not a free ticket to ride. There are a number of key things I do when I speak at events: I will always:

- get a full briefing on the event, the purpose, the full details, the likely audience and their needs and if appropriate, make additional

- suggestions on how to promote the event or even collaborate with another group (I don't force this issue, I just offer the opportunity)

- tailor every presentation for the audience, regardless of my personal preferences and I never make it salesy

- with the event organizer's permission, I will offer a prize for a prize drawer and also give guests a way to reach me directly after the event (if I have presentation slides, I include a 'contact me for x' message)

- with the event organizer's permission, I will bring along my pull up banner, books, business cards etc for people to see (you may also like to give a small gift or voucher to every guest)

- follow up with a thank you for inviting me immediately after the event and complete any other follow up, if possible, within 24 hours

Again, I do not have any expectations that I will secure business from every speaking event. Sometimes I find that absolutely nothing happens and then other times, all sorts of things happen.

If you are very busy, you may not be able to say yes to every request and you may have to decline some invitations. Selecting a suitable criteria for assessing each request can be difficult.

For example, you may not be paid to speak at an international conference, but in theory, this could potentially provide you with a higher level of status on the speaking circuit or within your industry. If you are very successful, a local community group may not be able to afford a speaker's fee, but they may be really inspired and appreciative of your time.

As a general rule, I say yes when I can. I see speaking as another opportunity to inform and educate people and I am passionate about sharing what I know, so for the most part, I enjoy it!

What I do find frustrating, as I have indicated previously, is when I am expected to pay a large amount of money to attend a conference when I am delivering quality information to the other participants. I figure that the caterer is paid for the food, the venue is paid for the room, why can't the speakers at least attend for free even if they are not paid for their content? But I digress once again!

Most of the time, participants are not aware that speakers have had to pay a fee to speak, certainly the general public are not usually aware. As a result of 'paying' for these 'opportunities' to share my hard earned knowledge, I try and make the most of the experience beyond the date of the event.

As a general rule, I audio record my presentation and put my slides and the audio recording on my website so that other people who could not attend can still benefit from my presentation. I don't worry about other people receiving my intellectual property - because it is constantly changing and updating so I am not losing anything with this strategy. As I have said before, I tailor every presentation for that audience. In some respects, it drives me to continually produce new content.

I also promote the fact that I am speaking at selected events to my networks and then after I have spoken and published the details online, I share it around my networks, social media and online platforms This way, I can reach my target audience again and gain additional immediate dynamic value. I also create lifetime value because the content is published on my website where it cannot be removed at a later date (or if it is, you will find it on http://archive.org)

I also reference other relevant presentations on that page as well. So if I have spoken at the same event in previous years, I also link to those presentations. This has had the added benefit of reducing my website bounce rate as people stay on my website for a lot longer. Also, anyone considering me for a speaking engagement can also check out my previous presentations.

Where appropriate, I am now recording my presentations on video. As you can imagine, this involves a bit more work, but again, it provides lifetime value.

If I have secured some personal email addresses from the event, I also forward all of this information directly to those people. I also usually invite them to connect with me personally on LinkedIn. Some speakers then put these new people into their Customer Relationship Management cycle and try and entice them through their usual sales funnel but as a general rule, I let social media fulfill this duty as I don't want to be seen as annoying or pushy.

Ultimately, I am doing all of these things to secure bigger and better opportunities in the future.

If you are just starting out in business, this speaking strategy can make you very well known very quickly. When I started working for a local real estate agency, I lined up a range of speaking gigs and within six months, it seemed that most people in the local area who met me at a networking event knew that I was in real estate! Not only that, I was promoting the entire business at the same time. This also triggered their busiest sales period in 25 years! (Mind you, I did also develop a fairly significant newsletter, events, social media and content production campaign at the same time).

If you have to make a choice between running free events, paid events or speaking, I would suggest you start with the speaking opportunities first. I would encourage you to create quite informal free events to get the ball rolling (again, on a regular time and date basis) as soon as possible and then once these get established, go for the paid events.

It really takes commitment to be successful with events, even if you are just the speaker. You need to make sure that you leave a good impression because you are really in the spotlight on these occasions. You need to be well prepared and allow plenty of time to get everything organized and arrive on time on the day.

However, the rewards can be phenomenal. I have had some people contact me after an event and explain how I have changed their life, for the better. I consider myself fortunate to be given the privilege to speak in front of people, so I do my best to give them amazing value. I don't hold back.

In fact holding back can give you a bad reputation. I recently attended a free ra-ra event and then went to a follow up four hour workshop provided by one of the speakers where I paid an amount of money that was well beyond my normal budget.

At that four hour workshop, approximately one hour was spent providing useful content - the other three hours were spent promoting the four day program available for thousands of dollars. To make matters worse, we were not even allowed to network with the other participants.

This presenter lost all credibility with me and in fact has made me dislike her whole approach to business. I would never recommend her program and if someone asked me about her course, I would tell the person about my experience. As far as I am concerned, this was not a fair exchange and in fact, it was false advertising.

Finally, before you commit to speaking at an event, you may like to check out the background of the organizers or organizations associated with the event. If they have a different value system to you, there is a chance that your presentation will not be well received by the audience or that your own reputation could be damaged by being involved. The opposite can also occur - your reputation can be enhanced by being a presenter (and it is even nicer when they ask you to be a special speaker).

One final comment I will make is to be careful with your time. I have often had to go through a very lengthy process to be considered for a speaking opportunity (particularly if it is interstate or overseas) and then after spending an enormous amount of unpaid time on this process, either not been selected or had the opportunity cancelled (through no fault of my own).

Of course I have to take this on the chin and keep going, but it can be very annoying to invest all of that energy and effort for a zero result. There is no such thing as a sure thing until it actually happens! You need to be careful not to feel resentful.

I would also like to add that what most people want from an event is to be entertained - so if you can use some safe humor that doesn't offend or make fun of anyone, I say go for it! I don't know anyone who doesn't enjoy a good laugh! My maternal grandmother used to say, "I don't mind if someone is laughing, even if it is at my expense, they are still laughing!"

Finally, remember that to really maximize the opportunity, it may be a good idea to share the details of the speaking engagement through some of your networks (either before or afterwards) - see Section 13.5 for some suggestions.

Action 87: *Speaking at events is a great privilege and it can generate some amazing opportunities for you and your business. It is an excellent strategy if you are starting to promote your business in a hyper local context or location and if you are able to record the event, it can also give you lifetime value. Just be aware of the specific preparation you need to complete and the pitfalls*

13.4 Teaching

I don't believe the saying that "Those who can do and those that can't teach." In fact, to be a teacher today, you have to be able to do and be able to teach. That is because the world is changing so fast that if you don't have any experience in the 'real world,' you run the very real risk of being completely out of date very quickly.

In fact, the way I see it, the more people who can both work or be in business and teach, the better. In this situation, the teacher can provide real life examples in class and keep the content fresh and relevant. As an individual person, it encourages the teacher to constantly stay on trend and up to date because the last thing that the teacher wants to happen is to be shown up by the students that may have already done some research prior to class!

I teach because I enjoy teaching. It doesn't pay that well, let me tell you. But I see it as a great way to give back and the students constantly inspire me to do better, to find an easier way to explain things and they challenge me in new ways so that I constantly bring back new ideas to my business. Their ideas and contributions to class help each other too. I encourage networking within each class and I invite students to keep in touch and tell me what happens after they have completed the course. I then feed that information back into future classes.

A real drawback though is the time spent preparing or following up after class. This time is not usually paid either. To keep up to date, I also need to spend quite a bit of time attending events, reading new research and updating my teaching resources. I guess that I do it because I am passionate about it, but to be fair, it is well beyond the scope of most hyper local businesses.

One small but quite useful benefit from teaching is the profile it helps me generate online. For each of my teaching roles, I have a profile page on a very reputable website, with links to me personally. This provides fantastic link juice but also significant credibility when someone searches for me online.

I also see it as an excellent strategy if you are planning some form of semi-retirement from your business or if you have sold your business but would like to keep sharing knowledge and mentoring others. You may consider tutoring too. This is potentially easier as you are dealing with a much smaller number of students and the demands of a classroom don't exist.

Rather than live teaching, you may also like to consider creating an online course on one of the online course platforms. This is a newer idea and in some areas, there is a lot of competition for very similar content. If you are teaching at a teaching institution, they are responsible for securing class enrolments - if you teach online, you are going to need to do a lot of the promotion yourself.

However the biggest benefit is that you will teach the class once and then multiple people can enjoy the class at anytime, usually 24 hours a day, seven days a week, anywhere in the world. You can choose to provide it free of charge or for a fee and naturally, you can also improve the class over time based on feedback. For most hyper local businesses, I would not recommend this as a first step in their marketing, particularly as so many people like to just jump onto YouTube and see what they can find for free.

But if you ultimately want to showcase your knowledge in a more structured format, a self hosted online course or an online course on a course platform could be the way to go.

Action 88: *Teaching, either live and in person or online can be a good way to maintain your expertise and gather new ideas for your business. It can also help you reach your target audience and give you an opportunity to give back*

13.5 Expos, Trade Fairs And Conferences

Have you ever noticed that these types of events usually attract either mostly the same exhibitors every year (because they have an allocated budget and/or gain ongoing value from participating) or new exhibitors every year (because the people last year got burnt and never want to do it again)?

It can be extremely expensive to be involved in one of these types of events, so you really need to gain maximum value from being involved. You need to look beyond the cost of the stand or publicity you will receive and really analyze the real benefit to your business. You might like to think about:

- how much promotion is guaranteed (don't assume that what they did last year will happen again this year - I made that mistake!)

- how much work you will need to do to prepare for and attend the event (including all of the additional staff you will need to have at the event)

- what items you will need to buy or hire for your setup at the event (including insurance)

- the time you will allocate before and after the event (including bump in and bump out and any official functions or briefings)

- the long term value of your involvement (website links, journal publications etc)

- how many people from your target audience will engage with your presence (just turning up is not enough - you may need to do more than give away chocolates or merchandise)

- how many people in your target audience will remember you and your business after the event (and will they remember you favorably or unfavorably - I remember one major sponsor representative who spoke on stage and her presentation was terrible)

- what real data and analytics will be provided by the organizers (either before the event or after the event). As we all know, statistics can lie and be made to say what supports their argument rather than what actually happened or will happen

It always concerns me when a business starts out with some seed funding and then they assume that if they blitz every expo, fair and conference in the next 12 months that they will instantly be known and used by their target audience. I still believe it takes time to get known in the marketplace as for the most part, it is a very 'noisy' place nowadays.

I also see participating in expos, trade shows and conferences as an 'above the line' marketing activity - when your business is reasonably well established in its own right and you want to increase your brand perception in a more public context.

It can also be a way to maintain your brand and showcase some of your new innovations, especially if people expect to see you there each year. It can also be a good idea to experiment with a hyper local context or location event where the entry costs are a lot lower and you can experiment with your ideas before taking on the bigger shows.

In many respects, you are becoming an 'investor' in the event and for that reason, it is for your benefit as well as the other exhibitors for you to actively support the event. You could:

- promote the event on your website and through all of your online and social media channels

- support their social media efforts by liking or following their presence on the various online platforms (you may also like to like or follow other exhibitors too)

- mention that you are going to the event through your online platforms and networks

- share the event with your followers or connections

- register for the event to find out what happens to other registrants when they register

- use the official event hashtag in your posts, comments and shares, before, during and after the event

- when the organizers distribute content via social media, like, comment and share it

- add the details of the event to your email signature

- conduct an email marketing campaign through your lists

- look at the list of exhibitors and consider personally contacting them and looking at ways you can support each other

- particularly if it is a free event, encourage everyone you know to register (so that they get the reminders) and share it around their networks

- put out your own media release or run your own publicity campaign (you may like to ask them for a copy of their media release so that you can tie in your message with theirs)

- ask the organizers if there is any other way that you can help them promote the event and its outcomes before or after the event

As I have said, you are essentially an investor in the whole concept, so it is in your interests to help them attract the right target audience, not just pay a fee and expect them to do everything. If you really want to maximize your opportunities, you will need to make sure that they do everything that they promise and that you follow up with everyone you meet or interact with as soon as possible after the event, preferably more than once.

A once off email to everyone who attended is worth very little. Ideally, you need to encourage people to be connected to your business on an ongoing basis. If you have added them to a mailing list, make sure that they receive good quality information on a regular basis.

I also encourage you to connect with people via social media as sometimes they will unsubscribe from a mailing list but they will be happy to remain connected via social media.

Action 89: *Expos, trade fairs and conferences usually involve a very substantial investment in time, money and resources. Make sure that you carefully evaluate the real benefits (rather than the sales pitch) and if you do decide to participate, adopt an investor approach and make every effort to support the organizers and the other exhibitors and guests as much as possible before, during and after the event*

13.6 Online Summits, Podcasts And Webinars

Real time and pre-recorded summits, podcasts and webinars are generating a lot more buzz nowadays. They are usually pushed on to people by using a time deadline and they can sometimes be 'free for a limited time' to encourage people to take action immediately. If you don't take action, they then offer you an 'all access pass' for a certain fee and again, put a time deadline on it. If you miss it, they then offer another time driven option. Alternatively, they are run on a regular schedule (more common for podcasts).

The main benefit of this form of marketing is that it is a one-to-many marketing tool that allows the consumer the opportunity to enjoy the experience in a location of their choice (and sometimes a time of their choice). It also enables them to do something else at the same time and drop out if something else crops up.

Having access to a recording after the event can be helpful (I have used this option many times), but apparently a lot of people do not listen to recordings, so you may like to re-purpose the content in another way to maximize its potential as a marketing tool. You may even like to re-release popular recordings.

This digital recording strategy is very good for engaging a hyper local context and giving you access to a much broader location base - so it may be ideal for expanding internationally, particularly if you choose a good local time option and market your activity within that location.

Some businesses are very canny and they make a webinar seem like it is about to be broadcast when it is actually a pre-recording that has been used multiple times. I managed to see through this technique, so I wouldn't encourage it, but it is an option.

I won't go into all of the technology options here as they are constantly changing and the ways to promote these summits and webinars is also extremely diverse (but can be similar to ordinary live events unless you are wanting to target new international locations).

Many of the summit, podcast and webinar hosts like to invite high profile speakers to their events and this can create more overall interest in the event or the recording or the group hosting the events.

Rather than hosting a summit, podcast or webinar, you might like to reach out to some hosts and ask to be a guest speaker! This can work particularly well if you have some content that is useful for their target audience (it is a bit like the Speaking strategy mentioned in Section 13.3).

It can take a lot of effort to host and organize a continuous lineup of speakers and whilst you may not be able to secure an immediate spot in a regular program, you may be able to book a spot in a future show (but again, you may like to use the strategies mention in Section 13.5 to help promote your appearance and perhaps mention that you are willing to share the show details through your networks).

I have another client who hosted her own weekly radio program for many years. In the end, she stopped the program, but she didn't replace it with another way to keep in touch with her target audience. Suffice to say, her business leads have dropped considerably.

As I have said with hosting regular free events in Section 13.1, whatever you decide to do, make sure that it is manageable for you to complete on a regular basis and that it doesn't overconsume your time, energy or resources. It is better to start off with something small and modest and grow than to start off with something huge and then collapse in a heap afterwards. If you can start with something huge, good on you, but make sure that you have all of your systems in place to make it work (it is a bigger risk, but some of the very first online summits were very successful).

Like most things, these types of initiatives go in cycles of popularity. Too early and no-one gets involved and too late, and everyone is already fatigued by the concept. That is why you really need to think about your target audience and their needs and the variety of ways you can re-purpose the content in both dynamic and lifetime ways so that you can gain the maximum value from your efforts.

Action 90: *Online summits, podcasts and webinars can be used to generate dynamic and lifetime content - but they need to be aligned with the needs and preferences of your target audience. Like most initiatives, make sure that you can maintain the momentum over time or alternatively, consider being a guest on someone else's show*

14. Media Marketing

The media landscape has evolved and changed enormously in the recent past. Ordinarily, it was expected that the content collected by journalists would be completely impartial and independent and if necessary, expose wrong doings and stimulate change within our society.

This activity was traditionally funded by advertising sales - mostly classified advertisements and sometimes a subscription (television) or publication (newspaper or magazine) fee. If you want to find out what content still works today, check out the newspapers and magazines that still exist - they are doing something right!

This reduction in advertising revenue has had an impact on journalism, in particular, investigative journalism. Some people will argue that all jobs have changed and we all have to do more with less, but when there are less checks and balances over what is investigated and what is published, that will change what is eventually published.

Let's look at a quick example. In the past, an editor would meet with a group of journalists and they would discuss stories and make decisions about what would be explored and how they would go about it. In most cases, a journalist would not consider interviewing a victim of a tragedy, particularly if that person was a child or in deep emotional distress. Now, without the editorial meeting and strategy decided first, a journalist could take matters into their own hands and inappropriately carry out their duties.

In a rush to get a story ready for publication, they may also rely on unverified online content rather than official records and information. With less time to review a story with an editor or sub editor, again, there is a bigger chance for error. Naturally, with this much time pressure, a journalist is likely to be very relieved when they receive a good quality story that is fully produced with all of the correct facts readily accessible, provided it is not simply a sales story. It helps if the story quotes multiple people, not just you.

Providing this detail for a journalist does not guarantee a story being published, but it sure makes it a whole lot easier.

I have had very little success with sharing a media release via media release distribution services (remember that search engines do not like duplicate content either). That said, I have found one local service that helps content rank immediately for a modest fee.

However, I have found that building relationships with journalists and editors who specialize in your hyper local context or location is very worthwhile.

You can then work in partnership with the media. Help journalists out by sharing notable achievements (especially for hyper local locations - if you have won a state, national or international award, that is very newsworthy).

I also encourage you to be helpful overall and not just try and plug your own business. Help them by sharing leads and stories that may be useful in their role. Keep them posted on developments and invite them to join you at selected events that will help them gather more stories and make more useful connections. Realize that the person in the role may change frequently, so make sure you always know who the current person is in that role and keep in touch with them.

Media marketing is a longer term strategy and again, to secure maximum value, you need to make sure that you re-purpose your coverage.

Look out for opportunities too - actually read or watch content produced by your target publication and think about ideas you can pitch in the future. If you are well informed, you have a better chance of meeting the journalists' needs.

A word of warning though, this technique is not for the faint hearted. There is a chance that if you do this the wrong way, you can look like an idiot in a story. Be prepared for the tough questions and have correct (and preferably independent) stats (statistics) and facts to back up your story. Be ready to provide high resolution images (300 dots per inch) and further details instantly as you will need to respond to media requests as soon as they are received.

Do not expect the journalist to provide you with a copy of the content they produce, but make sure you do obtain a copy of the final story for your records (even if you simply take a voice recording on your phone of a radio interview whilst the phone is on airplane mode).

Make sure that when you provide the details of the story on your website, social media and online platforms that you fully credit all of the people involved. If you are involved in a television or studio interview, see if you can take someone with you to take a few happy snaps as well (or kindly ask the producer to help you out).

As with every other business exchange, say thank you - personally and as soon as possible after the exchange. It is also a good idea to provide succinct but informative details of any feedback you receive.

Action 91: *The media landscape continues to change and the best way to secure media coverage for your business is via a direct relationship with journalists and editors in the publications that are of most interest to yours and their target audience. Be ready with independent and verifiable information and answer any requests immediately. Say thank you at the time of contact and after publication and re-purpose your content with full credits included*

14.1 Editorial

I have already provided a few clues as to how to secure editorial content, but now it is time to think about where you could secure editorial content in a hyper local context or location. There are a huge range of locations, some easier to sneak into than others, but again, you need to be strategic about reaching your target audience. You may also like to start with some publications that are less stringent as these help build your profile and get you started.

When considering your choices, look at the following factors:

- circulation (both offline and online)

- readership demographics (some items are more or less likely to be read than others, regardless of their circulation or distribution)

- dynamic versus lifetime value (and the ability for you to reproduce an archive copy on your website)

- amount of engagement with the content (either offline or online) - comments, responsiveness to comments etc

- your ability to share it through your networks easily

- the readers ability to share it through their networks

- the results it may be able to secure in online search

- whether they include a link (text or live) to your website or social media

- the amount of control you have over the content and its accuracy

- whether it is located next to a direct competitor or advertiser

So let's think about all of the locations that can publish factual information about your business in your hyper local location:

- local newspapers, bulletins or newsletters produced by well recognized organizations (media, business groups, government, schools etc)

- event listings (one of the most under-utilized resources around)

- local directories that need some local content as well as listings

- programs, event guides, festival programs

- tourist information brochures and guides
- white papers, reports, journals, fact sheets
- books, ebooks
- radio, podcasts, audiobooks
- videos, television programs, films
- blogs, forums and relevant websites
- student projects, community initiatives, local information portals

A good way to find out what might work for you is to review the editorial media coverage that has been received by other well-known local businesses. When you search for their details, where do they appear? Perhaps you can borrow a few ideas?

You might even come up with a few other ideas and you may also be able to partner up with a few other businesses and gain a group story. It never hurts to ask. What is the worst that can happen? They say no! But they might say yes!!

Action 92: *Editorial content is worth pursuing provided it still meets your overall marketing objectives and reaches your target audience. There are many different local options and it is a good idea to try out some easy options first to build your portfolio*

14.2 Advertorial

As mentioned above, with the lack of resources for quality journalism, advertorials are starting to appear more frequently. It is very tempting to incorporate a strong sales message in your written content, but you are far more likely to have your content read if you provide something that is genuinely informative, educational or entertaining (or all three!).

Remember that most people will respond to a good quality image and apparently pictures with a human face are more appealing than images without a face. Many newbies to the world of advertising try to include too much information in the space available, so try to focus on the main message rather than a lot of detail.

You may also like to:

- share a relevant story with stats and facts
- avoid cliches and slogans

- use quotes and formatting similar to what a normal editorial story would look like in that publication

- use headlines to break up the message and make it scannable

- include something familiar or memorable to make the content stick in their mind and be easily recalled at a later date

- arouse the reader's emotions to make them want to take action

- provide a solution, finish on a good note and include a call to action

Once again, you might like to have a look at other advertorials that have been published, particularly if they have appeared more than once (because in theory, they must be working). Also consider a package deal where you can either have the same content repeated or a similar spot secured with fresh and new content (perhaps forming part of a series but with a theme so that it looks familiar to the frequent reader).

If you really want to go all out, consider paying for advertorial in a very reputable publication directly aligned with your target audience and meeting all of the factors suggested in Section 14.1. In this case, make sure that at least 70% of the message is good quality content and no more than 30% of the content is promoting your product.

Unless you have a healthy advertising budget, I would normally suggest that you aim for free editorial content first. As a general rule, editorial content is more likely to be read and it is classified as more valuable than advertising content (and therefore more likely to convert to a good branding result for your business).

However, if your main goal is sales and you are able to negotiate a good rate and it does actually lead to sales, keep it going for as long as it keeps working (you may have to tweak it along the way).

Action 93: *Advertorial is becoming more popular, but to be effective, you still need to make sure that at least 70% of the message is good quality content and no more than 30% is promotional. Try and keep the style and formatting similar to the rest of the publication and include something familiar and memorable to increase its recall value*

14.3 Publicity And Public Relations

The people who provide communications, public relations (PR) and publicity opportunities are often viewed very negatively by journalists. Most people in the media prefer to speak directly to a business owner rather than their agent, but good agents can help advise you on what to do to reach a journalist.

Some of these PR people have generated a bad reputation for 'spin' - always putting a positive angle on a negative situation. However, I am sure we don't have to worry about that issue because I am sure that by now, after reading this book and getting so many reminders, you are now on the road to running a fully ethical business (even if you didn't in the past).

PR people have also been known to suggest crazy stunts or occasions that are used solely for the purpose of generating publicity. I remember seeing a well known celebrity on a news and current affairs program dressed in the latest release pyjamas that were launched that day by a well known fashion designer.

I would hardly consider that news or even current affairs, but it certainly received a lot of promotion in the advertisements leading up to the program and as you can imagine, advertisements for the pyjamas appeared in the television breaks. Very unfair to every other pyjama maker and in my view, it completely ruined the credibility of the television program.

I also believe it is much easier to generate publicity from something that is already occurring. For several years now, I have participated in an annual business festival and this program help promote every business that has secured a spot in the events program. Sure, it takes some effort to fill in the application and have my events approved, but all of the publicity generated by the festival team automatically helps my business. In fact it has been so successful, that each year I have had to find a second venue and host a second event because I have received so many event registrations.

Don't discount the idea of small bits of publicity either. It never ceases to amaze me when someone tells me that they have heard about me or my business from a miniature detail on an obscure post on a poor performing website or a tiny five line piece in the local newspaper.

What you must do though is always respond as quickly as possible (and appropriately), to bad publicity. If you are at fault, make sure you apologize first, provide details of how you are going to fix the problem and what you will do in the future to make sure that it doesn't happen again.

Do not say 'no comment." If you are not at fault, in my opinion, it is important for you to still apologize for any confusion and clearly state the facts and details, answer any questions and be willing to respond to further enquiries. Make sure that the business owner or most senior person available is the only person who responds on behalf of the business to the media - don't let staff and other associates accidentally give a mixed message.

To stay on the ball, I also suggest that your business subscribe to Google Alerts at http://google.com/alerts. Set up alerts for your own name as well as your business name (in quotation marks so it only finds that specific information). For example, "Sue Ellson" and "Camberwell Network".

Action 94: *Make sure that any publicity you generate is appropriate for your business. Start with small opportunities first and always respond to bad publicity as soon as possible in an appropriate way. Subscribe to Google Alerts to find out what is being said about you and your business online*

14.4 Responding To A Current Issue

This can be a very effective way to piggy back on another story or theme that is generating a lot of buzz at a particular point in time.

For example, one of my clients offers financial services to families when it is time for their elderly parents to move out of the family home and into elder living or care accommodation. I heard about a story that was going to appear on a very well known current affairs program later that day, so I recorded the program and watched it live. I immediately wrote an article that not only summarized the story in more detail, it also provided further information that was not included in the television program (like the full address and website details of all of the residences mentioned) as well as links to other useful information related to the topic.

Naturally, I also linked to the high ranking television program's website - to the exact story page where a visitor could watch the program at any time. This article immediately appeared in online search results so anyone who may have heard the story from a friend the next day would have been very likely to see my client's story appear first in online search results.

The story itself had a catchy headline, "Retirement Heaven." Four years later, that article still comes up on the first page of online search results, even though it hasn't been touched since. The current affair television program article is long gone.

By latching on to current topics of discussion, you have a chance to capitalize on the interest in that topic. When a big announcement is made in your industry, be willing to make an informed statement and share it through your networks as soon as possible. Include a relevant image and if you can, let the local press know about your perspective on the topic.

Be a little bit choosy though. You don't want to respond to issues that are not related in any way to your business or your core values. If you respond to every issue on a regular basis, you will not be taken seriously. But if you provide thoughtful and informative analysis, backed up with stats, facts and substantial experience, there is a good chance that you can jump on the publicity or topic bandwagon and secure some featured content as a 'first responder.'

Action 95: *Watch out for current issues or topics that are related to your business or core values and consider sharing factual content that refers to the issue as soon as possible so that you can jump onto the current publicity or topic bandwagon*

15. Community Marketing

Community marketing is one of my absolute favorite ways to market my businesses. I really value the opportunity to share my business value to members of my local community and support them in their efforts too. I have found various ways to get involved - through sporting groups, faith groups, activity groups (scouts), community houses (local classes), council events and so much more.

I started Newcomers Network in 2001 and at the time, it serviced the city of Melbourne. I started Camberwell Network in 2012 but it was designed to only support the suburb of Camberwell. I have not dedicated anywhere near as much time and effort into Camberwell Network, but I have found a way to sustainably manage this social enterprise and support many other local business owners in the process.

I have also been able to keep it running effectively even when I am extremely busy writing or doing other work. Conversely, because of the enormous amount of work associated with Newcomers Network (which expanded nationally), I have had to put that on hold at different times when my other commitments have been more important.

I first mentioned Camberwell Network back in Section 2.9 of this book when I was talking about hyper local recruitment. The model for the Camberwell Network enterprise is quite simple.

There is an expression that if you can't find the right network for your purpose, create one - and that is what I did.

I started off with slightly grander plans but it has morphed into something extremely simple. It involves me creating an email newsletter that I send out once a month with the details of as many events as I can find that are occurring specifically in Camberwell. I have become so efficient at finding these events, I can compile and prepare the email for sending in just over one hour.

Once a year, I set up the monthly events on various event listing websites. I also pay to host a Meetup Group in the name of Camberwell Network. The people who register to attend the monthly Camberwell Networkers gathering on the third Wednesday of the month from 5:30pm - 7:30pm at a bar inside a very nice restaurant are also added to the email newsletter mailing list, as well as anyone who just turns up at the event. I also invite these people to connect with me on LinkedIn.

I also share some other posts on Facebook and do a few little things on Twitter, LinkedIn and Google+.

So all up, including travel time and my time at the event, I probably spend an average of about one hour per week to provide this community service at virtually no cost apart from my time and a few small expenses. It has opened the door to paid work, speaking invitations, editorial media coverage and invitations to join working groups and economic development initiatives.

Whilst this is my personal way to help the community and efficiently and effectively donate my time and expertise, I am sure that you can think of ways that you can help your community through your skills or your business. Even if you do not set up something yourself, you can still support other people's initiatives and make a different type of contribution.

For example, I am pleased to report that I am constantly surprised by the generosity I have received from local businesses when I have represented the local church for their upcoming fete. I visited a few local shops and the donations I received, after a polite request, were phenomenal. In return, I made sure that the church acknowledged these contributions in a variety of ways.

I made sure that every single business or individual that supported the fete was personally recognized and featured on the church website (for some lifetime value). We also prepared some nicely crafted Certificates of Appreciation and hand delivered these. We also made sure that the signage at the event mentioned that the products were donated by XYZ Business and so on.

I encourage you to either keep up your community marketing or find ways to get involved! There are so many tangible and intangible benefits.

Action 96: *You and your business can select your own way to support your local community efficiently, effectively and sustainably. This will lead to all sorts of opportunities and a range of benefits*

15.1 Networks

As you can probably tell by now, I really value networks. I have shared the details of Newcomers Network and Camberwell Network and now I would like to share another example - this time a network that collects a fee for each transaction.

I have recently joined a marketplace distribution service where an organization allocates a certain amount of money for their individual clients to spend and each client then goes into the marketplace distribution portal and selects the various products and services they would like to purchase with their spend amount.

To make sure that the products and services are reputable, the marketplace distribution service goes through a rigorous process of making sure that all of the suppliers provide excellent quality and legitimate products and services and that each business is compliant from a regulatory perspective.

The marketplace distribution service also works hard to secure organizations that have groups of individual clients ready to create their own personalized product and service packages. In return for creating and developing this marketplace distribution service, the portal collects a 15% commission fee on each transaction.

In this collective model, apart from making sure that your own business is compliant and meets the marketplace distribution service criteria, a much smaller enterprise specializing in one aspect of a service can form part of an overall package and help individuals choose exactly the range of products they are seeking rather than be limited to a pre-determined package one size fits all service offered by a larger enterprise. Clients can choose to do things themselves (with tools), with someone or have something done for them.

In many respects, this is simply a more formalized and structured network hub. However, I think it is an excellent way for multiple independent enterprises to form a collective resource, particularly if it is for a hyper local context or location. That said, the person setting up the hub in the first place usually has to invest a lot of time and energy to make it all happen and it doesn't take five minutes - it involves an awful lot of negotiation and commitment, even if it is only done on a small scale.

Personally, whenever I decide to participate in these types of networks, regardless of how much work I receive, I always make an effort to support and develop the network providing the qualified referrals. I don't have to do this, I choose to do this. Why wouldn't I want to help them be successful, because if they are successful, I will get more work, not less! This approach has also helped me secure some excellent professional development opportunities.

So whether you choose to be part of a free network, a more formal network or a fee for service network, I encourage you to personally select the networks that are aligned from a values, business and target audience perspective. I have refused to join some networks (although I will occasionally visit them for special events) because they are not aligned. There is nothing wrong with those networks, they are just not the right fit for me and my business.

Also be aware that there may be a time when you are ready to leave a network and find another more aligned network. Make sure that you leave on good terms and wish everyone the best.

Action 97: *Free, formal and fee for service networks are a great way for your business to connect with customers, clients and businesses so that collectively, you can benefit as a result of the connection*

15.2 Bartering

Bartering is a way to negotiate a better price but also to decide on a different model of exchange between individuals and businesses. There are some actual trading schemes that allow people to collectively pool their contributions and then swap their value with other suppliers. These systems can be a little bit tricky to monitor on an ongoing basis and they don't always work for some businesses.

For example, if your small bartering pool had 25 gardeners and 10 accountants, I am quite sure that each accountant would not be able to exchange their services with an average of 2.5 gardeners each. I have also heard stories of people securing a lot of 'credit' and then never being able to fully redeem their contribution.

So in short, this is not one of my favorite marketing ideas for hyper local marketing as in my mind, there is too much room for error or dispute at a later point.

That said, it could be a way for a Cooperative to exchange value. There are also different currencies, time, money etc. For example, one hour with a solicitor might be worth $500 and the same $500 could involve 10 hours of gardening. Some would argue that this is not an entirely fair exchange (regardless of the study and commitment to learning that it took for the solicitor to gain their qualification) and they may barter the arrangement to five hours of gardening as a reasonable exchange for one hour with the solicitor.

When I was a new mother, there was a babysitting group that offered tokens that could be earned and spent - so this meant that the bartering was for one limited service rather than different services.

Whichever idea you consider for your business, make sure that you feel comfortable with the value proposition and the reliability of its operation. Personally, I like exchanges to be super simple and matched as closely as possible to the time of the transaction. It makes life so much easier.

Action 98: *Bartering is a way to negotiate and exchange value in different ways, either with the same products and services or with different products and services. Before you consider this marketing idea, make sure that the model you select will be fair and reliable*

15.3 Exchanges

I have negotiated several direct exchanges with people, particularly when they require consulting services but do not currently have the cash to pay for the service. I have really enjoyed a few special treats that I would never have experienced if it wasn't for the exchange, including business coaching, music concert tickets, therapeutic massages and holiday accommodation.

Naturally I cannot afford to remain in business by living off of exchanges! So this is definitely not a marketing strategy I would use on a regular basis. However, it does help my client or customer enjoy an opportunity that otherwise, they would not have access to. I see it as another way to provide a community service.

In special circumstances, I also consider providing a little extra value, particularly if the person has demonstrated an extra effort towards achieving success or I know that they also help others without a payment.

If you decide to help others in this way, I would also like to encourage you to remind the person that this is something a little different than usual and that you normally operate in a different way. It is important for the person to respect and value the opportunity and for you to maintain your self worth and value.

Unfortunately I have fallen into the trap of giving a little too much on occasion and it has only led to resentment because the person receiving the value did not appreciate it, did not value it or did not return the value they promised.

If you do decide to make an exchange, make sure that you are comfortable with the agreement at the time. If you are a little uneasy, it is usually a sign that it is not a fair exchange and it could easily lead to misunderstandings and disappointment in the future.

Action 99: *Exchanges are a way to share value in a different way when a client or customer cannot make the usual payment arrangements. However, make sure that you feel completely comfortable with the exchange agreement and its likely completion before agreeing to the exchange as your value may not be returned*

15.4 Local Suppliers

This is one of my truly favorite marketing ideas. Wherever possible, I source local suppliers for all of my purchases in my personal and business life.

There are many reasons - the environment, the convenience, supporting my local businesses, keeping my money in my community, encouraging sustainability etc.

I even try to do this when I know that it would be cheaper to source supplies from a distant location. Ethically, I feel that it is important to support local producers, manufacturers and suppliers.

It can also save a lot of time and effort. How much easier is it to go to a local newsagent on your morning walk than to get in a car and travel to a discount office supplies chain store? When you spend the money at your local newsagent, you are helping that store stay in business. When you spend your money at a big chain store, you are often helping a wealthy senior manager or shareholder pay for their holiday house in the south of France!

Also, when your local shop owner knows you, they can make quality recommendations and refer your details to other locals - and when you think about how much business is done by referral, why wouldn't you allocate some of your marketing budget to buying local!

Action 100: *Wherever possible, source your products, services and supplies from other locals. Not only is it a more sustainable and environmentally friendly option, you may also end up with more referral business*

15.5 Location Sharing

I have already touched on this subject in Section 7.1 when I talked about sharing a commercial kitchen when it wasn't busy.

There are many different ways to share locations. You could operate on an exchange basis with someone who lives locally and has an office at home and also in the city. On the days when they are working from home, you may be able to share their office in the city.

A lot of local shops have special rooms available for special functions. When these are not in use at peak times, these venues will often welcome a free networking event that will attract patrons to the venue at a peak time (as mentioned in Section 13.1).

Warehousing needs can vary a great deal and you may be able to find a local residence that has spare space that you could hire for short loads rather than full loads. This can be very helpful when you are in a very busy trading period and you do not have the time to go to a larger warehouse that is further away.

For example, a business associate of mine has moved into a new home that has a huge area under the house (fully lined) that would be ideal to lease or lend to a local business as it also has separate direct access.

At one stage when I was working from home on my own for most of my week, I started to feel very isolated and disconnected from the world of work. So I dropped off a one page letter in the mail boxes of local businesses (within walking distance) to offer my services on an as needs basis. I picked up a perfect casual job that lasted about six months and in the end, was very glad to go back to my own space - but to get over that hump in my personal psyche, working somewhere else really helped!

All of these opportunities to share a location will require you to make direct contact with people and businesses close to where you live. That is a good thing! Don't be shy. You are building community and sustainability and what is the worst that can happen - the person can say no. But they may say yes!!!

Try not to put your beliefs on to someone else. They may or may not like the idea. They may have never thought about it. They may want to work on a trial basis first to see how it goes before making a longer term commitment (I would encourage this approach because it gives both of you a way to get out).

Whatever you do, please approach the idea respectfully and with full consideration and respect for the other person. Explain how you are willing to make it work for them. For example, if you are asking for a free venue, explain how you can help their business, what you will do to promote their venue, what information you can pass on to guests etc.

Please do not expect everything for free either. There may need to be a consideration for the exchange and I would encourage this, especially after the trial period has concluded. Even if the exchange is not monetary, it is a good idea to check in with the person and make sure that it is still okay to continue on with the present arrangement at least every six months - and if it is for free, make sure you regularly thank them and acknowledge their contribution and do what you can to support their business.

There are other models of sharing - co-working spaces, hot desks, serviced offices etc and these may also be an option.

Apart from potentially reducing your overheads, by sharing your business location, you have an opportunity to regularly meet new people, receive branding in a different location and also profile other businesses in some way. You have an opportunity to be a part of your community and this is a great way to build your brand. Overall, I think it is a good hyper local context and location marketing idea.

Action 101: *Consider talking to other local businesses about ways that you can share space, either for payment or for some form of exchange (branding, promotion etc). Check in at least every six months to make sure that it is working well for both parties*

15.6 Naming Rights, Sponsorships And Advertising

I must admit that when I go for a walk in a park and I see a statue to some long dead person, I usually wonder why something permanent was established in one person's honor. I am not denying their contribution in any sense, it just seems a little egotistical to me.

Some years ago, I went to a ceremony in a very large church and saw rows of placards announcing people who had made a contribution to some church fund and again, I thought, how egotistical - the decision should be faith based, not marketing based!

Anyway, I digress. Here we are talking about marketing your business. The point I would like to make though is that if you are going to select naming rights as a way to market your business, you may like to think about how that will appear in the minds of your local community - if it is egotistical, I would consider another way to attach naming rights in a location that may be considered more suitable.

There are various locations where you could consider naming rights, sponsorship or advertising:

- your building or premises
- an event or festival you sponsor or host
- a publication, guide, white paper, research project etc
- a local sporting facility or team
- hand made or manufactured products
- a street name in a new development (it has been done before!)

Alternatively, you may like to find somewhere that will advertise your business in a location with a lot of foot or vehicle traffic - so it is not naming rights as such but if you have a continuous (but vibrant) presence there, the location may be associated with you for example, XYZ corner.

In most cases, naming rights usually requires some form of payment in return for exposure and branding. If the item or activity you are associating with is strongly connected with your business, it can be a nice fit.

I must admit that when a local sports stadium changes its name every few years thanks to a new sponsorship or naming rights agreement, I find it a little annoying. Advertising is also something that can have very little impact unless it is repeated many times.

Have you also noticed how print, radio and television advertisement costs decrease significantly on a proportional basis over time? Naturally they would like to entice you to spend more, but they also realize that for it to work, it needs time (I usually suggest that even an online digital marketing campaign will take at least six months to really work). As a general rule, I avoid advertising as I have had a miniscule return - but then again, I guess we can all learn from our mistakes!

I find that editorial content (that aims to inform, rather than sell), works much better.

Donations (disguised as sponsorships), will only work if the organization receiving the sponsorship provides some direct value, reciprocity or engagement in return. So if you have paid for sponsorship, make sure that you receive all of the items promised and that the organization really does its best to promote you when they have an opportunity (even if it is just Liking your posts on digital media and printing your logo on their marketing or printed collateral).

If you decide to implement a naming rights, sponsorship or advertising strategy, I encourage you to aim for a longer term agreement so that you can gain some real value. I have found that once off promotions, as a general rule, rarely produce long term results.

Action 102: *Naming rights, Sponsorships and Advertisements work best when they provide coverage for an extended time frame and are even better if there is a sense of engagement and reciprocity with your business*

16. Incentive Marketing

No doubt you have heard of the concept of encouraging someone to take action by using either a carrot or a stick - from the concept of making a horse do what you want - if you use a carrot, the horse will follow you, if you use a stick, the horse will be forced to move.

So in marketing, you or your business can use an incentive as a proverbial carrot to entice your clients and customers to purchase your products and services.

Large retail stores have used this approach with 'loss leader' products for years. They put a special discount price on an everyday item and place it right at the back of the store so that when you go in to buy the heavily discounted item, you might be tempted to buy something else at the same time.

There are many other ways to incentivise your clients and customers. You really need to know your target audience well and what problems they really want to have solved. By making it crystal clear that you can solve their problems, you are incentivizing them to purchase.

There is also an expression that people move, in the sales funnel, from being a 'prospect' to a 'suspect' and then to a 'customer.' An incentive can also help convert a prospect to a suspect or a suspect to a customer - it gives the person an extra little reason to consider what you have on offer.

If the incentive is very closely aligned to their needs and wants, it can really speed up the process. Alternatively, it can simply make them aware of an extra option.

Many of us have heard the expression 'would you like fries with that' when someone decides to buy a hamburger. The shop assistant is not asking if there is anything else you would like, they have created a phrase in just six words to help you visualize yourself eating fries at the same time as your hamburger so at that point, you are not thinking about what else to choose so it is quite easy to slip into saying 'yes.'

So this is the concept of traditional incentives - an extra reason to make a buying decision or in some cases, a reminder as to why you made a buying decision (if they give you a bonus afterwards). Incentives after a purchase may encourage you to go back again and can generate repeat business.

Action 103: *Incentives can be used to encourage people to be attracted to your products and services or help them move along the sales process more quickly. If they are provided after the transaction, it may also encourage them to make another purchase*

16.1 Competitions

Competitions seem to go through a lot of different cycles. It seemed that they were extremely popular on social media for about two years to try and encourage everyone to like a business page on Facebook, but when the algorithms changed and likes did not necessarily generate sales, Facebook competitions slowed down considerably.

In a hyper local context or location, I believe that the best competitions are ones where the person entering the competition has a real sense that they have a good chance of winning something fairly soon after entering the competition and it is likely to be a real competition.

So the competitions that I like to run are the ones that occur at an event. I usually ask people to complete their event evaluation whilst we collect the last few entrants to the competition (which means that evaluations actually get completed) and everyone is in the room and knows that someone in the room will definitely win before they all leave.

Another competition that I used to coordinate was a 'lucky square' competition. Each person at the sporting grounds on a Saturday afternoon would purchase one or more squares on a board of 100 squares (so $200 would be collected). We would then give one lucky person $100 and put the $100 in the fund raising account for the sporting association. What I really appreciated about this competition is that we didn't have to create or source a prize each week, the people entering the competition created the prize! They also looked forward to the chance to win $100, every week, for only $2 (and they also knew that it was more or less a donation to the sporting association). Some weeks I managed to fill up two 100 square boards. Ultimately, I didn't do it every single week because I did manage to receive a few other donated products to make the weekly competition a little bit more interesting.

Your business may have been invited to participate in a raffle or a lottery as part of a large fund raising project. I am not convinced that this type of donation leads to any genuine business brand recognition - but it may be a good way to show that you are willing to support a local school, community group etc. I guess that in most cases, you could write off the cost of your donation as a tax deduction - but you do need to be careful, because if the word gets out, you may receive too many requests for donations!

A competition that engages a person in some way is much more likely to be remembered. For years, coloring in competitions have encouraged people to color in a picture (and these are often displayed as well). So it generates some buy-in from the participants. It also works for photography and art competitions too.

Your business may also like to sponsor a competition - like a sporting race or a prize for the best XYZ. So rather than the prize go to someone based on luck, it is based on merit (but you need to find some unbiased judges!).

If your business is part of a shopping precinct, competitions that encourage people to do something within the precinct (find something, go to multiple places etc) can also be a great way to generate some engagement.

Like all marketing ideas, you need to make sure that the competition you associate with is related in some way to reaching your target audience or is related to your overall values, or that you are happy to just provide a donation.

If the competition is quirky, unique or memorable in some way and it also has the possibility of going viral online, then it could potentially be quite effective at sharing the details of your business brand to the wider community.

Action 104: *Competitions that are timely, encourage participation or engagement and can potentially go viral have the potential to be effective at sharing your business brand to your target audience and beyond. Alternatively, you can consider making a donation in alignment with your values*

16.2 Gamification Programs

Gamification is something that has been implemented in a lot of online learning to encourage people to complete tasks and aim for higher scores to 'beat' other participants or to secure higher levels of recognition or gain access to more complicated tasks. Essentially, it is trying to incorporate the concept of a game or playing into the learning process.

Gamification has been used in some industries to the point of corruption in my view. For example, gambling. I am dead against gambling of any sort. To me, that is not a business, it is a rip off and people can easily become addicted to it thanks to the manipulation of the various gambling machines. Enough said.

However, I think that gamification can be a very useful marketing tool in business because it can increase the novelty, variety and interest in products and services.

If your client or customer participates in a particular activity and they complete a task (or purchase), then you could give them an opportunity to participate in the next part of the game.

Let's look at a retail store where the customer could potentially purchase several items from different sections of the store. For example, if it was clothing and they purchased something from the Spring, Summer, Autumn (Fall) and Winter Collections, they could be entitled to choose an accessory of their choice to the value of $50. If this game was attached to 'Collection Preview' in-store events, then they may be able to receive an extra bonus if they can attend two or more preview events per year. If they also join the $1,000 club ($1,000 spend in a year), then they may receive another prize (discount or item). The goal with this process is to keep them involved in the game in a range of ways throughout the year but also to make it fun.

If you are in a service based business, you can still reward certain behaviors and incorporate a game philosophy into your business. Perhaps you can let people know that you will recognize some form of achievement every month and then put that person in the 'draw' to win the main prize for the year. You may be able to incorporate a gamified application, assessment or tool to help them gather the service they need from you and your business. You can even invite them to participate in additional game activities.

Games usually have a set of rules and requirements, but they also usually include an element of challenge or incentive for completion. So you need to include some form of reward along the journey to keep the players in the game. I think it also a good idea if the first few challenges are not too difficult so that the person can get involved fairly easily, but they still need to be encouraged along the way if they want to win the 'real' prizes.

Naturally if you are running any sort of game on a larger scale, you need to have it set up in such a way that it is relatively easy for you to maintain. If the data or information is collected automatically through your business, that will help. If it requires manual entry, it might not work.

You may decide that rather than come up with a complex automated system, you may choose to just incorporate the philosophy of surprises and fun every now and then to make doing business with you just a little bit more interesting. A little bit of unexpected (but appropriate) fun is usually always well received.

Action 105: *By applying the principles of gamification into the marketing of your business, you can increase the novelty, variety and interest in your products and services. Ideally, it is best if your gamification process is automated. Alternatively, you can simply incorporate some appropriate unexpected fun on a regular basis*

16.3 Loyalty Programs

Loyalty programs come in all shapes and sizes nowadays from printed store loyalty cards through to incentive based complex international loyalty points programs.

From a hyper local context or location perspective, I would like to encourage you to consider a loyalty program where you work either within your business or with other businesses close by. This will help connect your business to other businesses in unique and complementary ways and can even foster business relationships that eventually become either joint ventures or strategic alliances.

Loyalty programs are a great way to test whether or not something will work over the longer term. They can be for a time limited period (to encourage participation before the deadline arrives) and they can be varied depending on the purpose of the loyalty program.

You can achieve many different objectives too. You can:

- encourage people to 'bring a friend'

- reward frequent purchases

- showcase other complementary products and services (in your business or from another hyper local business)

- generate interest in a longer term relationship rather than a one-off sale

- build your brand, particularly if people share the good news about their rewards

The best aspect of a loyalty program is the time aspect - it enables you to lengthen your relationship with your valued clients and customers by creating a process for them to follow to secure additional rewards. It doesn't suit every business though because it can appear trite and as if the business is trying too hard (in this case, a more personalized recognition program would be better).

Action 106: *Loyalty programs provide an opportunity for you to extend your business relationship with your valued clients and customers. In a hyper local context or location, it gives you an opportunity to work with complementary businesses and help each other over the short or long term*

16.4 Relationship Marketing Programs

If your business has invested in a quality customer relationship management (CRM) system, there is every chance that you will be able to easily identify some VIP (very important person) individuals that are supporting you and/or your business.

This could include customers, clients, suppliers, distributors and any other stakeholders associated with your business. (including consultants, mentors and advisers) Recognizing their value to your business is important - for you and for them.

By personally selecting and rewarding these people in a personalized way, you are much more likely to receive unexpected benefits (which should not be your main motivation, but if it helps, go for it).

There are people that regularly assist me in unique and inspiring ways and I regularly make an effort to personally acknowledge their contribution to my success (by speaking to them directly).

I also like to do what I call 'state the bleeding obvious.' You are in your business most days of the week (if not in reality, definitely in your thoughts). It is so easy to forget to remind clients and customers about what you do and the benefits they have received. Sometimes, you need to describe what has just happened or follow up with them after the transaction has occurred to ask how your products and services have helped them.

In some respects, it shouldn't be necessary, as I said before, it should be bleeding obvious! However, it is a reminder to help your client or customer say thank you and to reinforce in their minds what you have done for them. It gives both of you an opportunity to recognize an exchange and build the relationship.

As I have said, to build the relationship, the more personalized it is, the better. However, it doesn't always have to be personalized - it could be 'automatic' but by having your system in place, it continues to build the relationship.

One way I do this automatically is by producing quality content and then distributing it through various online platforms and social media. This content has the potential to pop up in a news feed of my past or future clients and customers. So in this small way, I am able to keep in touch with people and maintain my business relationship without having to contact each person individually.

However, I do try and make an effort to make sure that my messages are not repetitive and I always try and provide information even if there is a 'sales' component included (like details of an upcoming event). This helps maintain, for the most part, a genuine sense of contribution rather than commerce.

Over time though, what builds a relationship the most is consistency. Consistently doing what you say you will do. Delivering what you say you will deliver. Completing what you say you will complete (and on time too). Consistency is what is most likely to maintain a relationship.

Under promising and over delivering is nice to throw in now and again (saying you will do something by a certain date but completing it ahead of time). However, if you over promise and under deliver more than twice, you can be sure that your clients and customers will not feel comfortable and are more likely to shop around elsewhere because they have lost trust in your ability to deliver what you have promised.

Again, when recognizing your good quality business relationships, you have the opportunity to work collaboratively with other complementary hyper local businesses - so once again, I encourage you to do so.

Action 107: *Relationship Marketing Programs help you recognize your good quality business relationships and also remind individuals of your value and build and reinforce the relationship. A key ingredient of business success is consistency*

16.5 Thank You And Gratefulness Initiatives

I really do not want to believe that the only way we will ever learn to say thank you and to be grateful for what we already have is to have a program that forces people to say thank you and be reminded to be grateful of what they already have.

I come from a family that insisted that I telephone everyone who sent me a gift on my birthday to say thank you. When I got off the bus, I was taught to say thank you again. If anybody ever offered me any form of courtesy, yes, say thank you. I understand that in some cultures, you can be perceived as weak if you extend this type of courtesy, but call me old fashioned, I still believe it is extremely important.

Too much of our lives today is artificially created and in my view, it is easy to lose sight of what is important and it is also way too easy to forget about all of the things that we do have. There are millions of people in the world who simply cannot even read this book.

From a marketing perspective, thank you comes in many forms. Obviously, when a transaction is conducted in person, it is fairly easy to say thank you, but you have many other opportunities to remind people that you appreciate their business:

- after they have attended an event, send a thank you for coming message

- after they have reached a milestone - dollar spend, anniversary of service, quantity of products

- when they provide a review or feedback of any sort

- when they do something out of the ordinary for you (your suppliers or manufacturers)

- for no reason at all - just because you felt like saying thank you

There are also many different ways to say thank you:

- privately and in person or via a direct message or card

- publicly on social media or an online platform (good to Ping them at the same time so that they are alerted to the post)

- via a review website for their business

- with an appropriate gift (product or service) delivered directly or in person

- by nominating them for an award or formal recognition

- by providing a Certificate of Appreciation, Completion, Achievement etc

- by finding out how you may be able to help them in some way and delivering that assistance

When you provide details of your gratefulness, I encourage you to provide specific information - for example, "Thank you for supporting our recent community charity event to raise funds for the school sports program. We really appreciated your product donation for the auction, your assistance with promoting the event, your support by selling tickets to people in your network and it was great to see you on the night having so much fun. We look forward to working with you again in the future and once again, thanks for your support! The event raised a total of $5,453 and we couldn't have done it without you!"

Personal gratefulness is also important. If you have left a job or career to go into business, it can be easy to forget about the joy of business when you go through a difficult phase and it can be very easy to reminisce about the 'comfort' of a 'normal job.'

At times like this, it is essential to reflect on all aspects of the choices you have made. There will always be pluses and minuses in every situation. Ultimately, you will choose which set of choices are more appealing.

For the most part, I believe that most people try and choose the best solution at the time they make the choice. If you have to make a significant decision and you are under stress, it is best to wait until you have had a good night's sleep, a healthy meal and a moment to weigh up all of your options first (perhaps with some professional assistance if a more careful analysis is required).

No doubt you have heard of some very inspiring stories where people have overcome incredible challenges to recover from a significant setback. In most of those situations, there is usually a person or other people around that person helping them along the way. Don't forget that there are usually many free and low cost options around if a challenge arises, so please, don't be too proud to ask for some help if you need it.

Action 108: *There are many ways to acknowledge and thank people and businesses for their contribution to your success. Remember to acknowledge what you can be grateful for and make significant decisions by calmly evaluating your choices. Ask for extra help if you need it*

17. Future Options Marketing

I guess that none of us really know what is going to happen in the future. As I write this, these are just my ideas on some options that I believe are possibilities (not certainties) based on my experiences up until now. It will be interesting to look backwards in the future and see if they actually did happen!

- **Interactive Marketing** – I suspect that there will be more marketing opportunities that enable a client or customer to be involved in an interactive sense in their purchase. We are part way there now with making selections from a range of choices, but I suspect with tools like 3D printing, we will be able to have much more scope in the range of options we can include in products. For services, I think that there are likely to be more automation funnels to sort people to a particular provider rather than requiring individuals to manually sort through all of the providers (similar to the comparison services now but much broader and more sophisticated)

- **Immersive Marketing** – I believe that there will be an opportunity for clients and customers to become almost part of a business like the staff where they are more connected to operations and they will have a more persuasive influence on what is offered for sale. Over time, we have moved away from an overall market driven economy driven essentially by key influencers (like mainstream media) into a market where individual collectives are determining what is provided. This could be a step in the right direction to help save the planet if people start to choose to be socially and ethically responsible for their purchasing decisions

Action 109: *Interactive and Immersive Marketing Opportunities are likely to enable people to be more actively involved in their purchasing decision and it may lead to more socially and ethically responsible purchasing decisions*

- **Collaborative Clusters** – an extension of a local community, I see collaborative clusters as being collections of like minded people who connect either physically within a small geographic radius or internationally through technology but they do so with some over arching principles that allows them to provide niche products and services to members within the group and selected clients and customers who are regularly involved in the decisions of the cluster. It will be a more egalitarian environment and the role of leadership may be rotated or be more of a balancing role rather than a directive role

- **Behavior Based Tribes** – I can see collective groups of individuals coming together with various technologies based on their behaviors and these tribes will be able to generate unique opportunities to constantly create continuous improvement. They will be motivated internally by the need to constantly develop and grow their own opportunities because they will trigger off the creative minds of the other people who have some congruent behaviors. This will essentially be a safe environment where the collective can experiment without risk or fear of failure. There is also a saying that 'your vibe attracts your tribe'

Action 110: *Collaborative Clusters and Behavior Based Tribes are likely to come together to make decisions as a group rather than as individuals. This can potentially lead to more egalitarian societies and continuous improvement.*

- **Alternative Payment Models** – There have been many different models of exchange over time – products, services and payments. When credit cards first appeared, there was enormous fear and apprehension and we are now moving to a society where almost every financial transaction can be completed with our mobile device (including withdraw cash from an automatic teller machine). As technology constantly develops, I can see that more individual marketplaces could quite easily be created and trade could technically occur within those markets rather than within particular countries. International trade may seem like a ridiculous concept as essentially, all trade and transactions could be done internationally. This has other implications in terms of collecting tax and revenue for local communities, so I imagine that regulators will still be keen to make sure that these marketplaces are monitored and regulated for some time yet (and rightly so as a true market economy driven by greedy humans could easily see a collapse in society).

Action 111: *The variety of ways that payment can be made for an exchange is likely to continue changing and country borders dissolve with international trade*

- **Device Independent and Open Source Technology** – For a number of years now, internet marketers have promised the concept of a location independent working life, where essentially you can be in any location and still earn a living through your connection with the internet. Personally, I prefer to stay connected to my local community and travel when I choose, but the next level on from this is a society where we can be device independent – where we do not have to have a particular model of a device to be able to continue our productive activity. I would also like to see a world where we have more open source options so that more people can live a modest lifestyle (I would also like to see some levelling off of the super rich but that is another story!)

Action 112: *A trend from location independent to device independent is likely to occur as more open source technology is developed and shared and made more accessible to all citizens*

- **Wearable Technology** – We are already seeing wearable technology in the marketplace and with the huge amount of data that this type of technology can generate, the sky is the limit in terms of what marketing we may have to 'turn off' to live a normal life in the future. When I look back at old photographs of cities where the only real advertising was a sign out the front of the shop and now we see LED screens and lights in virtually every store, station or place where people gather or regularly go past, I shudder when I think about how much content is going to be 'forced' onto me with wearable technology. But mark my words, I believe that there will be specialist consultants in this area fairly soon!

Action 113: *As wearable technology and other marketing devices enter the market, there will come a time when consultants will need to provide advice on how to maximize these tools and people will need to learn how to turn off constant marketing messages*

- **Middleware Integrations** – I really admire people who craft software and hardware that can perform so many amazing functions. Alas, as a person in business, it is very frustrating to have to use multiple different systems that do not talk to one another and in the case of customer information, have it accumulated in so many different locations. I believe that in the future, there will be more middleware software programs that will allow different operating systems, online platforms, social media, databases and applications to 'talk' to one another so that a business can essentially secure one source of truth

The over arching principle that I believe these ideas can achieve is a more seamless customer or user experience. There will be a certain level of artificial intelligence developed through these tools as machines will be learning as they receive and process data and information.

As Isaac Asimov declared in his three laws of robotics, a robot must not allow a human to be injured, it must not obey an order by a human to harm another human and it must protect its own existence provided it doesn't harm a human being. Whether or not humans will create robots or technology that can do these things or abide by robotic laws is a philosophical argument in itself.

Action 114: *In the future, marketing will continue to evolve and offer business many different ways to reach and secure sales and process payments. The most likely outcome is that there will be a more seamless customer or user experience based on previously collected data and information thanks to integration technology*

18. Marketing Measurement

Computers have increased our ability to measure our marketing much more effectively than we could have ever imagined 100 years ago. However, like a lot of statistics, the data can lie. Computers are fantastic for processing information, but they are not so good at storing so many different aspects of a business transaction (at the moment).

As you well know, the human body has so many different ways to collect, store and process information, way beyond technology at this point. If I had relied on data from my computer, I would never have survived this long in business.

What I have been able to deduce, after thousands of hours of experience in the real world is way beyond what is stored on my digital records. So until we have a device that can plug into my body and distill all of that data - and process it effectively, I have a sense that humans will still be involved in marketing decisions!

What can help you as a business owner is the ability to look at information and analyze it effectively. You need to be able to interpret the insights not just by qualitative numbers, but also on qualitative information that you collect from everyone associated with your business, including your clients and customers.

You will need to challenge yourself sometimes and consider experimenting a little (always a good idea to start on a trial basis first). Then test and measure again before proceeding to a larger scale. Also remember though that the goal posts are regularly changing, so you need to be able to adapt to the changing rules of the game. This is particularly true in the online world as algorithms appear to change weekly.

Action 115: *When measuring your marketing, look at both quantitative and qualitative information and trial and test before moving to larger scale implementation. Be aware that algorithms in the online world are constantly changing and your business needs to be ready to adjust accordingly*

18.1 Digital Asset Value

At present, I believe your most valuable online digital business asset is your website because it is something that you own and can control and develop (provided you abide by local laws and regulations).

However, your overall online presence can be developed in many ways – as discussed in this book. The dollar value that can be recorded on a balance sheet in preparation for a sale is still something that needs to be refined. Beyond assigning a dollar value for each engaged client or customer, there are many variables that need to be fairly calculated to demonstrate the value to a business.

For example, for you personally, via other online platforms, you have the ability to:

- share your message directly with your connections, followers etc

- encourage your followers to share your messages through their networks (virality). If you have developed a particularly strong influence in the marketplace, you are much more likely to have your content shared

- have your content ranked in generic online search results

- attract new clients and customers by publishing on a platform that reaches your target audience

- secure coverage on highly ranked or high priority websites which can actually increase in value over time

- develop platforms for ongoing engagement based on your past involvement

- be searched and found within the platform based on your past contributions

So as you can imagine, if you are no longer part of the business, this 'digital asset value' can be lost - which is why a number of business purchasers will make it a condition of sale that you remain associated with the business for at least 12 months after the sale.

Secondly, there are the digital assets of the business - the online profiles and platforms that have been created in the name of the business. These digital assets generate their own traffic and presence, but they also require a certain level of maintenance. If you have been in business for some time and you have maintained a constant presence, activity and engagement, this is far more valuable than a static profile and it can generate marketing traffic on an ongoing basis. If you have secured a good level of authentic engagement with your target audience, this is particularly valuable (although again, it is at the mercy of an algorithm change).

If you want to prepare your business for the day when you will not be there (sale, acquisition, transfer etc), then you really need to keep some records of your digital assets' performance. Many of these statistics are only available in real time, so if you do not keep a record, you will not be able to justify their value.

For example, you will need to collect, at least every 12 months, but preferably every six months, the details of your raw numbers of followers, connections, etc and some of the other significant measures (for example, how many views per 90 days or direct leads etc). A simple Excel spreadsheet is sufficient. Apart from keeping this record, consider how you are performing and whether or not you need to adjust your marketing activity to improve your business results.

Action 116: *To prepare your business for the day when you will not be there, keep a record of the most important online statistics that are only available in real time in an Excel spreadsheet every six months. Review your results and look at ways to improve your business results*

18.2 Goodwill

As they say in recruitment, past behavior is an indicator of future performance. So if your business has regularly been generating a certain level of profit over time, then there is a reasonable expectation that this level of profit could be maintained in the future.

I heard a fantastic story recently. An accounting practice decided that they wanted to change their client demographic and they only wanted to look after businesses that had a yearly bill of $5,000 or more. They were more than happy to refer their clients on to other local practices who would be happy to accept their business.

Interestingly, a majority of their clients were being billed at around the $3,000 per year mark. They simply said, "That's okay, keep doing what you are doing and we will pay the $5,000." They were so impressed with the level of service they already had that they did not want to go elsewhere and they were prepared to pay a significant premium to maintain it.

Businesses offering luxury products never battle with another business on price. When a person chooses to buy a luxury vehicle, they don't ask whether it will be extra if it is red - they just tell the salesperson they want a red car and then they find out the price. It is not always possible to start out in business in this way, but if you create a perception of value, it is surprising to see how many people will pay for that perceived value. Technically, any reliable car could move a person from one place to another, but some people choose to travel in a luxury vehicle and they are happy to pay for the privilege.

For balance sheet purposes, the amount of goodwill is usually based on a variety of factors, but it is an intangible asset - based on the purchase price less assets and liabilities. So if you buy a company for $10 million dollars and it only has a total of $1 million dollars in current assets (liabilities already deducted), then the business has $9 million dollars in goodwill value. The purchaser basically expects that the business is worth spending $10 million dollars because they believe that the intangible assets of the business will keep generating a profit.

So naturally, your goal is to build the goodwill value of the business so that if you decide to sell it, you can attract a better sale price. So you need to constantly be on the lookout for ways that you can increase the value of your business and marketing is a key component because it can increase your brand awareness and perceived value.

Action 117: *Marketing techniques can be used to improve your brand awareness and perceived value and ultimately raise the level of goodwill value when the business is sold, acquired or transferred. Always be on the lookout for ways that you can increase the value of your business*

18.3 Performance Assessment

How do you calculate what has worked with your marketing and what hasn't worked with your marketing?

Some assessments are actually very difficult to complete and you actually need to take a leap of faith because you know full well that there is no direct return on investment, but you know that the particular activity needs to be maintained.

For example, I encourage all of my clients to regularly add new content to their website and their online profiles on social media and online platforms. If you look at the direct statistics and the number of views received for each post, you could easily say, "it wasn't worthwhile."

However, that activity is what keeps a business appearing in search results, because you are updating your digital assets on a regular basis. One of my clients was very conscientious in the beginning and posted very frequently, now she only has to maintain a base level of activity to maintain her results.

Advertising, when incorporated with your marketing activities is something that is again, often very difficult to track and measure. In fact, I am not a big fan of advertising, I prefer to go down the editorial route as it has more credibility. That doesn't mean that it is easy to obtain and some businesses prefer the 'quick and dirty' approach of advertising and if it leads to ethical sales, then why not!

Online advertising is a little easier to assess than printed advertising as most advertisers offer a way for you to login and see what has happened. That's great, but if views don't lead to conversions, again, you need to ask yourself, "Is this activity worthwhile?"

You also need to monitor your complaints and how you have responded to them. You also need to monitor people who just disappear - they don't formally complain, but they stop doing business with you - why? Up to 80% of customers will leave because of a perception of indifference rather than a complaint - so if you want to maintain the relationship, stay in touch every three months.

Ultimately, any marketing activity will be useless if you do not provide the client or customer with the products or services they expect to receive. So part of your performance assessment should look at whether or not your products and services do meet their needs and if the person would be willing to provide a referral in the future. Feedback and reviews, even negative ones, can give you some clues as to how to improve in the future.

Action 118: *After selecting and implementing your marketing activities, you need to find ways to measure their performance and their ability to ultimately lead to conversions. Some activities will not be able to be measured, but they will need to be maintained. Your results can give you clues as to what to improve in the future*

18.4 Performance Improvement

After measuring your marketing results, you can now identify ways to improve your performance.

For example, if you find that your marketing efforts have led to a significant increase in website traffic but you have not made any extra sales, then you need to look at your website and work out ways for it to be easier for a person to purchase your products and services.

If you find that people are constantly trying to beat you down on price, perhaps you are not explaining your value adequately. I have an expression that I regularly use, "If you don't tell, you can't sell." If my clients do not now how I can help them, why would they come to me?

To be continually on the lookout for ways to improve can be exhausting, especially if you are willing to bend and flex with every minuscule insight. What is more important is for you to be very clear about what it is that you do and then assess any feedback you receive in relation to your vision and mission.

For example, you could have one person who comes along and says, "You should do this instead of that." But everyone else could be saying, "We love what you do, keep it up." Which statement is more reliable? Of course, it is the one shared by multiple happy clients and customers.

That doesn't mean that you should ignore the isolated anecdote. It simply means that you should investigate it in more detail before reacting or changing any of your current policies or procedures.

You also need to look at what works well for you and finesse it from time to time. Perhaps you have an excellent referral process in place, but how is it tracking - have your results gone up or down over time? Is there anything else that you could do to help your referral partner? If it is one of your best marketing strategies, could you consider more referral partners going forward?

It may also be time to end some marketing ideas. Perhaps the classified advertisement in the local printed guide book is simply irrelevant because the circulation and readership has dropped too much. Whilst you may not be able to justify the classified advertisement spend, perhaps there is some other way to support that enterprise - do they have an online version? Could you advertise there instead?

Every successful business owner knows that they must grow, change and adapt to market conditions. Likewise, every marketing idea also needs to grow, change and adapt.

I believe that the future of business involves a lot more collaboration rather than competition, a lot more democracy rather than hierarchy and global learning but local action. Ultimately, I would like to see a lot more collective hyper local communities.

Action 119: *From time to time, you will need to assess your marketing initiatives and look for ways to improve their effectiveness and conversion rate. Make sure that you base your decisions on statistically relevant information but also be open to small tweaks based on specific feedback.*

18.5 Top 20 Tips And Techniques

After reading through the book (or skipping to this section), I would like to share my top 20 tips and techniques for helping you to market your business hyper locally.

1. As a business decision maker, you need to be able to define your target audience and the clearer you are about your ideal client, how they can be reached and how you can serve them effectively, the closer you are to success

2. Managing expectations is one of the most critical success factors for a successful business. Remember that people who receive good products and services will tell a few people. People who receive bad products and services will usually tell lots of people

3. With up to 85% of business being sourced via a referral, your business needs to build a strong relationship with your existing customers and clients over time so that they can become your target audience ambassadors, willingly representing you and your business in various situations

4. To increase the potential size of your target market, consider international markets and connections, increasing demand through education, contributing to your community and adopting a growth mindset

5. I truly believe that a lot more enterprises could be value and purpose driven if more people had faith in the giving process rather than the taking process. Rather than viewing every other enterprise as a competitor, think about how they could be a collaborator. How can you help each other and your community? After all, in most cases, you will be serving either a different target audience or the same target audience but providing a different product or service

6. Before selecting a marketing idea, consider assessing the idea via a marketing idea viability test and measure the concept against a range of criteria. Once selected, even if the idea is not 100% perfect, be committed to making it a success but also be willing to let go and move on if it doesn't go according to plan

7. Creating and publishing search engine optimized content allows you to attract good quality search engine results. Ideally, your business should create a mix of dynamic, evergreen and historically useful content that has been enhanced with additional digital media

8. It would be easy to think that generating something that goes viral is the key to business success - however, that is like being a musician who is just a one-hit-wonder. If you want to drive conversions rather than just traffic, you need to consistently provide content that has the potential to be viral but also actionable. At the end of the day, making something popular is good for your vanity, but it is not necessarily good for your business

9. The time I spend on my business is at least as valuable as my earnings, but as a general rule, I prefer to take the long term approach and create a digital asset that automatically generates leads rather than take the short term approach of a digital expense that has the potential to quickly increase in cost

10. Membership of a professional body, industry group or association has many intrinsic and extrinsic benefits - provided you get involved and make use of the opportunities on offer. Remember to update your details every six months and plan what you will do each year in advance

11. To market your business hyper locally, you will need to manage multiple databases and implement business processes that capture the details and attention of your clients and customers as effectively as possible. Ultimately, you will need to reach out to people in a variety of ways, so do what you can to make the collection and management of data as efficient as possible. When reviewing the results, look for the most relevant information related to your location and context and make well informed decisions

12. To find suitable joint venture and strategic alliance opportunities hyper locally, you will need to find out how other hyper local businesses around you operate. Always start with a trial and test approach where either party can leave the arrangement before making an ongoing commitment. Consider representing international organizations at the local level and also using this approach to expand your business in the future. It is not the size of the community that makes a difference, it is your approach to meeting the people in the community that makes a difference

13. Following up with existing clients and customers can often be a more effective marketing technique than constantly trying to find brand new clients and customers. Consider implementing some automatic follow up processes into your business and respond to useful feedback with appropriate improvements

14. Identify hyper local, local, national and international awards that your business can enter either now or in the future. Collect information, maintain your best activities and continuously develop unique and inspiring initiatives that help your customers, clients and the industry. After entering the awards, promote your involvement across all of your marketing and business channels

15. Formally or informally recognizing your customers, clients or other businesses can be a very effective strategy for acknowledging their contribution to your business success. You can incorporate recognition in your everyday business processes or participate in more formal recognition programs. Recognition marketing is a tool for acting on past behaviors

16. Your reputation will ultimately be revealed by your values. Successful business owners are prepared to be authentic, vulnerable, proactive, apologetic and responsible. Even if your reputation has been damaged, it is possible to recover, so I encourage you to live courageously

17. Create a reliable system for collecting feedback from your clients and customers and respond with the appropriate actions as required. Do not react emotionally to uncomfortable or unreasonable feedback. Keep a record of changes you have made to re-affirm your commitment to continuous improvement and show this list to new employees and contractors

18. Speaking at events is a great privilege and it can generate some amazing opportunities for you and your business. It is an excellent strategy if you are starting to promote your business in a hyper local context or location and if you are able to record the event, it can also give you lifetime value. Just be aware of the specific preparation you need to complete and the pitfalls

19. Wherever possible, source your products, services and supplies from other locals. Not only is it a more sustainable and environmentally friendly option, you may also end up with more referral business

20. I believe that the future of business involves a lot more collaboration rather than competition, a lot more democracy rather than hierarchy and global learning but local action. Ultimately, I would like to see a lot more collective hyper local communities.

Action 120: *Review the Top 20 Tips and Techniques and make an effort to complete at least one of these in the next month*

19. Full List of 120 Actions

Section 1: Our Global Village

Action 1: Define your niche business idea based on a realistic assessment of market demand and personal ability. If there is no existing or future demand, there is no business opportunity

Action 2: Marketing, selling and networking are part of being in business. Accept that 20% of your time will be spent doing tasks that are either just outside of your comfort zone or necessary rather than fun. Aim for contentment rather than happiness

Action 3: Regardless of the reasons why you are in your current location, do your best to learn and adapt to the norms of the local community. Understand that it is normal to take some time to feel like a local, but there are many ways to connect with locals and make new friends

Action 4: Hyperlocal marketing is marketing that is designed to reach a defined area - that could be a geographical radius from a central point or a defined group of people connected by context, geolocation or time. Now is the time to define your target audience

Action 5: There are many benefits to creating a hyper local marketing strategy. Write down the three main reasons that will help you and your business in the future, based on your values

Section 2. Personal Context

Action 6: Identify what has happened up until this point with you and your business and identify any false beliefs and personal blockages. Acknowledge your past achievements. Focus on using your strengths to learn new skills and complete some actions now, soon and later. Review, reflect and record what needs to be done and find someone else to keep you accountable for taking action

Action 7: Whether you are new to your own business or you have been running your business for some time, you need to be able to manage yourself and source people, systems and processes to overcome your challenges. Make sure you create your own personal identity within and with the people around you. Describing your value is part of your personal branding

Action 8: Managers are task driven and Leaders are vision driven. As the business owner, decide whether you will be self employed or in business. Remember that managers and leaders need to be able to supervise people, processes and performance. Make sure you have enough knowledge to make effective decisions for long term results

Action 9: Consider which succession planning or exit strategy you will use when you are no longer a part of your business and consider this objective when selecting your marketing strategies

Action 10: Review how you spend your time each week and see if the majority of your time is aligned with your highest values. If it isn't, start making small changes today as a lot of little changes will ultimately lead to some big changes

Action 11: Review how other people currently contribute to your community and choose ways that you can contribute in the future based on your skills, talents and abilities. Make realistic and manageable choices for implementation within the next six months

Action 12: Understand that to be a successful business owner, you need to abide by ethical principles in both your personal and business life. On your business journey, you can source assistance from people, processes and business models. Ultimately, your goal is to self regulate your actions for the benefit of your community and the planet

Action 13: Whether you are just starting out in business or you have been in business for a while, you will need to think about your staffing and outsourcing requirements and be able to identify reliable sources of new recruits. If you manage this process effectively, you can also reduce your total costs and source more referrals

Action 14: It is possible to find good staff and contractors via hyper local recruiting based on geographic location or context. Real world groups enable real life assessment and accountability, online tools enable a wider reach and alternative verification methods. Remember that you cannot be an expert in every aspect of your business but you can manage every aspect of your business

3. Business Context

Action 15: Consider the current level of demand within your local context to make a valid risk assessment of your business. If necessary, re-evaluate what is worth keeping in your range of products and services

Action 16: Make sure that your business products and services match market demand and are in alignment with your values. If you need assistance to clarify your business direction, seek some professional advice

Action 17: Consumers now have a much greater variety of ways to select and purchase products and services. As a business owner, you need to be able to build a buying relationship over time and provide the best touch points that will lead to a sale. Some of these touch points are likely to be facilitated by mobile or online technology

Action 18: Developing a sustainable business can help create a positive impact on the local environment, community, society or economy. Combining mass production systems with hyper local systems can create a more egalitarian share of resources and lifestyle. Business owners need to combine the best of both worlds to leave our planet in good condition for future generations and accept full responsibility for managing all aspects of their business, not just the marketing

Action 19: Clarify the exact nature of your business and how you will differentiate yourself from other enterprises. Understand that the world is constantly changing and that you will need to continually learn grow and adapt - with professional assistance if required

Action 20: Ultimately, pricing is dependent upon dollar cost value, perception value and convenience. How you price your products and services needs to be aligned with your business costs and market conditions. If you can incorporate a 'currency' or 'recency' value, this can maintain demand for your products and services

4. Product And Service First Or Target Audience First?

Action 21: When selecting your products and services, always think about the needs of your target audience. Provide low, medium and high cost options so that you can create a natural pathway to a bigger total spend over time. Manage expectations at all times as bad news is spread further than good news

Action 22: With up to 85% of business being sourced via a referral, your business needs to build a strong relationship with your existing clients and customers over time so that they can become your target audience ambassadors, willingly representing you and your business in various situations

Action 23: Identify other quality sources of clients and customers by doing some research in to what is available in your local area or context. Make sure that each source either has a high volume of participants, high online authority or a direct link to your target audience. Maintain the accuracy of all of your profiles over time and review each option's suitability as a client source every six months

Action 24: Identify ways that you can maintain the relationship with your clients and customers over time. Always maintain your customer service standards and incorporate customer relationship management processes in your business processes so that it is automatically implemented for most of your transactions

Section 5. Market Analysis

Action 25: If you are planning to operate a business in a particular location, you need to understand the local geospatial data and make an informed choice before selecting your site. If you have already chosen a site, investigate what other opportunities might be available in the future by collecting reliable local quantitative and qualitative data

Action 26: To increase the potential size of your target market, consider international markets and connections, increasing demand through education, contributing to your community and adopting a growth mindset

Action 27: Every business needs to respond to changes in the economy and find ways to constantly improve over time. Aim to make at least a 1% improvement on a regular basis

Action 28: Complete an online competitor analysis for at least one business that is competing for the same target audience. As a minimum, visit their website, right click with your mouse, view the source code and see how they are optimizing their content. Visit http://archive.org for historical website information. Ultimately, look at multiple competitors' online presence across various platforms

Action 29: As you complete research on other enterprises in your location or context range, identify enterprises that may be suitable for a collaborator arrangement. You may be able to share referrals, economies of scale or mutually agreed exchanges. By adopting a giving philosophy, even if there is no direct benefit, you will find that over time, you will receive more

Section 6. Location Context

Action 30: Rather than worry about the challenges of a particular location - either offline or online, look for quantitative and qualitative data that can help you make better marketing decisions

Action 31: Source reliable local data and information to make informed choices. Do not make decisions based on assumptions or anecdotes. The process of sourcing reliable information can lead to new sources of ideal clients

Action 32: When selecting your business name, see if the domain name with the right extension is also available so that you can attract more relevant traffic to your website. Likewise when you establish a presence on an online platform, see if you can select the same profile name

Action 33: Select the best online platforms for your target audience and business objectives, ensuring that you have the time and resources to keep your profile current and effective and keep a close eye on the results - both tangible and non-tangible

Action 34: Your collective marketplace presence can be challenged by clients and customers and you need to have a clear strategy for resolving issues quickly, respectfully and fairly based on multiple factors. Be willing to apologize, find out the facts and deliver a solution without reacting emotionally and fairly assessing the risk

Section 7. Market Presence

Action 35: Setting up quality real estate is an essential component of your marketing strategy. It is a way to showcase the value and benefits rather than the price and features of your products and services

Action 36: If you are going to start implementing a hyper local marketing approach in your business, don't just think about ways to attract people to your products and services, think about ways that your premises can be acquired hyper locally and seek professional advice to optimize the space into an effective tool for your business

Action 37: Make sure that your website meets minimum Google requirements and has the essential components to stand up to the rigour of judgment from people who have either found your website on their own or been referred to your website by someone else. Understand that your website will constantly evolve over time and it is a good idea to start with a Minimum Viable Product and improve with revisions later

Action 38: A personal Authority Website in your own name can provide additional interest, referrals and opportunities for you and your business. It can be very brief and just provide a basic outline of your background or it can showcase you as an authority within your industry and/or profession. Select your goal and go for it

Action 39: Before selecting a marketing idea, consider assessing the idea via a marketing idea viability test and measure the concept against a range of criteria. Once selected, even if the idea is not 100% perfect, be committed to making it a success but also be willing to let go and move on if it doesn't go according to plan

Action 40: Every marketing idea or business initiative that you implement in your business needs to be valuable within your current context (currency), recently created if a new challenge has appeared (recency) and relevant in relation to your business values and target audience (relevancy). Avoid wasting time or money on ideas that ultimately are not aligned with your business goals

Section 8. Online and Digital Marketing

Action 41: Do not be tempted to implement shortcut search engine optimization techniques that have the potential to be black listed in the future. If you do, you will usually pay to have them added and have to pay again to have them removed as well as recover from any penalty that may occur

Action 42: Make sure that any content you publish on behalf of your business is search engine friendly and enables people to have a good user experience. Good quality content can ultimately lead to actionable behavior that leads to opportunities for your business. Wherever you have an opportunity to provide details, tags or descriptions with your content, do so

Action 43: Search engine algorithms assess multiple criteria to assess the relevance of your website for the search engine index and search engine results. Understand these principles when creating and updating your website to help your enterprise attract additional traffic and ultimately, conversions

Action 44: Creating and publishing search engine optimized content allows you to attract good quality search engine results. Ideally, your business should create a mix of dynamic, evergreen and historically useful content that has been enhanced with additional digital media

Action 45: When you identify content that has performed well for your business, make an effort to amplify its impact by adding even more value, updating your call to action and providing more effective actionable suggestions. If people respond with a Comment or a Share, make an effort to respond personally

Action 46: If you can generate content that encourages viewers to share it through their networks, you can significantly increase content views, engagement and conversions. There are many different ways to create content that has the potential to go viral - so think carefully about your target audience and what sort of behavior you would like to trigger before publication and use different tools to test and measure what has the greatest potential to go viral

Action 47: Be aware that you and your target audience are generating signals based on your measured behavior. There are various tools you can use in your business to track and connect with your target audience including cookies, tracking pixels and other measurement tools

Action 48: To market your website hyper locally via website links, look for websites that offer a range of search engine benefits based on the concepts of relevance, authority, ranking, search engine optimization, influence, performance, indexing, popularity, reliability, conversions and currency (updated regularly)

Action 49: When asking for a link to your website, make sure you do your research and personalize your request, clearly outlining how some value can be exchanged. Remain polite, even if the answer is 'no.' Remember that you can still link to them even if they do not link to you

Action 50: Your online performance can be improved if you focus on benefits rather than features, but remember to meet the needs of your target audience and provide them with the specific details they need to finalize a transaction

Action 51: Your online conversion rate can be increased if you provide the appropriate amount of choice for your selected target audience. If your enterprise can do this well, there is a very good chance that your website will also perform well in online search results for that target audience

Action 52: Make it easy for your clients and customers to complete their transaction online. You need to have a website that works well and provides the person with the safe and reliable experience they expect. The benefit to you and the customer is that if you provide this experience, your website is also likely to perform well in organic search results

Action 53: Be vigilant and aware about the most significant changes that are occurring online and be ready to adjust your online presence accordingly. Whilst hyper local marketing relies more on referral techniques, if you would like to independently attract search engine results, you will need to be far more strategic, particularly if you are competing in a high frequency or high volume marketplace

Section 9. Paid Marketing

Action 54: Before embarking on a paid marketing initiative, start out with what you know will work, even if there is a lower profit margin because if you are paying per click, you can quickly churn through a lot of cash. Adopting a startup or organic growth model can help you develop a viable business. Future paid marketing ideas need to pass the Marketing Idea Viability Test

Action 55: Search Engine Marketing (SEM) should only be considered as a hyper local marketing or general marketing strategy if your website successfully converts traffic to sales. Your SEM certified partner needs to work with you to maximize your ability to reach your specific target audience for the best cost per click (CPC) rate. All SEM needs to be carefully measured to ensure that there is a return on your investment

Action 56: Social Media Marketing (SMM) should only be considered as a hyper local marketing or general marketing strategy if your spend successfully increases your brand awareness and/or sales. Your SMM qualified and successful advisor needs to work with you to determine the most effective techniques for your purpose (content marketing may be more helpful than sponsored advertisements). All SMM needs to be carefully measured to ensure that there is a return on your investment

Action 57: The best hyper local online advertisement opportunities have the potential to support the local enterprises and the local community. These online advertisements are likely to be more effective it they can be maintained on an ongoing basis and if they can enhance business relationships and encourage referrals. Larger scale online advertisement opportunities need to be examined much more carefully to ensure that there is a fair exchange and a reasonable cost per client or customer acquisition

Action 58: Good quality aggregator websites with a large database and high traffic volumes have the potential to lead your target audience directly to you, provided you do your homework first and optimize your profile and any of the other features they offer as part of the aggregator service. Consider both local and international aggregator websites but make sure that you can still independently measure your results before subscribing to either a free or paid service

Action 59: Membership of a professional body, industry group or association has many intrinsic and extrinsic benefits - provided you get involved and make use of the opportunities on offer. Remember to update your details every six months and plan what you will do each year in advance

Action 60: Consider sourcing some locally created products and services to share as gifts with your clients and customers. You can choose different options for each part of the sales cycle and you can also provide products or services from your own business

Action 61: There are many ways that your business can provide a donation to your local community and there are also programs that may allow you to receive a donation. Be creative in the way you give back to your community by examining any areas of your business where you have excess capacity and by looking at local causes or charities that share common values where you can both benefit from working together

Section 10. Database Marketing

Action 62: To market your business hyper locally, you will need to manage multiple databases and implement business processes that capture the details and attention of your clients and customers as effectively as possible. Ultimately, you will need to reach out to people in a variety of ways, so do what you can to make the collection and management of data as efficient as possible. When reviewing the results, look for the most relevant information related to your location and context and make well informed decisions

Action 63: Email newsletters can be very effective for maintaining and building relationships with your hyper local contacts, clients and customers. Make mindful choices about the purpose, setup, frequency, format and content and be consistent with your distribution schedule. Make allowances for plain text viewers, incorporate video links and consider aligning your cycle with a live activity

Action 64: To find suitable joint venture and strategic alliance opportunities hyper locally, you will need to find out how other hyper local businesses around you operate. Always start with a trial and test approach where either party can leave the arrangement before making an ongoing commitment. Consider representing international organizations at the local level and also using this approach to expand your business in the future

Action 65: To form a successful partnership, you need to make sure that you and the other person or business can maintain your accountability, performance and dedication, despite changes in circumstances. Always start with a trial and test approach first and before making an ongoing commitment, make sure that you both understand exactly what you are agreeing to. Alternatively, consider working in parallel or on a transaction basis

Action 66: If / then scenarios can be applied in a hyper local context or location, but you need to make sure that you base your sequences on reliable information that considers the nature of your clients and customers and how they may feel if they are put on an automatic marketing sequence. That said, it is never too early to think about business processes you can automate in your business

Action 67: Following up with existing clients and customers can often be a more effective marketing technique than constantly trying to find brand new clients and customers. Consider implementing some automatic follow up processes into your business and respond to useful feedback with appropriate improvements

Section 11. Program Marketing

Action 68: Marketing programs usually require some level of effort and commitment to implement. However, they can help improve your business processes and lead to ongoing benefits to your marketing channels, brand presence and business reputation. Carefully evaluate the program with independent research before purchasing a marketing program

Action 69: Identify hyper local, local, national and international awards that your business can enter either now or in the future. Collect information, maintain your best activities and continuously develop unique and inspiring initiatives that help your customers, clients and the industry. After entering the awards, promote your involvement across all of your marketing and business channels

Action 70: Affiliate programs need to be carefully assessed before implementation and ideally should offer a complementary product or service. At all times, you need to preserve your relationship with your clients and customers. Good quality affiliate programs have the potential to help both businesses and the local community both directly and indirectly

Action 71: Formally or informally recognizing your customers, clients or other businesses can be a very effective strategy for acknowledging their contribution to your business success. You can incorporate recognition in your everyday business processes or participate in more formal recognition programs. Recognition marketing is a tool for acting on past behaviors

Action 72: A well designed rewards program can encourage repeat behavior, access new clients and customers and potentially go viral. Make sure that the rewards you offer will be well received by your ideal clients and customers. Wherever possible, source the rewards from within your own range of products and services of from a hyper local context or location

Action 73: Surveys, quizzes and research programs can help your business and the community collect a range of useful qualitative and quantitative information that can be used either to start or develop a business. I also recommend working with academia and sharing your findings internationally so that you can improve your business brand

Action 74: Formal accreditation and certification programs are worth securing and showcasing, maintaining and improving and potentially developing in your hyper local context or location. They are not a guarantee of business success, but they are an important piece of the business puzzle that can be a catalyst for continuous improvement for your business and for clients and customers

Section 12. Public Marketing

Action 75: Public marketing can be intentional and unintentional, online and offline and can be shared within a hyper local context or location. Bad news can also travel fast, but it usually only lasts for the duration of the media life cycle. Your business needs to be prepared to manage the issues associated with public marketing techniques

Action 76: Public Marketing can be obtained by curating, composing or contributing content to online and offline publications (including your own website). Aim to have good quality informative, educational or entertaining content published where your target audience will see it

Action 77: Identify the best review websites and add your business details so that you can receive reviews. Encourage your clients and customers to add reviews and respond appropriately to reviews as soon as possible

Action 78: Recommendations need to be adequately showcased in a public way to provide maximum value but make sure you have the author's permission to list them publicly first

Action 79: Good quality referrals that lead directly to business require you to make sure that your online and offline content meets the due diligence requirements of your prospective client or customer. Be curious and always look for ways to provide referrals to others and make sure that you always say thank you for referrals you receive

Action 80: Your reputation will ultimately be revealed by your values. Successful business owners are prepared to be authentic, vulnerable, proactive, apologetic and responsible. Even if your reputation has been damaged, it is possible to recover, so I encourage you to live courageously

Action 81: Make an effort to secure a range of quality testimonials from well recognized individuals. If authorized, include a link to their online profile so that people can verify the testimonial and/or take a video. Publish the testimonials on your website and where appropriate, on your online profiles

Action 82: Create a reliable system for collecting feedback from your clients and customers and respond with the appropriate actions as required. Do not react emotionally to uncomfortable or unreasonable feedback. Keep a record of changes you have made to re-affirm your commitment to continuous improvement and show this list to new employees and contractors

Action 83: There are many different ways you can be an advocate in your hyper local context or location. Use your unique gifts to find a way to help another person or group by completing a lot of little positive actions over time. You will benefit and so will your community

Section 13. Events Marketing

Action 84: Before attending an event, think about the real cost to you and your business including the time to travel to, attend and then follow up after the event. You can potentially reach more people, but the risks can also be higher, especially as more people appear to be fickle and reluctant to commit

Action 85: Free events work best if they are regular, easy to coordinate and attend and you treat them as a brand awareness and information gathering exercise. They are also very effective at building business relationships in a non threatening environment

Action 86: If you have chosen to run paid events, make sure you understand the commitment and action steps involved. Events can be a tool for opening up opportunities through the event promotion and referral systems you use

Action 87: Speaking at events is a great privilege and it can generate some amazing opportunities for you and your business. It is an excellent strategy if you are starting to promote your business in a hyper local context or location and if you are able to record the event, it can also give you lifetime value. Just be aware of the specific preparation you need to complete and the pitfalls

Action 88: Teaching, either live and in person or online can be a good way to maintain your expertise and gather new ideas for your business. It can also help you reach your target audience and give you an opportunity to give back

Action 89: Expos, trade fairs and conferences usually involve a very substantial investment in time, money and resources. Make sure that you carefully evaluate the real benefits (rather than the sales pitch) and if you do decide to participate, adopt an investor approach and make every effort to support the organizers and the other exhibitors and guests as much as possible before, during and after the event

Action 90: Online summits, podcasts and webinars can be used to generate dynamic and lifetime content - but they need to be aligned with the needs and preferences of your target audience. Like most initiatives, make sure that you can maintain the momentum over time or alternatively, consider being a guest on someone else's show

Section 14. Media Marketing

Action 91: The media landscape continues to change and the best way to secure media coverage for your business is via a direct relationship with journalists and editors in the publications that are of most interest to yours and their target audience. Be ready with independent and verifiable information and answer any requests immediately. Say thank you at the time of contact and after publication and re-purpose your content with full credits included

Action 92: Editorial content is worth pursuing provided it still meets your overall marketing objectives and reaches your target audience. There are many different local options and it is a good idea to try out some easy options first to build your portfolio

Action 93: Advertorial is becoming more popular, but to be effective, you still need to make sure that at least 70% of the message is good quality content and no more than 30% is promotional. Try and keep the style and formatting similar to the rest of the publication and include something familiar and memorable to increase its recall value

Action 94: Make sure that any publicity you generate is appropriate for your business. Start with small opportunities first and always respond to bad publicity as soon as possible in an appropriate way. Subscribe to Google Alerts to find out what is being said about you and your business online

Action 95: Watch out for current issues or topics that are related to your business or core values and consider sharing factual content that refers to the issue as soon as possible so that you can jump onto the current publicity or topic bandwagon

Section 15. Community Marketing

Action 96: You and your business can select your own way to support your local community efficiently, effectively and sustainably. This will lead to all sorts of opportunities and a range of benefits

Action 97: Free, formal and fee for service networks are a great way for your business to connect with customers, clients and businesses so that collectively, you can benefit as a result of the connection

Action 98: Bartering is a way to negotiate and exchange value in different ways, either with the same products and services or with different products and services. Before you consider this marketing idea, make sure that the model you select will be fair and reliable

Action 99: Exchanges are a way to share value in a different way when a client or customer cannot make the usual payment arrangements. However, make sure that you feel completely comfortable with the exchange agreement and its likely completion before agreeing to the exchange as your value may not be returned

Action 100: Wherever possible, source your products, services and supplies for other locals. Not only is it a more sustainable and environmentally friendly option, you may also end up with more referral business

Action 101: Consider talking to other local businesses about ways that you can share space, either for payment or for some form of exchange (branding, promotion etc). Check in at least every six months to make sure that it is working well for both parties

Action 102: Naming rights, Sponsorships and Advertisements work best when they provide coverage for an extended time frame and are even better if there is a sense of engagement and reciprocity with your business

Section 16. Incentive Marketing

Action 103: Incentives can be used to encourage people to be attracted to your products and services or help them move along the sales process more quickly. If they are provided after the transaction, it may also encourage them to make another purchase

Action 104: Competitions that are timely, encourage participation or engagement and can potentially go viral have the potential to be effective at sharing your business brand to your target audience and beyond. Alternatively, you can consider making a donation in alignment with your values

Action 105: By applying the principles of gamification into the marketing of your business, you can increase the novelty, variety and interest in your products and services. Ideally, it is best if your gamification process is automated. Alternatively, you can simply incorporate some appropriate unexpected fun on a regular basis

Action 106: Loyalty programs provide an opportunity for you to extend your business relationship with your valued clients and customers. In a hyper local context or location, it gives you an opportunity to work with complementary businesses and help each other over the short or long term

Action 107: Relationship Marketing Programs help you recognize your good quality business relationships and also remind individuals of your value and build and reinforce the relationship. A key ingredient of business success is consistency

Action 108: There are many ways to acknowledge and thank people and businesses for their contribution to your success. Remember to acknowledge what you can be grateful for and make significant decisions by calmly evaluating your choices. Ask for extra help if you need it

Section 17. Future Options Marketing

Action 109: Interactive and Immersive Marketing Opportunities are likely to enable people to be more actively involved in their purchasing decision and it may lead to more socially and ethically responsible purchasing decisions

Action 110: Collaborative Clusters and Behavior Based Tribes are likely to come together to make decisions as a group rather than as individuals. This can potentially lead to more egalitarian societies and continuous improvement.

Action 111: The variety of ways that payment can be made for an exchange is likely to continue changing and country borders dissolve with international trade

Action 112: A trend from location independent to device independent is likely to occur as more open source technology is developed and shared and made more accessible to all citizens

Action 113: As wearable technology and other marketing devices enter the market, there will come a time when consultants will need to provide advice on how to maximize these tools and people will need to learn how to turn off constant marketing messages

Action 114: In the future, marketing will continue to evolve and offer business many different ways to reach and secure sales and process payments. The most likely outcome is that there will be a more seamless customer or user experience based on previously collected data and information thanks to integration technology

Section 18. Marketing Measurement

Action 115: When measuring your marketing, look at both quantitative and qualitative information and trial and test before moving to larger scale implementation. Be aware that algorithms in the online world are constantly changing and your business needs to be ready to adjust accordingly

Action 116: To prepare your business for the day when you will not be there, keep a record of the most important online statistics that are only available in real time in an Excel spreadsheet every six months. Review your results and look at ways to improve your business results

Action 117: Marketing techniques can be used to improve your brand awareness and perceived value and ultimately raise the level of Goodwill value when the business is sold, acquired or transferred. Always be on the lookout for ways that you can increase the value of your business

Action 118: After selecting and implementing your marketing activities, you need to find ways to measure their performance and their ability to ultimately lead to conversions. Some activities will not be able to be measured, but they will need to be maintained. Your results can give you clues as to what to improve in the future

Action 119: From time to time, you will need to assess your marketing initiatives and look for ways to improve their effectiveness and conversion rate. Make sure that you base your decisions on statistically relevant information but also be open to small tweaks based on specific feedback

Action 120: Review the Top 20 Tips and Techniques and make an effort to complete at least one of these in the next month

20. Bonuses

To access the free Special Bonus Offers from this book, you will need to join the 120 Ways Publishing Membership Program at http://120ways.com/members

You can select the free Personal Membership Program or consider an Upgrade to the Professional or Premium Membership Program.

The free Special Downloads that you will automatically have access to in the Personal Membership Program include:

1. **Marketing Idea Viability Tes**t

2. Excel Spreadsheet file of all of the **Links** mentioned in this book

3. Comprehensive **Website Project Briefing Questionnaire**

4. List of our **Currently Most Popular Search Engine Optimization Techniques**

120 Ways Publishing Membership Program - Valid for ALL Books!			
*Correct as at 23 Aug 2016	**Personal**	**Professional**	**Premium**
Free Email News (Value $100)	√	√	√
Free Lifetime Access to Later Edition Summaries (Value $250)	√	√	√
Free Lifetime Access to Special Download Files offered in the books (Value $150)	√	√	√
Access to Questions & Answers Summaries (Value $500)		√	√
Access to How-To Instruction Videos and Audio Recordings (Value $1,500)			√
Total Value	$500	$1,000	$2,500
Investment	Free	$39 a year*	$59 a year*

The pricing for the Professional and Premium membership levels may change in the future but we will always do our best to keep these as affordable as possible and still provide maximum value.

The best part of the 120 Ways Publishing Membership Program is that if you become a member, you will also have access to all of the other equivalent products from our other books!

Previous Books: 120 Ways To Achieve Your Purpose With LinkedIn
120 Ways To Market Your Business Hyper Locally

Join the 120 Ways Publishing Membership Program right now at

http://120ways.com/members

Index

This index was manually created to give you direct access to many important topics in this book. If you have a digital version of this book, you can also search for topics by keyword.

The index quotes Section Numbers rather than Page Numbers.

120 Ways to Achieve Your Purpose With LinkedIn 4, 7.3
120 Ways To Attract The Right Career Or Business 4.1, 5.5
3D printing 17
80/20 1.1

above the line marketing 13.5
academia 11.5
academic qualification 11.6
Accelerated Mobile Pages Project https://www.ampproject.org 8.2
accountability 10.3
accountability partner 2.1
accreditation 9.5, 11.6
achievement 2.1, 2.3
acquisition 2.4
acting 12.4
activity based office design 7.1
activity groups 15
Ad-Blocking software 8.9
adaptive business 12.6
admit mistakes 12.4
advertisements 8.8, 9.3
advertising 7.4, 8.6, 14, 14.2, 15.6, 18.3
advertorial 12.1, 14.2
advertorial content 8.6
advocacy 12.7
advocate 4.1
affiliate marketing 10.2, 11.2
affiliate programs 4.2, 7.3, 11.2
agents 14.3
aggregator 9.3, 9.4
aggregator website 8.7
agreement 15.3
Airbnb 9.4
algorithms 6.3, 8, 8.1, 8.2, 8.4, 8.6, 8.7, 18, 18.1

alternative payment models 17
ambassador 4.1
amplification 8.4
analyze information 18
anecdote 6.1, 11.5, 18.4
animations 8.3
apologize 2.2, 6.4, 12.2, 12.4
apps 8.3
artificial intelligence 8.1
assets 18.2
assumptions 6.1
attraction power 4.2
audio recording 13.6
audiobooks 14.1
authority website 7.3
automation 7.4, 16.2
automation tools 6.3
award judges 16.1
award programs 11.1

backlinks 8, 8.1, 8.7
backups 6.4
bad news travels fast 12
bad reputation 6.4, 12.4
bad reviews 12.2
balance sheet 18.1, 18.2
banner ads 9.3
bartering 15.2
behavior 3.2, 8.6, 11.4
behavior 8.6
behavior based tribes 17
benefits 7, 8.8
billable hours 2.8
biography 7.3
black hat techniques 8
blame 2
blockages 2.1
blog 7.2
Bluehost 7.2, 11.2
Boolean Search Operators 8.9
borrowed authority 7.3
bounce rate 8.8, 13.3

brand 4.2, 6.3, 8.5, 11, 11.2, 12.4
brand penetration 4.2
brand recognition 11.4, 12, 13.1, 13.5, 15.5, 16.1, 16.3, 18.2
branding 7.4
business 2.3
business coach 2.1
business context 1
business ethics 2.7
business friend 4.1
business incubators 4.2
business processes 10.4
business sale 18.1, 18.2
Business to Business (B2B) 11.3
Business to Customer (B2C) 11.3
buy local 3.2, 9.6, 15.4
buy locally 1.4

cache 7.2
café 3.1
calculated risks 12.4
Camberwell Network 2.9, 10.1, 15, 15.1
carrot and stick 16
cash flow 3.5
cats 8.5
cause 12.7
celebration 2.2
celebrity 4.2
Certificate of Appreciation 15, 16.5
certification 9.5, 11.6
certified advertisement partner 9.1
challenges 16.5
chambers of commerce 4.2
change 2.5, 3.1, 3.4
change register 12.6
chaos 4.3
charity 13.2
charity 16.5
choice 3.2, 8.8, 16.5
circulation 14.1
clarification 3.1, 3.4
classified advertisements 4.2, 14, 18.4
clichés 14.2

click resistant 10.1
cloud 10
clutter 7
co-working spaces 4.2, 7.1
coaches 3.4, 10.3
collaboration 2.5, 5.5, 7.3, 12.4, 16.4, 17
collaborative clusters 17
collaborator analysis 5.5
collect feedback 12.6
collective model 15.1
collective presence 6.4
comfort zone 1.1
comments 8.4
commercial real estate 7.1
commissions 12.4
commitment 7.4, 10.3, 13.2
committee position 9.5
common good 2.6
communications 14.3
community 2.5
community development 2.7, 15, 15.5, 17
community houses 15
community marketing 15
community service 15.3
companion 4.1
comparison service 9.3, 12.4, 17
competition 2.7, 7.4, 8.9, 11.6
competitions 16.1
competitor analysis 5.3, 5.4, 5.5, 8.2
competitors 4
complaints 4, 6.4, 13.1
complementary business 11.2, 12..4, 16.3, 16.4
complementary website 9.3
composing content 12.1
conferences 13.3
conflicts of interest 10.3
confusion 4.3
congruency 4.2
congruent behavior 17
consistent behavior 12.4, 16.4
consulting 3.1

consumer behavior 3.2
consumer choice 3.2
content 7.3
Content Management system (CMS) 7.2
content marketing 8.3
contentment 1.1
continuous improvement 3.3, 11.1, 11.6, 17
contributing to others content 12.1
convenience 3.5
conversational queries 8.1
conversions 8.4, 8.5, 9.1, 9.2, 12.4, 18.4
cookies 8.6
cooperative 15.2
cooperatives 2.7, 4.2
cooperativism 2.7
Corporate Social Responsibility (CSR) 9.7
Cost Per Click (CPC) 9.1, 9.3
Cost Per Thousand Impressions (CPM) 9.2, 9.3
councils 15
courage 12.4
courses 13.4
courtesy 16.5
cover up 12.4
Crazy Domains 11.2
credibility 8.5, 12.2
criticism 12.4
crusader 4.1
culture 2.5
curating content 12.1
curiosity 12.4
currency 3.5, 7.3, 7.5
current affairs 14.3, 14.4
current issue 14.4
customer experience 17
customer relationship management (CRM) 4.3
Customer Relationship Management (CRM) 4.3, 10, 10.4, 13.3, 16.4

data 6.1, 8.6, 10, 11.5
database 1.3, 10.5
database marketing 10
databases 6.3, 10, 10.1, 10.2, 10.4

David Jenyns 8.8
decision making 2.3, 2.4, 11
decisions 16.5
dedication 10.3
demand 3, 3.1
democratized information 2.5
demographics 8.6, 14.1
device independent 17
differentiation 5.5
differentiators 3.4
difficult customers 12.4
digital asset value 18.1, 18.3
digital assets 7.2, 9.1
digital disruption 3
digital expense 9.1
digital media 8.3
directories 4.2, 8.7, 14.1
disappointment 7.4
disaster 12.7
discounted logistics 10.2
discounting 3.5, 4.3, 9
discounts 7.3, 11.3, 13.2
distribution 1.4, 3.3, 10.1
diversity 2.8
domain name 6.2, 7.2, 7.3, 8.2
donation 16.1
donations 9.7, 15.6
dragons 3.4
due diligence 4.1
dynamic content 7.2, 8.3, 13.3, 13.6, 14.1
dynamic value 10

economic development 2.7, 15
economies of scale 1.4, 3.3
editorial 12.1, 14.1, 15.6
editorial content 8.6
education 7.4, 12.4, 14.2
efficiency 2.8
egalitarian environment 17
egotistical 15.6
email 11.3
email mailing lists 10

email newsletter marketing 10.1, 10.4
email opens 10.1
email signature 10.1
email systems 10.1
emails 6.3
endorsement 4.2
engagement 7.3, 8.3, 8.4, 8.6, 9.2, 10.1, 14.1, 16.1, 18.1
entertainment 14.2
entrepreneur 2.4
entrepreneurs 12.4
environment 3.3
environmentally friendly 1.1, 1.4, 15.4
ergonomics 7.1
ethics 2.7, 3.1
event guides 14.1
event venues 13.1
Eventbrite 13.2
events 13, 13.5, 16.2, 16.5
events marketing 13
evergreen 1.3
evergreen content 2.4, 7.2, 8.3, 8.4, 12.5, 13.3
exchange 15.2, 15.3, 15.5
excuses 2
exhibitions 13.5
exhibitors 13.5
exit strategy 2.4, 10
expansion 3.3
experience 18
expert 7.3
exploitation 2.7
expos 13.5
external links 8.1, 8.7

Facebook 6.3, 7.3, 8.4, 8.6, 9.2, 11.3, 12.4, 15, 16.1
Facebook group 9.2
Facebook page 9.2
fair exchange 4.3, 6.4, 15.3
faith groups 15
fake reviews 12.5
false assumptions 4.2
false beliefs 2.1, 3.4
family 2.5

family business 3.1
featured content 14.4
features 7, 8.8
feedback 2.2, 3.1, 4, 4.3,, 10.5, 12.2, 12.6, 18.3
first responder 14.4
first right of refusal 5.1
fit out 7.1
fixed messages 7.4
focus groups 4
follow up 10.5
formal recognition program 11.3
framework 11.2
franchise 5.4, 7.4
franchise 7.4
free advice 1.4
free events 13.1, 13.5, 13.6
Freeloader 9.5
friendship 4.1

games 8.3, 16.2
gamification 16.2
generating content 12.1
generations Intro
geolocation 7.2
geospatial data 5.1,
gifts 9.6, 16.5
gigs 13.3
giving rather than taking 5.5
giving referrals 12.4
global village 1
globalization 1.4
goodwill 6.4, 18.2
Google + 6.3, 15
Google AdSense 9.3
Google AdWords 9.1
Google Alerts 14.3
Google Analytics 6.3, 8.5
Google Plus 8.4, 8.7
Google Search Console 8.2
Google Webmaster Tools 8.2
government grants 2.7
government regulation 2.7

grandfathering 11.6
grapevine 6.4
gratefulness 12.7, 16.5
growth 3.1, 5.2, 9, 11.1
guru 7.3

happiness 1.1
hash tags 5.4, 6.3, 13.5
headline 14.4
hidden sales team 10.5
high authority website 4.2, 8.1
high ranking website 8.1
higher authority website 8.7
hire for attitude not aptitude 10.2
hourly rate 2.8
HSBC Bank 11.5
HTML Code 5.4
http://archive.org 5.4, 13.3
http://archive.org/web 5.4
hyper local marketing definition 1.3
hyperactive 1.3

ideal client 4.2
identity 2.2
if/then process 4.3
if/then scenarios 10.4
immersive marketing 17
incentive marketing 16
incentives 11.4
incognito mode 8.6
incognito search 5.4
indexable content 8.3
industrial age 3
industry qualification 11.6
influence 18.1
influencers 4.2, 8.2, 11.3
informal arrangements 10.2
information 14.2
initiative 11.1
innovation 7.5
inspiration 13.1
Instagram 6.3

intellectual property 2.5
interactive 8.5
interactive marketing 17
interactive technology 8.3
interlinks 8.1, 8.7
international business 1, 5.2, 10.2
international marketing 13.6
internet browser extension 8.5
internet marketing 17
investor 13.5
IP Address 7.2, 12.2
Isaac Asimov 17
iterations 10.4

jail 12.4
job interview 2.9
joint ventures 10.2
journalist 11.3
journalists 3.4, 9.3, 12, 14,14.2, 14.3

Kangaroo Island Intro, 1.2, 12
keywords 6.2, 7.2, 8.2, 8.9,12.4
know like and trust 1.4, 4.1

landlords 6
lead generation 6.3
leadership 2.3
leadership role 12.7
leads 14
leasing 5.1, 7.1, 15.5
legal agreement 5.5
legal agreements 10.2
liabilities 18.2
lifetime value 8.4, 10, 13.6, 14.1
lifting your game 11
Like, Comment or Share 8.4
linear 3.4
linear 10.4
link juice 13.4
LinkedIn 2.2, 2.9, 6.3, 8.7, 9.3, 12.2, 12.3, 12.4, 12.5, 13.3, 15
links 8.3, 12.1, 13,5
liquidation 2.4

listening 2.1
load time 8.3
local 1.2
local community 1.2, 2.6
local customs and traditions 1.2
local information 6.1
local suppliers 15.4
location attachment 1.2
location by choice Intro, 1
location context 6
location independent 1, 17
location of choice 13.6
location sharing 15.5
location specific 6.2
long term campaign 15.6
long term vision 10.1
lose face 6.4
loss leader 16
lottery prize 16.1
loyalty program 16.3
lucky square 16.1
luxury products 18.2

machine learning 8.1
magazines 14, 14.1
mailing list 13.2
maintenance 7.2
making a difference 1.2, 12.7
management 2.3
managing expectations 4
market demand 1
market share 3.3
marketing collateral 12.3
Marketing Idea Viability Test 7.4
marketing measurement 18, 18.4
marketing spend 7.4
marketplace distribution service 15.1
mass production 1.4, 3.3
material wealth 2.5
McDonald's 4
measurement tools 8.6
media 8.7, 14

media release 13.5
Meetup Group 9.3, 15
Melbourne SEO Meet Up Group 2.9
memberships 9.5
mentor 2.7
mentoring 9.5, 13.4
mentors 3.4
merchandise 9.6
merchandising 7.1
merger 2.4
meta descriptions 8.1
middleware integrations 17
milestones 16.5
mind map 2.1
Minimal Viable Product (MVP) 7.2, 8.8, 9
minimalist approach 1
mistakes 2.2, 6.4, 13
mobile devices 3.2, 6.2, 7.2, 8.2
monopolization 2.7
moral compass 2.5
motivation 2.2
motivation 8.8
moving messages 7.4
multi-tasking 2.8
multimedia content 8.3
multiple locations 1.2
multiple strategies 4.2

naming rights 15.6
needs versus wants 2.5
negative reviews 12.2
neighbors 6.1
net worth 1.1
Network marketing 11
networking 4.2, 12.7, 15.1
networks 1.1, 15.1
newcomers 1.2
Newcomers Network Intro, 3.1, 6.2, 7.3, 11.5, 12.7, 15, 15.1
newspapers 14, 14.1
niche 1
No Comment 14.3
noise 7.4

non executive director 2.4

occupational health and safety 7.1
one % better 2.5, 5.3
one-to-many marketing 13.6
one-too-many 4.3
online course 13.4
online performance 8.8
online platforms 4.2, 5.4, 6.2, 6.3
online presence 6.2, 7, 8.2, 8.8
online profile 6.3, 8.7
online real estate 8.6
online research 3.2
online reviews 12.2
online search 8.8
online shopping 3.2
online summit 13.6
open source technology 17
organic growth 9
organizing events 13.1
outcomes 8.8
outsource 1.1
outsourcing 2.8, 2.9, 4.3, 10.2
overthink 3.1

package 15.1
page visits 8.8
pages per visit 8.8
paid events 13.2
paid marketing 9
partnership approach 10.2
partnerships 5.5, 10.3
passion 3.1
pay to play 6.3
paying for traffic 9.1
paying it forward 12.4
payments 17
perception 3.5, 4.2, 7.4
performance 2.2, 2.9, 10.3, 11.1
performance assessment 18.3
performance improvement 18.4

performance management 2.8
perseverance 2.2
personal ability 1
personal information 10
personalization 4.3, 8.7, 10.2, 10.4, 11.3, 11.4, 16.4
philanthropic donations 9.7
photographs 14
photos 7.3
ping 16.5
pitch 14
pity party 2
planning 2.1
plugins 7.2
podcasts 13.6
policy 2.7
portal website 8.7
portfolio 7.3
post nominals 11.3
PR 14.3
precedent 6.4
predictions 8.1
predictive analysis 4
premium products
presentations 13.3
pricing 3.2, 3.5, 7
pricing 3.5
pricing 7
pricing levels 3.3, 3.5
primary and secondary keywords 5.4
privacy 3.2, 7.1
pro bono assistance 9.7
proactivity 12.4
product lifecycle 3.5
productive outcome 6.4
productivity 7.1
professional association 1.3
professional associations 8.7
professional bodies 11.6
professional development 11.6, 15.1
profit 2.5, 3.3, 3.5
Program marketing 11
promotion 13.5, 15.5, 15.6

property selection 3.2, 5.1
prospect 16
public company 2.4
public marketing 12, 12.1
public recognition 16.5
public relations 14.3
publications 7.2, 14.2
publicity 13.5, 14.3
purchasing 3.2
purchasing power 10.2
purpose 2.2
pyramid schemes 11

qualitative information 5, 18
quality real estate 7
quantitative information 5, 18
quick wins 11
quizzes 11.5
quotes 14.2

ra-ra events 13, 13.3
radio 13.6
raffle 16.1
react emotionally 6.4
real world groups 2.9
receiving referrals 12.4
recency 3.5, 7.5
reciprocal links 8.1, 8.7, 9.4
reciprocity 15.6
recognition 2.2 11.1, 11.3, 16.2, 16.3
recognition marketing 11.3, 16.4
recommendations 3.2, 12.3, 12.4, 12.5
recovery 12.4
recruitment 2.8, 2.9, 10.2, 18.2
referrals 1.4, 2.9, 3.2, 4.1, 4.2, 4.3, 5.5, 7.1, 7.2, 9, 9.5, 10.2, 10.4, 11.2, 11.6, 12.4, 15.1, 18.4
refund policy 6.4
Reg Eustace 3.3
regional community 4.2
reinvent the wheel 8.5
relationship 6.4
relationship marketing 16.4

relationships 1.4, 4.1, 4.3, 14
relevancy 7.3, 7.5
repeat behaviors 11.4
repeat business 16
repurpose content 11.1, 13.3
repurposed 7.4
reputation 8.8, 10.2, 11, 12.4, 13.3, 14.3
research programs 11.5
research project 11.5
resentment 10.3, 13.3, 15.3
resilience 2.2
responding to reviews 12.2
responsibility 3.3, 6.4, 12.4
responsive economy 5.3
responsiveness 10.5, 12, 12.4
retail precinct 11.6
retention 2.9
retirees 2.9
retirement 14.4
return on investment 2.5, 7.4, 18.3
reviews 7.3, 12.2, 12.4, 12.5, 18.3
rewards 16.2
rewards programs 11.4
risk 6.2
risk management 5.5, 10.2
robots 17

Sales 101 10.5
sales cycle 10
sales funnel 16
saying no 4.3
scannable 14.2
search competition 8.9
search engine index 8, 8.1
Search Engine Marketing (SEM) 9.1
Search Engine Optimization (SEO) 7.2, 8, 8.1, 8.3, 8.7
search engine results 6.2, 8.2, 8.6
Search Engine Results Page (SERP) 8.2
search engine robots 8
search frequency 8.9
search results 6.3
self employed 2.3

self evaluation 2.1
self management 2.2
self regulation 2.7
semi-retirement 13.4
service 4.3
setup costs 9
share the love 10.1
sharing 2.5, 7.1, 8.5, 9.7, 12.7
Sheena Iyengar 8.8
shiny objects 3.4, 7.5
shop local 3.2
shop locally 1.4
shopping precinct 16.1
short term mentality 10.1
shout outs 11.2
signals 8.6
simulations 8.3
single shingle consultant 13.1
site location 5.1
sitemap 7.2
skills coach 2.1
smiling 1.4
SMS 11.3
snippets 8.1
social democracy 3.3
social investment 1
social media 5.4, 6.3, 10.1, 10.2, 12.4
Social Media Marketing (SMM) 9.2
solutions 14.2
SPAM 8, 10.1
speakers 13.2, 13.6
speakers fee 13.3
speaking at events 13.3
special offers 10.5
sponsored content 8.5
sponsored posts 9.2
sponsorships 15.6, 16.1
sponsorships 16.1
sporting groups 15
staff turnover 12.4
staffing 2.8
stakeholders 13.2

standard of living 2.5
standards 11.6
standing your ground 6.4
statistics 14, 14.2, 18, 18.1, 18.4
statue 15.6
store layout 7.1
story 14, 14.2
strategic alliances 10.2
stunts 14.3
style guide 7.2
subconscious motives 1.2
successful business 12.4
succession planning 2.4
support 2.8
surveys 4, 11.5, 12.5
suspect 16
sustainability 15.4
sustainable 1.1, 1.4, 2.7
sustainable business 1.3, 3, 3.3, 4, 8.8

target audience 4, 4.2, 4.3, 5.5, 6, 6.3, 7, 7.4, 7.5, 8.5, 8.6, 8.8, 8.9, 9.3, 9.4, 9.5, 12.1, 13.1, 13.2
tax deductions 9.7
teaching 13.4
technological age 3
technological era 4, 4.1
television 14, 14.4
testimonials 7.3, 12.5
thank you 2.3, 9.6, 12.6, 13.3, 16.5
the money is in the list 10
time management 2.5, 2.6, 13.3
total spend 4.3
tourist information 14.1
tracking pixels 8.6
trade fairs 13.5
traffic 9.1
tragedy 12.7
training 6.1
transferrable skills 7.3
transparency 10.3, 11.2
trial period 15.5
Trip Advisor 9.4

trust 7
tutoring 13.4
Twitter 6.3, 7.3, 15

under promise and over deliver 2.3, 16.4
unemployable 3.1
unique gifts 2.6
Unique Resource Locator (URL) 7.2, 7.3
unsubscribes 10.1
user experience 17
User Experience (UX) 8.8
usernames and passwords list 6.3

value 2.5, 3.2, 3.5, 7, 7.4, 13.2
value exchange 1
values 2.2, 2.5, 2.6, 3.1, 4, 4.3, 7.1, 10.3, 11.4, 12.4, 13.1
victim 2
Victorian Writer's Centre 10.1
video 8.5
videos 7.2, 10.1, 12.5
View Page Source 5.4
village to raise a child 1
VIMEO 10.1
VIP clients 10.5
viral content 8.5
virtual reality 8.3
vision 2.3
voice activated search queries 5.4, 8.9
voluntary work 2.5
volunteering 2.6, 9.5, 9.7

warehousing 15.5
wearable devices 5.4
wearable technology 17
webinars 13.6
website 6.2
website conversions 8.2
website design 7.2
website hosting 7.2
website layout 7.2
website ranking 8.9
website speed 8.8

website traffic 8.2
websites 6.4, 7.2
what gets measured gets done 11.6
white hat techniques 8.1
white label associate 10.2
word of mouth 7.2, 9, 11.6, 12.4
WordPress 7.2
work in parallel 10.3
work/life balance 3.3
workshops 13.3
World Bank 11.5
writing voice 6.3
wrong clients 1.4, 4.2

Yelp 12.2YouTube 6.3, 10.1, 13.4

Author

Sue Ellson BBus AIMM MAHRI CDAA (Assoc) ASA MPC

Sue Ellson is an experienced trainer, professional learner, consultant in practice and an Independent LinkedIn Specialist.

Sue was born in Adelaide, South Australia in 1965. Sue was married in 1985 and moved to Melbourne in Victoria, Australia in 1994. She had two children in 1995 and 1997 and was granted a divorce in 2006. Sue enjoys the simple pleasures of life – like being able to walk and breathing fresh air.

Sue has completed a Bachelor of Business in Administrative Management from the University of South Australia (2000) http://unisa.edu.au, is a Member of the Australian Institute of Management AIM (since 2001) http://aim.com.au, a Member of the Australian Human Resources Institute AHRI (since 2005) http://ahri.com.au, a Member of the Melbourne Press Club (since 2008) http://melbournepressclub.com, an Associate Member of the Career Development Association of Australia CDAA (since 2015) http://cdaa.org.au and a Member of the Australian Society of Authors ASA (since 2015) http://asauthors.org.

Sue has a varied range of professional experience in banking, training, recruitment, career development, human resources, marketing, networking, online publishing, social media and business. Sue's first enterprise, Newcomers Network was started in 1999 and her first website http://newcomersnetwork.com went live in 2001. Newcomers Network and Sue's close circle of local and international friends have helped her understand the needs of people from many different cultures and countries.

Sue joined LinkedIn on 21 December 2003. Sue has been consulting, training, speaking, writing and advising on the topic of LinkedIn since 2008. In 2012, she created Camberwell Network http://camberwellnetwork.com and in 2015, she created 120 Ways Publishing http://120ways.com.

More information about Sue is online at http://sueellson.com. LinkedIn connections are welcome at http://au.linkedin.com/in/sueellson

Google reviews are very welcome at https://plus.google.com/+Sueellson2

Sue Ellson - Topics

Sue knows how to gather information on a variety of topics, but is most passionate about:
> helping people achieve their purpose (career or business)
> utilizing LinkedIn and technology to achieve a purpose
> the successful settlement of newcomers, expatriates and repatriates
> the value of local communities and becoming more connected

Sue Ellson - Speaking and Training

Sue welcomes selected opportunities to be a keynote speaker, guest presenter, trainer or webinar guest at conferences, seminars and professional development events in Australia and overseas. Her previous presentations are listed at http://sueellson.com/presentations

Sue Ellson - Consulting

Sue provides personally tailored individual and group consulting services in Melbourne and via Skype, or with sufficient notice, in person elsewhere depending on availability. Her current services are listed at http://sueellson.com/services

Sue Ellson - Publications

Sue has written a variety of articles for many different publications and welcomes selected opportunities to provide exclusive written content. Her previous publications are listed at http://sueellson.com/publications

Sue Ellson - Media Requests

Sue has provided a range of content to newspapers, magazines and online publications and has been a guest on radio programs both in Australia and overseas. More information at http://sueellson.com/about

To Contact Sue Ellson

sueellson@sueellson.com
http://sueellson.com
http://120ways.com
http://newcomersnetwork.com
http://camberwellnetwork.com
http://au.linkedin.com/in/sueellson

Copyright

All text and technical diagrams copyright © Sue Ellson 2016. The moral rights of the author have been asserted. All rights reserved.

Photocopying and reproducing in print or digital format

If recommending the content in this book to friends, family, clients or colleagues, please keep in mind that the original rights belong to the author only.

The content has been generously provided and it is only fair that the reward be returned to the author to recover the cost of production, distribution and future editions.

If you wish to reproduce, store or transmit any part of this book, please email the publisher 120ways@120ways.com for written permission rights.

All quotations need to be referenced to Sue Ellson

Join the 120 Ways Publishing Membership Program NOW!

For free bonuses valued at $500
http://120ways.com/members

www.ingramcontent.com/pod-product-compliance
Lightning Source LLC
Chambersburg PA
CBHW070556300426
44113CB00010B/1281